Ramblings of a Rascal

Lawrence Stacey

The Lancashire Fusiliers in action at the Battle of Minden,
1st August 1759, Richard Caton Woodville.

*'I have seen what I never thought to be possible – a single line of infantry
break through three lines of cavalry, ranked in order of battle, and tumble
them to ruin!' – Marquis de Contades, French Commander*

Ramblings of a Rascal

LAWRENCE STACEY

First published in Great Britain in 2014 by LS Publishing

Copyright © Major Lawrence Stacey 2014

Edited, designed and produced by Tandem Publishing
http://tandempublishing.yolasite.com/

ISBN 978-0-9930617-0-7

10 9 8 7 6 5 4 3 2 1

A CIP catalogue record for this book is available from the British Library.

Printed and bound by CPI Group (UK) Ltd, Croydon CR0 4YY

Dedicated to our children
Warwick, Antonia, Danielle and Hugh-Oliver
Whom we have loved unconditionally since their first breath and
no doubt to our last sigh

And to the memory
of my Mother

Contents

‡

AUTHOR'S NOTE & ACKNOWLEDGEMENTS

As you will see, this book is no literary masterpiece. It was never meant to be so, as it is certainly not within my power to complete one. Indeed, it came about largely because my children and friends constantly nagged me to record my stories. One or two of my other contemporaries expressed doubts at my boldness, even my hubris, in wanting to write anything at all. They pointed out that 'We can all write such things,' and of course they were correct. Many have led far more interesting lives than my own, but for one reason or another they have chosen not to commit to paper. As I say, without the children, in particular Hugh-Oliver, I would not have sat down to it.

I have not in every story given the correct names, either because I have not been able to seek permission, or because I wished to spare someone's blushes over his or her involvement in my misspent youth. In recounting these stories I have relied on my imperfect memory. I hope the reader will be indulgent when this has proved hazy. In the many Army stories I have not used the 'f' word, merely the first letter of it. Obviously, swearing in the Forces was and still is endemic, but I didn't want to follow the example of American movies, when every other word is a profanity (we counted fifty-seven in a recent Mafia film before finally switching off for want of dialogue). After all, we can all swear if we wish, but it becomes boring and offensive if used so gratuitously.

‡

I am indebted to many people for bringing this book to fruition. To the lads and lasses of the north-east of England, to my home town of South Shields for my Geordie roots, and in particular to that other working-class enclave of northerners across the Pennines in Lancashire, for without the Lancashire Fusiliers (LFs) there would be no book. People so often say to me, 'Gosh you are just Barmy Army.' Far from it – I have in fact scant regard for the amorphous 'Army'. This is the Army that cares not one iota for its soldiers; and nor, generally, does the country at large care for it, although there has been a softening of late in the face of the thousands of limbless servicemen returning from our pointless wars. The Army will use you up and spit you out, with never another thought. What I and others like me treasure is, or was, our unique regimental system, dating back hundreds of years and respected all around the world. A Regiment boasted real territorial connections and a vital network of branches. My own Regiment had outposts throughout Lancashire, offering help, advice and above all comradeship. None of this had anything to do with the 'Army', rather a lot of big-hearted ex-XX men voluntarily giving up their time.

In Lancashire we have eight branches of LFs who come together regularly to support each other. Only recently I was reading that the widow of an ex-Lancashire Fusilier exiled to a southern county needed the regimental flag and accoutrements, for as she said, 'That was his wish, to be buried with XX regalia.' No sooner asked than done. This system is in its death throes, as our age group wastes out and our county regiments wither away in the face of the new mantra – *the big Regiment*.

It need not have happened; as one Oxford-educated German

officer said to me many years ago: 'Why is it that you British throw away that which we would dearly love to acquire?'

Why indeed? In the American Army, as in others, any stint of service ensures that you have access to military hospitals, PX stores or other shopping facilities at reduced rates, 10 per cent military discount for motor cars and, if you are lucky enough to live near an air-trooping facility, the chance to use it, if there is free capacity. None of these things are on offer to us. Policemen and policewomen claim overtime – not so our soldiers. Personally, I am not an advocate of Army unionisation and overtime but something more equitable should be done when one is working seven days a week and 365 days a year. Remember, in my day leave was a privilege not a right. Perhaps the time has come to amalgamate the Army and police, combining them into a paramilitary defence force with higher pay but no overtime, able to be used worldwide, though not with Tony Blair's gay abandon. The police should then be selected properly with a commissioned officer system along the lines of the armed services – indeed, in tandem – and in this way, hopefully, the corruption and numerous malpractices that have been so prevalent of late in their ranks would not occur, given correct and professional leadership.

However, back to what I should be about: those who have a hand in this book. Well, no greater thanks can I confer than upon Mrs Jackie Clarke, who has been a steadfastly constant companion in typing my copious sheets, giving advice and, after breaking both her wrists – simultaneously – managing to convince us all that getting back to the typewriter was therapeutic, indeed that I was doing her a favour! So thank you for your dedication. Also my own daughter, Danielle, who with the rapidity of a knitting machine has typed another tranche. This while running a hectic family of four young children. Female multi-tasking at its best. I am also indebted to my editor, Mr Sam Carter, for without his wise help and counsel there is no way this book would have come about. His actions were a great act of faith, which I hope I can repay. Also my great friend Mr Paul Clarke whose inspiration produced, in my opinion, a very apt title, and Mr Jon Wainwright for jacket design and illustrations.

Then there is my cousin's husband, Lt Colonel Tim O'Donnell, late 10th Gurkha Rifles, who corrected my Arabic for me. Major Bruce Lawson, late Royal Engineers, who nudged my memory about places and things all those years ago when serving in British Army of the Rhine (BAOR) and Borneo together. Mr Nick Mello, a proud member of 2 Platoon, A Company, sportsman extraordinaire and, at the same age as myself, his remarkable memory far surpasses mine in XX folklore – his help is appreciated.

To all I am indebted.

FOREWORD

By Bev Morgan

Lawrence and I joined the 1st Battalion XX The Lancashire Fusiliers in early January 1961. The Twentieth has a proud history. Formed in Exeter in 1688 following the landing at Torbay of Prince William of Orange, the future King William III, it boasts many battle honours and achievements. The burning of the White House by General Ross during the American War of Independence, the award of the Primrose Hackle by Queen Victoria following the Battalion's action at Spion Kop in the Boer War and the award of 'Six VCs before breakfast' at the Gallipoli landings in the First World War illustrate the diverse nature of its engagements and the part it has played not just in British history but all over the world.

In 1961 the First Battalion was stationed in Osnabruck as part of 12 Infantry Brigade, 2nd Division, British Army of the Rhine. Recently mechanised with armoured vehicles, it played a critical NATO role in Western defence. Training was of a very high standard and the Battalion was to win the highly contested Brigade Skills and Endurance Competition three years in succession. The period marked the height of the Cold War. It was against this background of intense military training that 'off the field activities' need to be judged, for young men faced with the enormity of fighting the Russians in a nuclear war had to seek outlets or go bananas.

On our first day our reception from our fellow subalterns was hostile to say the least, and for many nights we sought refuge in a bar in Osnabruck. It was a period when for the first six months a newly joined subaltern could not initiate a conversation, only respond to a direct question.

We shared an equally horrific initiation experience on our first Dinner Night when we somehow survived the rituals: being rolled up in a dust-filled carpet, turned upside down and nigh-drowned with beer for me. Submerged in cold baths in Lawrence's case – followed by the inevitable blackened balls...

But there our similarities ended, for whereas Lawrence was the Beauty I was the Beast. For whilst he was adored by all the regimental wives and pursued by all the nannies and eligible daughters in the garrison, I was playing rugby, skiing and shooting. Lawrence was, however, an accomplished cross-country runner and captained the regimental team. His running skills were key to self-preservation later in life. On one infamous occasion, Lawrence escaped through a bedroom window under fire from an irate husband who, unsportingly, had returned home earlier than expected from chasing terrorists.

Time moved on and I volunteered for secondment to the Northern Rhodesia Regiment, just prior to independence. Lawrence had meanwhile been selected to be ADC to Lt General Sir George Lea, late Twentieth, who at that time was Commander of the Armed Forces of Northern Rhodesia and Nyasaland.

On arrival in Rhodesia I was called for interview with the General by Lawrence. General Lea had a most commanding physical presence, well over six feet tall with a huge frame. 'The First Battalion is on operations against the Lenshina terrorists in the Luangwa Valley,' he said, 'it is of vital importance to the path to independence that they are defeated. You will be on active service – don't let The Twentieth down!'

With these words ringing in my ears I left his office and sought out Lawrence. There out in the huge grounds I discovered him playing hide and seek with the General's children.

Some months later, possibly through the General's influence, I was selected to carry the Queen's Colours on the Independence Parade. Following the Parade I had a brief chance to bid farewell to Lawrence before his departure for Borneo, where again his adventures with the fair sex proved more challenging than the terrorists, but I don't want to spoil the plot.

Our paths were to cross again when we both returned to England, succeeding one another as Regimental Recruitment Officers in Bury, Lancashire. We both took immense pride that The Twentieth boasted the highest number of recruits during the mid to late sixties, and it was no small irony when, shortly afterwards, as the newly formed 4th Battalion The Royal Regiment of Fusiliers, the 4th was disbanded. The same fate befell the 2nd Battalion just weeks ago, despite a march by former Fusiliers on Westminster coupled with a resounding win for an Early Day Motion opposing its disbandment.

Aside from The Twentieth one common love was 'our' Austin Healey 3000, which I sold to Lawrence for £400. They are now worth £30,000, and we both shed a tear just thinking about it.

And now the first metamorphosis occurred: my marriage to Pam at RAF St Clement Danes. Lawrence commanded the Honour Guard, who were resplendent in their Blues, setting an excellent example to the Royal Air Force. Pam's sole bridesmaid, Sallyanne, still recounts with graphic clarity her several narrow escapes from the intrepid youth in the grounds of RAF Bentley Priory, where the reception took place, given that Lawrence felt that his Honour Guard role entitled him to the spoils of war.

Sometime later I needed a place to stay in London to complete a Business Studies degree. Lawrence agreed to offer me accommodation, somewhat warily given that I had not been known to have the smartest of rooms as a bachelor in Quebec Barracks. To his surprise and to my own I found that marriage had changed me forever and I couldn't stop cleaning his already immaculate flat.

Times had changed. The boy wonder was meantime forensically involved in biological studies with every pretty young thing he met and was happy for me to be the housekeeper.

But finally, he too was to undergo a metamorphosis and as Pam changed me so too has Jillie changed him. The former Rake can now, with a most adorable wife, four children and eight grandchildren, reflect on how lucky he was to have met Jillie.

Lt Col B. M. J. Morgan MSc (Oxon) BA FCMA
September 2014

1

THE TRAP

The ending of the Second World War released millions of men back into the workplace, all competing for jobs and much-needed money to rebuild so many shattered dreams. Some had witnessed untold horrors, as within my own family. My uncle had entered the war at the age of eighteen, a handsome, carefree youth, full of vigour and life. He ended it an old and broken man, embittered by his time in the Japanese POW camp after the fall of Singapore in 1942.

He had been brutally tortured, starved and beaten. It took two years to bring him back to life and some form of sanity. We were told as children never to upset Uncle John for the consequences were dreadful, not only for him but those in his presence. His temple would swell to the size of a Jaffa orange and his eyes roll, culminating in violent shaking. He declared that he couldn't care anymore for anything, the niceties of life were dead to him and he would think only of himself in future. My prep school master had suffered the same treatment; both were lucky to be alive, but the latter realised this and became utterly philanthropic in his outlook on the world.

The war affected everyone in so many different ways, and who are we in hindsight to judge the feelings of those deprived, as they undoubtedly were, of the things we take for granted today?

Solders became spivs in a few cases, and why not? They saw so many profiteering from the war, people who had not suffered from its deprivations. Men bought bombers and converted them to freighters or passenger aeroplanes and became rich. Others entered the scrap trade and found success there; some were able to exploit the knowledge they had gained in the war and cleverly apply it. Others tried a miscellany of things, some laudable, some dubious, but all with the same purpose: to acquire wealth. The one I describe now I leave to your judgement.

I was probably ten or so when my mother read in a national newspaper of a fly-trap that was guaranteed to kill all flies. Up to then homes relied on the ubiquitous and disgusting brown spiral sticky paper which hung down from the ceiling in lengths of about 12 inches. Flies stuck to it and there they remained for days or even weeks, fascinating for small children, but my mother thought differently. For 2/- including postage (2/- = 10p) one was invited to send a postal order which would once and for all end the pestilence of flies. The deed done, she was pleased to see that the product arrived promptly in a brown paper package. So far so good. She unwrapped the product, which revealed two small blocks of wood. Lifting the top block revealed a printed piece of paper which gave instructions on how to use it. It read:

PLACE THE OFFENDING FLY ON THE LOWER BLOCK OF WOOD.
TAKE THE UPPER BLOCK AND BRING IT DOWN FIRMLY ON THE FLY.
THIS IS GUARANTEED TO KILL IT.

There is no arguing with this.

2

ARTISTIC BENTS

The reader will undoubtedly gather through the pages of this book that I am not overtly modest, and with this in mind I feel I must brag about my artistic prowess.

I think it was in the autumn of 1948 that I was encouraged to pursue my artistic muse. Mr Brown our prep school master was not like his colleagues, for instance he hardly ever wore his academic gown, only on special occasions and then probably under duress. His jackets were invariably loose, his corduroy trousers baggy and he always wore a bright cravat in lieu of the more formal tie – yet, in his way and looking back, I regarded him as sartorially casual. His grey-tinged hair belied a youthful, florid face and a rather lazy drawl was his manner of speech. However, he taught me to observe, to look at things in detail – an artist's eye, he said – and showed me how to use colours. Of course, at the age of eight I would not be as perceptive as I am looking back, but something must have clicked and in time I produced a painting of a large London omnibus, startlingly red but considered good enough to send off to the children's exhibition at the National Gallery. Sometime later I was told that I had won first prize in my age group and was presented with £25 … a lot of pocket money! However, this was not all, for in those days, the weekly pictorial news appeared squeezed between the main film in cinemas, known as the A film, and a lesser film, presumably with inferior actors or of shorter duration, known as the B film. Two newsreel companies competed against each other, one I remember being Movietone, and this said in a crisp, urgent voice: 'Lionel Gamlin reporting.'

The other was Pathé News and showed a cockerel crowing, both of course in monochrome. Now this is hard to believe but I appeared, I think, on the former newsreel, 'Lionel Gamlin reporting', and here I am paraphrasing, but it went something along these lines:

'Today, their Majesties attended the National Gallery and saw the artists of tomorrow.' (Actually they didn't see us but only our paintings but it sounds good.)

'Children of exceptional ability; here they admire the much loved London bus, the work of nine-year-old Lawrence Stacey who gains first prize. A name we will hear much more of in the future, no doubt. Good luck to him and the other talented youngsters.' Wasn't that wonderful and wasn't I exceptionally clever, you'll agree?

Well, what happened? Well, nothing really. I can just about draw a straight line but only with the aid of a ruler, but don't despair – all was not lost.

At the age of fifteen our holiday reading was *Great Expectations* by Charles Dickens. This I failed to read but I was taken by my mother to see the film at the local cinema the night before I returned to school. This ploy was standard, for I always got collywobbles as term time was approaching and I would be forced to leave my mother. I don't think I called it by this name at the time, but having consulted the dictionary it gives the perfect symptoms: 'abdominal pain, or nervous stomach', which was me. However, once at school I settled down reasonably well, although on this occasion apprehensive about the forthcoming test on the unread book. The test, however, was not forthcoming, but instead we were told to write an essay which I was able to crib perfectly from certain aspects of the film, the scene in the graveyard, I think. Anyway, here I could let my imagination take flight and I completed the essay and breathed a sigh of relief, at least I had not been caught out. Two or three months had elapsed, when one morning the headmaster announced at assembly that one of the pupils at the school had won the public schools essay prize – or some such title. This student, the panel had predicted, would have a fine future either in journalism or some form of professional writing. Would Stacey of the Fifth Form step up and receive a gold star and a handshake from the Head? This I did but I was totally bemused and somewhat bewildered. Brickbats I could take, but bouquets were hard to handle and few and far between. Later in the year I was to set a new house record for 'three of the best' twelve days running.

Well, what happened about the writing? Well, nothing really. No novels flowed from my pen or sensational headlines issued from a crackling telephone from our foreign correspondent in some far-flung corner of the globe – a few short stories perchance, but probably unread.

Never mind, this tale does have a happy ending and concludes as follows. I was at my club, 100, Piccadilly, London, some twenty years later when I entered the reading room to take in the Sunday papers. The room, I should point out, has nineteen-foot full-length windows giving a beautiful view of Green Park across the road. Here, every Sunday morning for as long as I can remember, various artists display their works on the railings and who should I suddenly see but my old mentor Mr Brown. I raced across to see him, and I still called him sir, of course. Little compensation, alas, for the fact that the club porter then wouldn't make an exception for the artist – he wasn't wearing a tie would you believe and I suspect the corduroys were the ones I had seen before. But it was wonderful to shake his hand and say thank you.

THE GEORDIE BOY, MADE GOOD?

As I mentioned, I was born in the north-eastern town of South Shields, in the County of Durham, on 6 March 1940. It will never be described with epithets such as 'pleasant', 'leafy' or 'beautiful', for it was blackened by coal from its collieries and noisy from the steam hammers of its dockyards, reverberating about the town. I can even recall the omnipresent smell when the whaling ships arrived with their gross cargo, to be carved up in dock, when the stench of whale oil enveloped us all.

I remember, too, the screeching hooters going on the River Tyne; these sirens announced the workmen's lunchtime and hundreds of men, their overalls dirtied by toil, would be disgorged from the yards to board the blue and white corporation buses, perhaps twenty in line, all going to different destinations within the community. It must have been a highly efficient drill, as I believe it was all completed within the hour. Their wives with careful preparation had a hot plate of food ready and waiting for them, it was consumed in double-quick time and the menfolk would board the bus which had by then completed its circuit on its return journey to the workplace. It also testifies to the fact that in the late 1940s and early 1950s the roads were traffic-free, giving the buses a clear run.

I remember the seafront, often windswept and forbidding as dark clouds rolled in from the restless North Sea, drenching the shoreline in torrents of rain. I still hear with a certain trepidation the sonorous mourn of the foghorns; to me it was the knell of witches, devils and death. The wealthier part of town had neat streets and gardens with some well-laid-out lawns; there was even a farm between the two parts of town. The farmer plied his wares in a well-turned-out horse and buggy with milk churns and ladle. In particular the cemetery seemed, with its floral borders and abundance of colours, a sanctuary of peace and beauty. Certainly at that age I did not associate it with death, just pleasant walks and my baby sister's Silver Cross pram, sprung, substantial, beautifully crafted with its golden carriage lines painted over its lustred black body. But this tranquillity was about to be brought to an end.

A Labour Government decreed that pre-fabricated houses should be built on our adjacent green fields and diggers and other building impedimenta soon began to despoil our genteel surroundings. To us five-year-olds this was seen as one gigantic fun fair, for with no health and safety rules and regulations one had novel climbing frames, wondrous missiles and weapons. Oil drums littered the site and these could be used for a miscellany of purposes, the tops making robust steel shields which were painted in authentic heraldic fashion. My highly imaginative and wayward (well, spoilt) sister Patricia, some five years older, had me locked in a pre-fab for many hours until a local search party eventually found me. However, our joy was short-lived, as those unfortunate people whose homes lay clustered in the industrial bomb zone of the war moved into healthier housing; for instance, all had bathrooms and lavatories inside the house and each had some form of garden, albeit small.

The children's background, however, was different, and if on occasion one was forced to run the gauntlet of the 'baddies', or 'slummies', then one could expect a beating. At the tender age of six I was usually on the receiving end of such affrays, but as I grew older I became more adept at dealing with such situations and during one confrontation I was proclaimed a hero, as I sat on a bag of cream cakes which were destined for some child's birthday party. My mother recovered the situation with a timely 5/- (or 5 bob as we would say) to the boy's parents.

Such, briefly, was the environment of my youth, but in spite of all that I have said, one should not presume that I am at all derogatory about the north-east, for its people make it an area of 'outstanding beauty' – obviously not in the sense of conventional grace or form but in their friendliness and down-to-earth approach to life and personal relationships. They are unimpressed by wealth, status and the flippancy of class distinction; they rather look to the inward man and see the genuine person.

In 1949 I travelled home at the end of the term – King's Cross, London to Newcastle. The journey north was one of exhilaration and joy; in reverse it was a morose experience which no child should go through. I recall that the train that steamed into the glass-covered station, hissing and puffing and generally remonstrating at its harsh exertions over a tedious journey, usually arrived at platform 2. On this occasion, due to engineering works, it came into platform number 9, a venue unknown to me. I therefore stepped onto the platform, somewhat bewildered at my unfamiliar surroundings, to confront a porter.

'Excuse me, sir,' I said, raising my badged school cap, 'can you take me to my mother who is waiting for me by the clock in the main station?' I was dressed in polished black leather shoes, long grey socks, punctiliously pulled up to the knees and restrained with garters. My blue blazer was also badged with the school motto, *Audi, Vide, Tace* ('Hear, See, Be Silent', something which

I have consistently failed to follow), and my cream shirt with detachable stiff collar was complemented by a two-tone dark and light blue tie (the collar, though, would have been liberally spotted with soot from the anthracite coal of the locomotive – in those days we were able to stick our heads out of the window and see the countryside flash by). Clearly not a local. I clutched a small case in my right hand (the heavy baggage, travelling under the misnomer of 'luggage in advance', arrived two or three days later at home). The porter led me to my mother who was standing sentinel at the clock, which I am assured is still there today. She was slim, pretty, high-heeled with lovely legs, in an eye-catching hat and I think a Russian-styled high buttoned jacket. She exuded charm and her green eyes and flashing smile displayed a genuine gratitude for the porter's thoughtfulness.

'Thank you so much for bringing my son to me ... you are so kind,' she enthused, 'thank you so much.'

His taciturn mien changed in the face of such overwhelming femininity.

'Hey missus,' he said, in his beautiful Geordie accent, 'Ee what a canny little lad, ee impeccable manners, ya know, canny lad, if, I tuck him home to the missus ya know ee, she would luv him the little bairn – just luv him she would.'

My Mother, proud of her prodigy, thanked him even more profusely, which prompted my earlier observation of being unimpressed by class.

'The only thing is missus, does the bairn have to speak like this for the rest of his life – it's a terrible affliction ya know.' He was in no way being unkind, just noting what he believed in. To non-Geordies, a good education was a way out of the industrial north with its hard manual labour, intermittent piece-work and its unhealthy atmosphere. But not so for the Geordies. Independent, proud of their heritage and achievements, and lackey to no man. Such a sign of upward mobility was not worth losing one's soul for, certainly not losing one's Geordie birthright for, and that birthright included the vernacular!

On another occasion, a good thirty years later, I took my children to the boating park, opposite the Grace Darling lifeboat of 1888 (rescuer of the survivors of the *Forfarshire*). There, three dear old ladies came to admire our children, all under six or so.

'Bonny bairns,' they remarked. There then followed a conversation of some minutes which terminated in the observation, 'Ee, ye not rooned these quarters, are ye?'

'Why do you say that?' I asked.

'Ee, well, yer don't half speak funny, hinny yer foreign or something, aren't yer?'

Traitorous me, a foreigner in my own land of South Shields.

4

THE KISS

I have always loved the fair sex. I suppose it must have started with my mother whom I always regarded as beautiful, but there again when she was widowed our home was very much female-orientated. I was bracketed between two ugly sisters, one approximately five years younger than me and the other five years older. We had a young Irish maid, Mary Pigott, whom we all liked, fair-skinned, with light ginger hair and blue eyes. Her mother, who visited us once, was terrifying, the nearest thing to a witch I had met aged five. She was wild with unruly black-wire-type hair, deep-set fiery jet eyes, an ample bosom and a loud, shrill voice which was alien to my ears, being heavily accented Irish. She told us, as a devout Roman Catholic, 'that Mary aged three had died and gone to Heaven, God rest her soul, but the Lord in his wisdom and love for children had returned her to earth to serve his needs' … in this case ours! My mother said that the diatribe delivered by her went on interminably regarding Mary's resurrection, needless to say we looked upon this young thing as divine (not that I knew the meaning of the word then) … a sort of modern day Nanny McPhee.

Mary was gentle, kind and loved her adopted family. Her only drawback was that she had 'nits', I think that's what we called them, so ever since 'nits' and ginger hair have been synonymous. So unfair to any ginger-haired person reading this who has not been bored so far, but if she had been dark-haired then I would have identified all dark-haired people as having 'nits' and that would be even more unfair as there are many more dark-haired people in the world than ginger. Oh shut up! I also thought that all girls were therefore beautiful (apart from my two ugly sisters), divine and gentle. I had no inkling that females had normal bodily functions, like us uncouth boys, even now with my wife and two beautiful daughters I find it hard to believe. Men belch and pass wind and are generally unwholesome and malodorous, whereas girls seem to smell of flowers and I imagine pass puff balls of exotic perfumes. I also observe my wife and my girls' hands, with long expressive fingers, slender like chocolate matchsticks and so vulnerable and weak; in short, pure and lovely. In all my time at home I knew nothing of what is now freely advertised on TV of the female cycle, probably only becoming aware of such things as an officer-cadet at Sandhurst.

Anyway, I have hopefully established the fact that my passion for women was founded on love and purity, that is until I went to public school and there discovered the maids. Generally speaking these were young girls, some Irish, many Cockney and local village types, and furthermore about our ages, fifteen to eighteen. The maids came out of swing doors like a cabaret act in our impressive wood-panelled, high-beamed dining hall, pushing their trolleys with a Monroe wiggle. They knew full well the effect they had on the older boys whose testosterone like sap from the trees was beginning to rise. The grand entrance was made towards the end of every meal to collect the piled-up plates at the end of the long refectory tables. Those older boys with seniority would say to the younger ones opposite, 'leave those dirty plates in front of you,' thus requiring the delightful Doris or the voluptuous June to bend over the junior boy's back, stretch over and collect the crockery.

June was plump, cheeky and pretty; she also wore no bra but was more than amply bestowed. The seniors therefore had a wonderful view of these magnificent mammary glands and would generally swoon and discuss the merits of June, Doris or whoever in a serious sort of way in the cloisters afterwards. I can't remember it being vulgar, more like discussing wine. However, this may not be all true, as I recall as a Fifth Former singing, 'June is bursting out all over,' as she leaned towards me. She smiled but it was all a set-up, for the duty master, Mr 'Henry' Hall, a tall, powerful man, was standing right behind and lifted me up by my right ear and led me out of the dining hall to be caned later. All this in front of those 'skivvies' whom I wanted to impress.

I went off June and turned my attention to Doris. She was slim and cute, with black, shortish hair and a strong Cockney accent which always seemed to be authoritative. I am told that this would be called 'lippy' in today's terminology. Doris was a better bet for she worked in my house, Burwood, every day polishing the beautiful dormitory floors where only slippers were allowed. She also made our beds, neater than any hospital with 45 degree tucked-in counterpane corners. These had the school crest emblazoned in the middle, as did the chamber pots which were always aligned perfectly underneath our identical beds. All shipshape and perfect, so unlike my two sons' dormitories, where untidy, lumpy duvets sport Batman, pop stars or other icons of similar frivolity. How unbecoming! With Doris in the 'dorms' one could of course sneak up and have a chat, providing Matron or one of the older maids wasn't around. (I only referred to them in the common vernacular 'skivvies' when they upset me.) One day I crept up to see her and I found her painting her legs brown to represent nylons … with Oxo cubes or something. This was a requirement when they went out with the American GIs down the road – indeed, for special dates their friends painted black lines down their legs to represent seams. This seemed silly to me as they told me they only went out with the Yanks to get silk stockings anyway, but presumably they were only given them at the end of the evening if they had come up to the mark! Silk stockings were still expensive into the 1950s, I am told. In fact, when pantyhose came out and one leg was laddered the girls would match up an odd leg from a previously laddered pair ... which wasn't fair in my opinion as they then had a double line of defence, actually triple, if you count the panties too. This could be a bit of a tussle, if I remember correctly.

My lust for the delectable Doris became unbearable but after all these weeks totally unrequited. One morning I slipped away and asked if I could see her that night in the village. My fecund, evil brain had come up with a splendid plan. There was to be a scripture Union meeting in the local village hall at 7 p.m. that night. Now it so happened that I was the only pupil doing GCE scripture and the Reverend Harry Hoskins (later BBC) thought that my suggestion of attending this not only worthwhile but divinely inspired – perhaps I would take Holy Orders! Indeed, so impressed was he by my religiosity that I was later awarded the senior scripture prize (*Robbery Under Arms*, Rolf Boldrewood and *Ben Hur*, Lew Wallace, 7 June 1955 ... I still have them!). He therefore contacted my very strict Victorian housemaster, Mr Walton (so senior and so old that he didn't even possess a Christian name), to ask if I could attend. Luckily this was all agreed and I therefore had a free hand to see my potential paramour. The scripture meeting began at 7 p.m. and I suspected that I would be free by 8.30. I would therefore meet her by a disused railway tunnel on a minor back road.

I felt a bit uneasy, for all the while that I was being directed towards pure thoughts of Jesus, my head was brimming with carnal thoughts of Doris! Perhaps a bolt of lightning would strike me down at the critical moment or the devil claim me and I would sprout horns or something – all these thoughts were jumbled in my brain. That was the trouble with religion – all the guilt. Now of course there is no dichotomy: sex first every time.

However, I am jumping the gun: there was a great deal of preparation to be done. I must borrow a bicycle for timing was important – I needed to be back in the dormitory by 10 p.m. If I arrived on time this gave me a good hour plus for my plan of seduction. I had some Cedar Wood aftershave, my collar stiffener of wire, an essential piece of equipment for our new flannel shirts (the detachable collars had been dispensed with) was new from Woolworths, some Brylcreem was acquired to maintain a magnificent quiff, so popular at the time – really vulgar in hindsight – and a friend of mine instructed me on how to do the banned Windsor knot, rather fat and just as vulgar as the quiff. The blazer in the Fifth Form was secured on the bottom-most button of the three, allowing the shoulder pads to be pushed back to give one accentuated broader shoulders (also banned). It was probably copied from the Teddy Boys of the time and in hindsight terrible. However, what I really needed to practise was the walk with the bicycle. When I was on school 'hols', I noted that all the apprentices and workmen in the Vickers factory at Byker, Newcastle-upon-Tyne, would stroll out of the gates chatting before mounting their drop-handle-bar 'steeds' for home. They had the knack of holding the saddle of the machine and pushing it in this way, the front wheel miraculously following a straight line. I had also perfected this strategy of coolness but the sit-up-and-beg bicycle that I had acquired for the night was unsophisticated and it didn't really know the form; try as I may I only got it right 50 per cent of the time. I could only hope it would be all right on the night. The other thing I had to bear in mind was the October night – should it be cold or raining, what then was I to do? My school cap also presented a problem; I would have to take it off jolly quickly, as a grown-up girl like Doris would certainly find it a turn-off. Lastly, I was advised to eat some cachous which came in a tiny painted tin – they represented the apogee of sophistication and must not be forgotten.

The stage was set then and I must have complimented myself on my sedulous preparation for the great seduction of adorable Doris. I remember nothing of the religious meeting, only, as I said, my guilt competing with my lascivious thoughts. I was up and away on schedule and cycled furiously, my heart pounding at the thought of my first sexual encounter. By now it was well and truly dark, which was good, as I thought that sex took place only in the dark. A light misty rain was beginning to fall as I rounded the insalubrious corner of this ex-wartime industrial area with the satanic tunnel barely lit by a nearby gas lamp. There stood the object of my desire, standing in a classical Soho pose, one leg thrown slightly forward supporting her body and the other propping up the tunnel wall in the form of a triangle. The glow of a cigarette-end traced a parabola from mouth to leg. In retrospect it was not the most romantic of settings but my young body was inflamed as I dismounted and with total nonchalance (but carefully orchestrated) threw the bicycle to the ground. My cap went into my pocket. She stood just inside the tunnel so we were at least dry. The cigarette had dropped to the ground as I eagerly took her into my arms. I don't think we spoke but my trembling lips were already hard pressed against hers and for seconds we were locked together as one. (Perhaps I should write for Mills & Boon…?) Everything had so far gone to plan and I knew that my unused power of osculation was a success, for I felt her tapping and then pushing on my shoulder … a form of surrender, I guess, a 'take me now' sort of thing. I knew that I would be a natural romantic. We broke for breath.

'Ere. Ere. Wot d'yer think yer bleeding doing then?' she panted.

'Well, I am kissing you Doris,' I replied, somewhat nonplussed.

'Yer bleeding wot, that's not snogging, yer got to open yer mouth and put yer bleeding tongue in my mouth and wiggle it about a bit,' she exclaimed with conviction.

I don't think in the darkness she could have seen my face turn ashen. She grabbed me again, reiterating, 'Now put yer bloody tongue in!'

I broke free. Oh, how horrible, I thought.

'Doris, I don't think I can do that,' I said, stepping backwards, collecting my bicycle, replacing my headdress and returning my blazer to the correct button … and with that I fled into the night.

Postscript

Doris didn't date me again but she left under my pillow a small handkerchief of hers with her lipstick on it. This was secured to the inside of my locker door with drawing pins, for lesser mortals to come and pay homage to – I suspect I never mentioned anything to my friends other than my success of course! The silk stockings acquired from the Yanks may have been free at the point of entry but were paid for nine months later. She left soon after when Matron noticed that she was putting on weight. Anyway, the song says 'A Kiss to Build a Dream On' – but for me a sad little story.

5

Trawler Days

At the age of thirteen, Terry Freeman's swearing was already deeply impressive. I was about the same age when first I met him, a real local lad, whose profanities were uttered in the strongest possible Geordie accent. His many bad habits were similarly legion. He had come knocking on our door one day, when I was away at school. He was probably casing the joint, but certainly selling something and of course my mother not only bought the dusters or polish or whatever it was but also invited him in and dispensed tea and biscuits. She told him that she had a son of his age and when he returned for the school holidays he would love to meet him. This was how I was paired with the unfortunate Terry.

I say unfortunate, but really it was I who suffered the most from this bizarre relationship. Terry became a semi-permanent feature in our household, sharing meals with the family and generally being my shadow. I should add that there was a role reversal as soon as we stepped into the outside world. Terry ran a gang of teenagers who seemed to be in fear of him. He would be equally at home with my mother as he was with twenty-year-olds, both men and women, who appeared to treat him with respect and regard him as their equal. He was clearly a leader as he would cosy up to those shady characters who confronted him on street corners and back alleys. I was unaware of drugs in 1953 and looking back I now think that he was involved in betting – 'runners' were employed as betting shops were illegal and did not exist then. I suspect that he was also a 'fence' for stolen goods and I would not have put it past him to do a little breaking and entering himself. We were, in common parlance, as different as chalk and cheese, in dress, in conversation, in interests and in background. He was at thirteen already a man of the world – a world I could neither enter nor understand. In comparison I was still a child; I still enjoyed playing with my electric train set ... it was just before my mother gave it away! As 'his shadow', when we were out in the big bad world, his older accomplices would nod and cast a dubious glance towards me.

'Wees he?' they would say confrontationally.

'He's alreet, div'n't wurry,' Terry would reply and continue the deal. The gang, when they were truanting from school, all smoked – indeed, it was essential to do so, as it was an undoubted mark of manliness. Smoking to us was a sin, and boys were expelled for even having a puff or two. This was a boundary I couldn't cross, as was their promiscuity, which was discussed in passing; whereas our class or age group discussed it and lived in hope, these people did just the opposite – barely mentioned it but seemed to have access to it. I suppose saying that it was a bizarre relationship doesn't even approach the magnitude or depth of division that existed between us.

I knew my mother's rationale in befriending Terry through me. She knew of his sad upbringing and thought that the example of a stable, secure and loving home might influence him for the better. Over time, I discovered that both his parents had been in prison – his mother came and went, for soliciting, drink and the like but his father was in for a long stretch. His only sister, who ran the home when their mother was inside, was on 'the game'. I thought that games were healthy and fun and I am sure that I didn't associate it with prostitution until a little while later.

One day, perhaps it was a special occasion, my mother told me that I should invite Terry for dinner. It was then I told her that I really didn't think this was a good idea. Terry was a Teddy Boy, a thug, both his parents were in prison and his elder sister hung around the bars on the quayside earning her living by sleeping with the sailors that still came into the docks. He wasn't of our standing and nothing that we could do or say would change him – he was the bottom of the heap. By this my mother deduced that I regarded myself as being at the top of it – both extremes she regarded as bad. The bottom strata may be involved in dishonesty, even thuggery, but this was brought about by poverty or misfortune, the premature death of the breadwinner, for instance. However, to put oneself at the other end of the social scale was just as indefensible, for so often it meant taking advantage of such a situation and it produced arrogance and snobbery. The ideal lay somewhere in the middle.

I can't remember whether Terry came for dinner or not – probably, my mother usually got her way – but I do remember, as if it was yesterday, her lecture to me regarding class. 'Darling,' she said, 'a gentleman is a man who can make a duke or a dustman feel at home and until you have mastered this art of respect for all then you are still a boy.' She told me that it had its practical side too. My deceased father, as a young midshipman-cadet, had passed the galley one day when he heard the steward say to the cook, 'This is the Captain's.'

The cook responded simply but effectively: 'Bastard,' he said, and spat into the soup.

My father had said that if he ever became a Captain he would always be nice to the catering staff! Well, I can see the logic behind that – but I hope that I have taken the lesson to heart that my mother tried to teach me that day. Certainly the practical lesson to reinforce the theory was extremely effective and took me by surprise.

‡

My mother in her wisdom had decided that I needed to be 'socialised', to see how the other half lived, to be thankful for what we had and to learn above all else the common touch. We were all brothers and had a common duty towards each other. To this end, she announced that she had got me a trip on a trawler. It was one of Irving's fleet from North Shields, a deep sea trawler, bound for the Icelandic fishing grounds. North Shields in 1955 was a veritable hive of activity – trawlers of all types prowled the fishing fields, returning from Iceland and the Dogger Bank with their catches. I can see the fish markets along the harbour – early morning affairs, where the middleman would come to purchase in bulk. The language of bidding was unknown to me – fast, staccato, signs, deals dealt, boxes full of fish slid away, money passing hands, all purchased in the blink of an eye. By 9 a.m. there was no evidence that there had even been a market at all, just a swilled-down quayside and empty boxes piled high. Even the seagulls had left to steal elsewhere. I recall all the trawlers as rusty, unpainted, neglected externally with a miscellany of buckets, trawling nets, wickerwork baskets of all shapes and sizes and derricks and equipment of every conceivable type. Some of the ships were puffing smoke and all were festooned with old tyres which rubbed against the adjacent boats as they rose and fell in the ever-moving sea. The occasional figure would emerge on deck to perform some necessity or other; all were in strange dress and uniformity of anything seemed an absurdity. It was a world unknown to anyone not involved in it and I was soon to be baptised into this rough and ready society. If one were to return today there is nothing, as if it had never been.

The day of my departure dawned and we left early in order that the ship could depart on an early tide. My mother, as ever, looked incongruously smart as she stood among the smell of fish boxes and the like. Her presence, I suspect, led the owner or manager to come and say hello. He was brutally direct as he said to her, 'Nice to meet you missus, now this lad of yours, ye realise he's on his own – in fact I'll go as far to say that as soon as he opens his mooth, he'll have a bloody fish hook in his back.' As I remember, she had smiled and said something to the effect that I would therefore have to tread carefully. No kisses were exchanged in this mightily masculine atmosphere. A dull, cloudy June day ushered us out of the harbour as the nightmare began.

The trawler was built around 1903 and had served in both world wars as a minesweeper. It had given valuable service but in reality it was now a rust bucket and by today's standards would definitely have failed its seaworthy test, for it had no modern amenities and refits in boats of this kind were probably unheard of, other than essential gear. I was shown to the very bow of the vessel and noted there was nothing between me and the sea, just the red-oxide-painted metal plates. The condensation ran down in rivulets and the big rivet nuts were neatly aligned along the plates. It was cold now but I could not imagine what it was like in winter, for there was no insulation and certainly no form of heating. The two-tiered wooden bunks were as sparse as they could be; even the dreaded Victorian workhouse demanded standards higher than this. The cabin, if one could really describe it as such, was so small that I rubbed shoulders with my companions as I placed a holdall containing toothbrush, washing kit and a pullover or two on the bunk. It was then I heard my own voice echo, 'Oh, my goodness I have forgotten my bed sheets.' To this day I remember the atmosphere froze, time stood still a little and my three crew-mates seemed to stop for an instant, not only for the crass remark but for the alien voice that made it. I was soon to find that the bunk beds were an irrelevance for on this trip at least, the palliasse and rough blanket (there was no such thing as a pillow) were seldom used for reasons which will become apparent. As the trawler steamed out of harbour, I was told that once over the bar the sea would become rougher, our voyage to the Icelandic fishing fields would take no longer than three weeks and was expected to be relatively comfortable at this time of year. I noticed the seagulls were our ever-present companions night and day but prolifically so when the nets were being hauled in. The crew were as odd an assortment of fellows as one could ever expect to meet, but there again what man in his right mind would ever subject himself to such harsh conditions? No film of Blackbeard and his gang could ever intimidate me in the future – I knew them well having met them all on 'the trawler'. Sad to relate I can't remember its name, but there again it had probably been eroded over the years as it took on the full force of North Sea storms during its long life of many winters. I was given a penknife which I was told was for gutting the fish. This was my first embarrassment for, try as I may, I could not open it. I think that I still may have it somewhere – it certainly was around for many years. The Skipper was a youngish chap, fair and athletic as he negotiated the gangways and ladders, bridge to deck and vice versa. Sometimes he washed and shaved, which was an unusual habit. The cook, always puffing on his woodbines, befriended me. He was small, a little pot-bellied, with balding ginger hair but he liked my company – perhaps because I did a lot of washing up, a good symbiosis for it got me out of gutting.

Undoubtedly, though, the man who I still remember vividly was André, an exotic name to find aboard such a worn-out trawler. André was the senior hand. He was, he thought, born about 1885 or marginally before, which put him well and truly into the Victorian age. He had been at sea since he was ten and had endured all kinds of deprivation, both in the Merchant and Royal Navy. He had been shipwrecked and had seen the globe in all its brutality in the hundreds of ports he had visited worldwide. He had also served in both world wars and survived to tell the tale of Atlantic and Arctic convoys. I wish that I could remember his tales for they were history then. He still had the strength of a much younger man and his work output was prodigious, as was his licentiousness. His ABC of life was simple: 'Ale, Baccy and C ... and if I can't get C then a boy will do.' If I had been brave enough to suggest that there was a trace of homosexuality in his philosophy he would undoubtedly have killed me, for that was disgusting, whereas his conduct was a matter of mere expediency!

André would stand legs straight but apart, bending over the fish, and gut for two or three hours without ceasing. He had a mischievous sense of humour for he chewed his tobacco endlessly and would always make a point of sitting next to me as we ate a hurried meal. Our crude wooden table had certain divisions in which plates and mugs could go in the event of a severe pitch or roll. My bread was invariably next to his on the flat and he would be ever so diligent in spitting out his 'baccy' right next to my bread, just touching the crust. I would watch as the bubbles of his saliva popped on my bread, and if I surreptitiously moved it, his hand (as he turned to talk to others) would move it again, transgressing my space, but making it appear a total accident.

It was André who showed me what to do when I cut myself gutting. It was simple really: cut out and wash the stomach of some unspecified fish, and lo it acted like an Elastoplast – well better really, for it could envelope a finger by rolling over the top of it like a prophylactic, similar to sheep guts and sausages. Which prompts one to ask why they were never used as condoms ... but André certainly used this method for cuts. It was also André who put me on the spot and caused me great confusion. I don't think he was being malicious, just mischievous and having a laugh at my expense.

We hadn't been long out of harbour, six hours or so, when the Skipper ordered the nets to be put over, huge trawls on either side of the ship, and I knew that I would soon be gutting, therefore my knife would need to be opened. It was to the cook that I turned. He made no comment but merely flicked it open – how could it be so simple? Trawling usually took about three hours, and at the end of that time the nets were recovered. The catch was good – indeed, considered exceptional, like the disciples by the shore of Galilee. It was accompanied by shouts of delight and great merriment and now work began in earnest. I was instructed in the art of gutting fish, and for someone who doesn't like the sight of blood I coped quite well.

First, I remember that the nets disgorged fish of every shape, size, dimension and colour. They came up to my knees, their mouths opening and closing involuntarily, thrashing their tails, wriggling and tumbling over each other in their bid to regain freedom. The smell became overpowering, the seagulls excited and me nauseous at the sight of guts and blood. My first fish, indeed all fish, felt like cutting through tinsel. I was told how to cut away the guts and these I threw over the side to the delight of the gulls, noisy, aggressive birds who swooped and caught them mid-air. The livers were thrown into a large drum to become the cod liver oil that as children we had been 'force fed' during the austerity of wartime;

it supplemented the crews' wages and was their perk. The gutting, packing, icing and storage of the fish completed, the decks were swilled down, cigarettes rolled and tea or a hasty meal taken and then it was time for the next catch to be sorted. The whole process was repeated again and again. The crew's morale was high even though sleep became sparse and meals rushed affairs. Later, I was to learn that the seafarers were extremely superstitious and the fact that they had a funny young boy aboard who seemed to bring them miraculous catches was a sign of good fortune ... a sure protection for the voyage. It was during one such gutting session, amid curses, laughs and general banter which went over my head, not only because of subject matter but also the dialect, that André turned to me and said,

'Hinny, have you ever f***** a skate?'

'I am sorry André,' I said, genuinely thinking that I had not heard him correctly.

'Have you ever f***** a skate, lad?'

I pondered the question carefully, as if trying to give the impression that I was counting ... camel, donkey, skate – if only they knew that at this stage of my life coition of anything was nil.

'No André, no ... I don't think so ... well ... no actually, never,' I said with embarrassment.

The crew all laughed riotously at my expense.

'Hey Skipper,' André addressed his cupped hand to the bridge, 'the lad's never had a skate.'

'Ah well,' came the reply, 'he's new crew so he can f*** the next one.'

I then lived in fear and trepidation of catching a skate. If only I'd known that I was a good omen, it may in some way have allayed my fear. The tiredness of the crew was offset by our continually good catches, until one day the dreaded cry came. In fact, I had just taken a mug of tea up to the wheelhouse for the Skipper when I heard, 'Hey Skipper, we've caught the f****** skate.'

'Haway, lad,' the Skipper said, grabbing my arm and swinging me down the ladder behind him.

André picked up the fish, a big flat one.

'Hinny, look at that. You'll never see a finer fanny than that,' and here he demonstrated with his hand.

Life on the ship came to a stop … it was like a Fellini film, and I recall it all so vividly, though in tones of black and white, probably because it was black and cloudy and the heavens lay low and brooding and a light rain was falling. The cook came out on deck, wiping his hands. The engineer, a Spaniard with a large-brimmed hat which he always wore, was followed by his taciturn apprentice from below decks. The engines, I think, had been cut for I seem to remember we gently bobbed on the surface just like a cork. The skate was held in front of me baring its delight. 'I'll hold it lad,' said a crewman, 'howay, now give it a go … its good, soft ya know, you'll enjoy it man, luvely like.'

I recalled what Mr Irving had said to my mother, about the fish hook in my back. I imagined the cabal all back in port, all swearing on oath to the fact that I must have jumped overboard in the middle of the night. 'Homesick' 'unhappy' and 'seasick'. What could the police do? They weren't there. The crew would cling together and present a united front. All this went through my mind as I saw the anticipation on their unshaven faces, a disparate group of men with their bloody gutting knives held limp, oilskins and wellingtons, balaclavas and home-knitted hats, a real hotchpotch of men expecting a show – me against thirteen or so. Had my mother really intended this lesson to be taught so well?

I looked at them defiantly and shouted, not too loud as I recall, but determinedly,

'You can all f*** off now.'

With this, I pushed aside the crewman and the skate and moved back to the gutting area. My friend the cook, still wiping his hands on a cloth, was the first to smile and turn away, then another laughed and yet another, soon all were laughing and those near me clapped me on the back. The spell had been broken – steam let off and the tension of all this hard work and sleepless nights forgotten. The good omen continued, for a twenty-one-day trip was completed in half the time, and we had to return to port as our holds were bulging to full capacity.

The sight of North Shields, not a town that would normally evoke a pulling on the heartstrings, hove into sight. Our battered little trawler with her intrepid crew was going home happy with the money they would earn, but no one was happier than me. I had learned a great deal about human nature, of men and their needs: much of this would reveal itself with hindsight, especially men's sexuality and basic aggressiveness, which I was to find the female species devoid of. The skate, incidentally, is a fish which procreates like us. Its fleshy vagina, I was assured, made the fish appealing to sailors of old, who reputedly strapped it to the mast. They justified its use when females went unseen for months on end. The landlubber may find this offensive but the sea is a cruel master and men became dehumanised serving in the navies of the world, when floggings were prevalent, and disease, bad food and death constant companions. I was to witness similar thoughts, if not actions, when soldiers emerged from prolonged duty in the jungles of Borneo. No, life on board a 1903 trawler was hard. Looking back there was only one lavatory on board and this I think was unused, as I remember removing rope ladders to gain access. The rusty door didn't close and the whole thing faced the Skipper's bridge. I think the crew went over the side!

Terra firma was a great experience when we eventually docked. I was given an oilskin bag to take home, filled with fish ... but not a skate! I remember feeling immensely proud and a real man as I stepped off the gangplank onto the quayside, for my gait was that of a real jack-tar, a bona fide rolling movement. The bus home presented problems as the fish, although very fresh, did seem to attract attention. Perhaps my fellow passengers noticed that this was no boy, but one who had now attained manhood. Anyway, I was wished well by my fellow crew members and, because I had brought them luck and good fortune, the Skipper's farewell remark was most gratifying,

'Lad, yer welcome back anytime.'

I suspect I was: years later I found that my mother had to pay for my privilege!

Postscript

I don't know what I told my mother – certainly not about the skate. However, years later at a fish market in Germany, I recounted my distasteful but true story to the fishmonger. 'Ah yes,' he said, 'perfectly true; that's why by law we always have to quarter [e.g. cut into four] our skates when displayed in shops.'

There was also a silver lining to my arduous trip, for when I took the Regular Commissions Board exam, a three-day test of leadership skills for RMA Sandhurst, my lecture was on trawling. The board thought that I had shown great initiative to put myself through such a task. So my mother's remedy proved effective, not only for the Army but hopefully for my relationships with fellow human beings in the future.

6

THE RELUCTANT
FLOWER SELLER

I have always been somewhat diligent in my mode of dress, and in that regard my youth was very different to that of my own children. I suspect there may have been an element of deprivation, for back in the 1940s clothes coupons were introduced and the population was encouraged towards thrift in all matters – as opposed to our profligate society of today, a truly throw-away and wasteful world, especially in the West.

I can recall an almost Dickensian scene in my home town of South Shields. It was 1945 and the war had taken its toll on the people of the north-east, who were certainly unbowed by the antics of Hitler but were nevertheless war-weary. They had suffered more than most for the area was still a major supplier of coal and shipbuilding on the Tyne, Wear and Tees had a worldwide reputation – in short, heavy industry did not make for green pastures and healthy people.

I was standing next to a forlorn figure, a boy of about my age of five years, with his mother who had also known better times. Their poverty was obvious for I recall the young lad having bare feet – perhaps, at best, he had some form of open sandals. He had no socks, no coat but a ragged pullover. In the heavy rain, as we patiently waited for the bus, both he and his mother shivered uncontrollably. It was approaching Christmas but few lights or decorations proclaimed that this was the case. My mother was clearly upset by the state of the pair – added to this the mother coughed badly, so I learnt later. It was obvious that money was non-existent and who was to say what terrible times they had experienced. My mother took off my blue Burberry and gave it to the little boy, pressing him to her in order to control the shaking of his puny body. She apologised profusely because I had lost the belt – a detail like that sticks in the mind.

What else took place I don't know, certainly my mother's handbag opened and no doubt some money was given under the guise of a Christmas gift or some such excuse. I suppose it was my turn to shiver but I was better prepared than he with stout leather shoes and long socks. Apparently, I had a Fair Isle pullover on, multi-coloured and very popular even in my teenage years.

My mother's largesse did not stop there, for when I was twelve she met me off the London train at Newcastle station. It was the end of the school term and with consummate diplomatic skill she told me that my prized possession – my wonderful Hornby double 0 train set – had been given to Mrs Flynn. She sometimes 'did for us' but what did it for me was that Mrs Flynn had eleven children and they needed a miracle Christmas gift, for poor old Mr Flynn had gone blind and could work no more. Whatever happened to my Duchess of Athol and shiny blue Sir Nigel Gresley, all streamlined and tactile, not to mention the carriages with their Pullman cars equipped with little lights and tables? Such possessions could not just be bought willy-nilly: my own set had been on order for nearly two years. My mother knew that since I was returning home for the holidays she could get anything past me – she was right, but then there were the tramps who were given tea and sandwiches ...

but that's another story. Anyway, what has this to do with flowers? Clearly not a lot at this stage, but the plot will unfold.

I have established my penchant for clothes, but what was true then and not so much today (if at all) was the fact that we genuinely wanted to emulate our parents or betters or – in my case – the establishment. In the Sixth Form at school one could wear a coloured waistcoat and carry a rolled umbrella; I was positively excited when I claimed my first bowler hat and riding mackintosh in preparation for my entry to RMA Sandhurst. As a young officer-cadet one was introduced to one's expensive West End tailor, London firms that went back to Nelsonian times – in my case Jones, Chalk and Dawson who proudly proclaimed that they had clothed six crowned heads of Europe. Impressively, they had Oates of Antarctica's letter when he joined the Inniskilling Dragoons prior to his departure for the South African War – and many more I am certain, but that's the one I remember. It was a wonderful and exciting time learning the folklore of the Regiment, and the tailors were the custodians of our traditions both dress-wise and social. They took a pride not only in their work but in the Regiment – 'Did you know sir, that Captain So and So was in the other day, he collected his ceremonial whites – you know he's on the Governor General's staff?' Here, they would announce some part of the globe totally unheard-of by me.

Now one is quite entitled to ask how some impoverished young man could have access to such an establishment. The answer is simple: first the patronage of the Regiment over a period of many years. You will go to such and such a tailor and as one was young and impressionable one would be foolish not to do so. You got the correct pattern and style and any deviation in your dress was then the responsibility of the military tailors, but there was a more practical reason too. A suit here would in all likelihood cost five to ten times more than the average High Street gentleman's fitter (remember the 50/- tailor?), but the regimental tailor had one great advantage – he extended a good deal of credit. The form was that the Army gave you an allowance when you were commissioned. In my case it was £145, which appears to be a reasonable amount in 1960 – but in point of fact it barely covered your service dress, let alone your Mess kit, blues and a host of other accoutrements. However, by paying this direct to your tailor you obtained almost unlimited credit once you had started your banker's order, for say £10 per month. With luck an overseas posting meant that on your return in two to three years' time you had a little nest egg. Far and Middle East tailors tended to be much cheaper, dealing with lightweight fabrics and low labour costs. The same was true of Africa where Indian tailors competed favourably with the others. To this end I was introduced by my regimental representative at Sandhurst to the esteemed establishment which has resided for many years in Albemarle Street, in the Savile Row area, the home of English bespoke tailoring. It was here that I got my first British Warm, a coat interchangeable for both civilian and military wear. It was both heavy and elegant, with leather buttons, epaulettes, slanted pockets and sword vent. The material was a formidable Crombie, an Aberdeen cloth noted for its warmth and with a heavy down surface, upon which my tailor traced his initials before my eyes. This he brushed away with his hand, declaring that a really excellent cloth was so deep that one could write on the down 'with one's finger'. His claim was correct for the coat, with heavy wear, was handed down to my elder son.

It was as a proud recipient of such a gift to myself that I now approach the point of my tale. I was standing outside my girlfriend's flat at the Brompton Road end of Knightsbridge, at the entrance of the tube station after walking down Piccadilly in my virgin garment. I had on a bowler hat, spit and polished toe-caps – in today's parlance polished shoes – and the specified unlined leather gloves. I felt every inch a gentleman and incipient Army officer. I stood erect but at ease next to Harry's flower stall, which had certainly been there since 1946 or perhaps prior to the war. Harry was then old to me, probably all of forty, flat-capped and Cockney; indeed, so strong was his accent that one may have thought that it was contrived. As I stood there admiring the blooms Harry said, 'She'll be ages yet mate – don't get back till well after 6.' He continued his banter with a customer before finally addressing me again,

''Ow 'bout looking after me stall while I grab a cuppa?' he pleaded. I knew this to be an untruth for Harry's breath declared that he was a great devotee of the local brewery and the hostelry across the way – now renamed the 'Glorious Gloucester's' I believe.

My options were negligible, as before I could reply he was gone. Still it was a pleasant enough evening watching the world go by, wrapped around in the warmth of my new coat. I stood with pride, convinced that my smart appearance made the world a better place – something that others could follow, a good example to the faint-hearted, espousing our fine military standards and our youth. I had been in this silly daydream for some minutes when suddenly a taxi stopped immediately in front of me and out stepped the most beautiful apparition, certainly no daydream here. She was dark-haired, with a white bejewelled turban which accentuated her eyes by making them almond-shaped and jet-black. She was as lovely as my pen is inadequate in trying to describe her. My heart jumped and probably missed a few beats just by being near her. She exuded female charm out of her every pore as she took in the bright array of the floral display. She opened her mouth and said in what can only be described as delicious tones, 'I would like those, please.'

Her accent only added to her allure and in my ignorance I judged it to be South American – probably because of the turban and Carmen Miranda.*

'Certainly, madam,' I said. I inexpertly wrapped the flowers, trying to prolong the encounter, but eventually I nervously took the money. Where had my confidence gone? I reverted to being myself, a boy not long out of school whose fine clothes could not as yet fit the man. She took the flowers, thanked me, flashing her dark eyes and a gratifying smile before re-entering the waiting taxi. I felt drained and quite exhausted – an opportunity missed but the truth was that she hadn't even noticed me. As my heartbeat returned to normal I noticed time had stood still, but now the external noises returned, engines, horns the buzz of the traffic. I realised how inconsequential I was, but with that feeling came a little ire.

Did she think all flower sellers wore bowler hats and dressed in expensive clothes – even if not paid for? Would she return to her hot and passionate homeland and report that English flower vendors wore bowler hats and dressed impeccably? It looked doubtful. I was still in this deflated mood when Harry returned, rubbing his hands and breathing alcohol all over me.

'Alright guv?' he cheerfully said. I replied that I had sold a bunch of those roses (all flowers to me are roses, if not dandelions, buttercups or daisies).

---

* A popular entertainer of the day. 'Ay ay ay – I love you very much.'

'How much?' he said.

'A shilling,' I replied.

'A shilling ... a bloody shilling?' he queried. 'They are 2/6 mate. That's 1/6 you owe me.' The evening didn't get any better. Beth returned only to announce that I had my dates wrong and she was going to the theatre ... with her brother. A likely story.

It's such a cruel world.

7

Batman

I have already mentioned my sartorial standards and even divulged the name of my favourite tailor. However, the snobbery of 'one's tailor' also extended to the hatter, and there were a handful of good military ones. My Regiment used the services of Herbert Johnson of Bond Street and the owner, I presumed, was a magnificent gentleman who had served as an infantry officer in the Second World War. I knew him over many years and was always in awe of his impeccable manners, strident good looks and total urbanity. I presumed him quite old, as he had silver-grey hair curling at the temples and the nape of his neck. We called him Mr Max, and of course he addressed his customers as 'sir', but I always felt uncomfortable about this and would have preferred a role reversal.

Herbert Johnson prided themselves on dispatching their hats all over the world and retained your hat size in the form of a 'last', together with other relevant details in their archives. A visit there was always a temptation for they not only had a vast collection of hats of all shapes and sizes but also off-the-peg hacking jackets, cravats, a host of colourful silk ties and handkerchiefs spotted and striped, the latter as big as tablecloths. A funny bronze/copper kettle-type machine steamed away in the corner ... but not for tea. Its purpose was to revive old and misshapen hats of Boer War vintage, and it was most effective.

On this particular visit I saw on the old model dummy a deerstalker – the type one always associates with Sherlock Holmes – and beneath it a most appealing cape. It was, Mr Max told me, Austrian Loden material, water- and wind-proof and ideal in rain and showers. In truth it was not unlike a military cape for it allowed unfettered movement of the arms. It was in an attractive green tweed, and although unusual for most men's dress I saw merit in it for the following reason. I noticed that, once seated in my motor car, an overcoat or a stiff rubberised Macintosh was liable to ruck up behind you, almost covering your head, restricting movement and straining the buttons. This had arm vents too and was absolutely super.

'May I try it on please, Mr Max?' I asked.

'Certainly sir,' he replied.

It was light to wear, giving one a pleasant feeling of being unencumbered; it was of waist length and had a wonderful flair to it. In short it was perfect, the one great deterrent being the price of about a month's spending money.

'Well sir, I have got to say it looks wonderful on you – truly elegant – yes, very smart indeed,' Mr Max said, his hand reflectively on his chin and slightly stepping back to see its full effect. He had consummate good taste, one only had to look around the shop to take in the ambience, so who was I to argue?

I took little time to make my decision and when he asked me if he should parcel it up, I replied to the effect that I was so excited I would wear it now – it was quite a cold day. My banker's order was readjusted, I placed my Herbert Johnson trilby on my head and threw the newly acquired Loden cape about my shoulders and secured the three buttons. Mr Max opened the door with its heavy brass handle polished daily, and we bade each other farewell.

Bond Street in those days allowed two-way traffic and it was always busy. I stepped out with my steel-heeled shoes clicking on the pavement, accentuating my military gait. As always, with our training, I walked with a sense of purpose, decisively and upright. I must admit that there must have been a slight vanity about me then, for I could not help looking at my reflection as I passed the many august shop windows that line Bond Street. To be honest they revealed an imposing military figure swaggering down the road (and what is wrong with a little swagger sometimes?). Yes, I had to admit I looked good, in fact, if I made such an impression on myself (and I was hard to please) what effect would I have on lesser mortals? They must find me quite ... *devastating*.

I was about to find out.

I had walked about a hundred yards when a rather large truck drew up alongside me, and as the traffic was somewhat sluggish we kept abreast of each other in irregular spurts. I noticed in the reflection of the window the driver's mate was admiring me ... well, certainly looking at me. I thought that the cost of my trilby would just about match his entire Sunday wardrobe – poor chap. The next reflection revealed him beckoning to me – he may have been an ex-national serviceman and wanted to compliment me. I turned to look at him and in an instant saw a rather pugilistic sort of man with a heavily tattooed but muscular forearm, cauliflower ear, in truth an uncouth character – but what was wrong with giving him a cheery hello? Time was against me, and before I could raise my hat and say hello, he leaned as far out of the cab window as he could and shouted: 'Who do you think you f****** are mate, f****** Batman?' The passers-by looked from him to me, and in that instant, in the tradition of Sir Walter Raleigh or a matador, I whipped off the cape from my shoulders in total humiliation.

I never wore it again but told my sister that I had bought it for her birthday and reminded her that our lovely mother always wore a cape – but obviously much more fetchingly than me!

Oh well. Pride before a fall and all that.

8

THE BOXING MATCH
THAT NEVER WAS

When we were at RMA Sandhurst we went through a rigorous and intensive two years of training. In essence it equated to a good three-year university course as our terms were longer, in all ten months a year. Anyway, university was barred to us as we had to join the Academy before we were twenty-one years of age. Many would say that the academic standard of a minimum of two A-levels, or the Civil Service Commissioners' examination, was not the problem – what most people failed was the Regular Commission Board (RCB) at Westbury, Wilts. This was a three-day affair, in which a board of officers tested one's leadership ability. We were all about eighteen or so and we had to wear numbers on our backs, so that the examiners, in theory, had no knowledge of who you were and could therefore exercise no favours if a serving officer's son came before them. Welbeck College accepted young boys at sixteen who took their A-levels and passed into the Academy for commissions in the technical Corps. They were, we thought, lucky as they avoided doing an RCB – but there again I wouldn't like to do science subjects, which was mostly their bent.

Once into Sandhurst, I probably thought that I could relax and enjoy the beautiful grounds and the pleasant life that further education brought. What a shock I was in for – it was like the Grand National, with every term a fence or two to test your mettle and trip you up. If you didn't get over the first fence, you couldn't jump the next hurdle and the threat of back-terming was ever-present. There was obviously all the military side of things to do – tactics, military history, weapons and weapon training, even down to book-keeping, in case one day you were unlucky enough to have to run an account. I had little aptitude for accountancy, and hated it.

There was also the academic side of life, which one rather put on the back burner if the military pressure became too intense. Unfortunately, this didn't apply to me as I chose to do sociology under Dr Terrence Willet. He was as keen as mustard to impart his subject to just five of us, but there again he had been until recently a serving Lt Colonel in the 'Gunners', or Royal Artillery (RA). However, he was then serving with the Army Air Corps as a pilot, and he had decided that before he left the Army he would take an external degree. This he did by getting in his flying time going to Bristol University to study. He didn't stop there, but also found time to marry, adopt two children and do a PhD on drink-driving which was serialised in the *Sunday Times*. Within five years, he had a professorship at Reading University, I think. Certainly, our study was based on their degree course. This was hard work.

I was also in the senior set for Modern Subjects under a superman, Lt Colonel Leyland, MA. Indeed, I came top throughout my year, with him gracious enough to reward me with the Modern Subjects essay prize. Three weeks later I was summoned to his study where he told me, to his embarrassment and my chagrin, that due to Sandhurst politics my prize had been withdrawn by the Commandant and awarded to a General's son, who was in the lower set. If Deakin (sorry, I don't know his Christian name) ever reads this … he may wish to buy me a pint … or even two!

There was drill, there was cross-country running, there was all manner of sport and there was boxing and it is to this that I now turn. All of us at some stage had to box; it was obviously a way of learning to look after yourself, developing some form of aggression while at the same time learning how to point score and adjudicate at matches. This, we were told, was essential, for on joining our regiments, we would probably have to organise inter-company and inter-regimental boxing tournaments and therefore needed to be qualified boxing judges. Now at some stage someone had told me that it was a real fag to be involved in this pastime, as it took a lot of your free time and much effort and it was probably the only test that you could fail without the authorities getting too upset. To this end I set out assiduously to make certain that I failed. At the end of every bout, which I didn't pay much attention to, I would return a spurious figure, but covering myself just enough to see that my cover wasn't blown. My boxing partner was one of my great friends and it was during a normal PT session that our instructor said, 'Mr Waters, Mr Stacey in the ring next.' It didn't matter that Robin, a handsome youth, was a different weight and 4in. taller than me – it was informal, just our squad, 'but get some punches in so the others can get some useful tips and be able to point score'. In truth we tried not to punch too hard while at the same time trying to look good.

The Army Physical Training Corps were, I should explain, a breed apart. They wore white singlets, edged in red with their Corps badge emblazoned on the front of the vest, and blue trousers, which were attached with elastic, I guess, which kept them in perfect shape and creased. They were all young (but older than us), neat, tidy and seemed to possess muscles denied to other people. In short, they were fanatics ... no, that's unkind, *dedicated* would be a better and fairer summation. Anyway, 'In the ring gentlemen', the PTI said, whereupon Robin and I started our 3x3 minute bout. Suddenly, there was a commotion in the gym as we were invaded by a delegation of foreign journalists, photographers and other hangers-on all explaining what was happening.

'Oh, flippin' hell,' remarked the PTI, 'they're not meant to be here until this afternoon.'

'Box gentlemen, give it all you've got ... go for it.' Not one to disobey orders, let alone let down the world's oldest and premier Military Academy, we boxed. At the end of the second round the gentlemen of the press were just that – 'impressed'. Now my particular sport then was riding and although my legs were strong with this and cross-country running, it was amazing how jelly-like they became after just a couple of rounds of boxing, but also my arms that became so heavy to pick up. It was seconds before the bell went for the last round that Robin's reach began to tell, for he landed a perfect right hook that swayed me on my feet, and is the only time in my life that I have seen stars, stops, crescents, moons and exclamation marks, all multi-coloured and jumbled together like a kaleidoscope. I still had time to think: this is just like the *Beano* comic, 'biff, bang, wallop' – before I finally slumped in my corner. Our nice PTI – I remember his face so well, but his name evades me – said: 'Congratulations, gentlemen ... well done, they went away very pleased to have seen such a set-to ... well done again.'

'What about me, staff?' I said, 'I've got a huge headache and we have exams this afternoon.'

'Don't worry, sir,' he smiled, 'some good news to cheer you up, you've passed the boxing test ... you are now an official boxing judge.' That was the last thing on my mind, feeling that I had just completed fifteen rounds with Muhammad Ali. I just wanted to die!

However, my short ordeal was pleasant compared to that which I am about to relate, for in the annals of RMA Sandhurst I am certain that I witnessed history on the night in question. As I said, all new officer-cadets had to do some boxing, and it was a key test. The boxing all related to something called 'Charlie George', the RMAS code for Character Grading. Were you strong, average or weak? If you were weak then you would be weeded out as unsuitable for officer training. I was lucky enough to get away with a few knock-arounds in the gym; some, however, were chosen to box in a gladiatorial fashion, and by this I mean very much in public. Mess nights were held every so often, formal dinners where one wore best bib and tucker, parade and inspection beforehand as we dined with the officers, after which it was a free-for-all, a drinking night. After dinner we all walked to the Sandhurst Hall for the gladiatorial part of the evening: 1,100 men, all fed and merry, the officers in their resplendent Mess kits, the Commandant, a Major-General with his retinue and the dinner-jacketed civilian lecturers headed by the Director of Studies. Centre stage was the boxing ring, professionally lit, Army Physical Training Corps (APTC) instructors, independent Army boxing judges, timekeepers, medical officers, ambulances and orderlies in attendance, as well-organised as any premier boxing match could be. The noise was deafening, and over the hall there was a blue stratum of smoke from copious cigars.

The evening was presided over by the most immaculate and impressive figure I had ever seen at that stage of my life. His name was Jacky Lord, known to us as Regimental Sergeant-Major J. Lord, MBE. He was the senior RSM in the British Army and a man where superlatives cannot be used too often. He was probably about 6ft 3in. tall, straight, dark-haired and probably handsome, but here I am unqualified to say, as I don't think that I ever saw him smile; but there again, I usually saw him on a parade ground where his strict disciplinarianism had to be to the fore. He was the quintessential military figure and bestrode his domain like a colossus. It was always said that when you called the NCOs 'sir', you meant it, but when they called you 'sir', it was because they had to, and in Jacky Lord's case this was certainly true. He had been a Grenadier Guardsman in his youth (well, still was) and had risen quickly through the ranks. Had he benefited from a better education he would probably have become a Field Marshal, for he was a natural-born leader who commanded everyone's respect … even if some may have disliked him. It is worth telling you this story, for the lecture he gave us had a great impact on me; well, on all of us to some degree and when one talks of hearing a pin drop it was true for the entire forty-five minutes of his talk.

Lord had been captured during the war and put in a POW camp, Stalag number unknown. He must have been an extremely young RSM, even given the fact that promotion came quickly in wartime for obvious reasons. Nevertheless, he saw that the British soldiers there were a disgrace: to their country, their regiments and their families. There were many older men in the camp who had been in the Army far longer and who resented this young buck, probably no more than twenty-five, who now entered their lives to disrupt things. He immediately set about changing their slovenly habits, ashamed of a once-proud Army being held in such low esteem by our enemies.

One can imagine the newcomer berating the parade and being confronted with line upon line of sullen, hostile faces, their clothes unwashed and uniforms disgraceful. Lord's first order therefore was to say that every man, without exception, would parade shaved and washed next morning. This done, he then demanded that the following day the POWs were to parade correctly dressed, uniforms patched, pressed, boots clean and metal polished. Morning parades were followed by barrack room inspections, lectures, drills and sports parades; very soon he had wood to make the rifles required for arms drill. Finally, he obtained musical instruments from a grateful German Commandant, who saw a camp well-run and functioning smoothly all due to the British NCOs. His biggest problem came when he ordered all soldiers passing a German officer to throw up a 'guardsman-like salute'. They objected to this, but never short of a solution, he added, 'You will look them straight in the eye and say to yourself, "Bollocks to you."'

It was an officer's duty in wartime to try to effect an escape, but not so for the NCOs and junior ranks. Lord was therefore able to institute a routine similar to an Army barracks back at home, where every man was kept busy with education, sport, drama and lots of physical training, arousing them from their lethargy and giving them back their self-respect. When the American vanguard reached the camp, they radioed back to their HQ to report that 'the limeys have beaten us to it.' For what they had seen were a thousand men on parade, with rifles (fake), a band playing and a Union flag already flying. But the Americans were of course mistaken, fooled by the good order of the British POWs. RSM Lord had called the parade to attention, marched out and given the salute. It is with this formidable figure in mind that I ask you to consider what took place next.

RSM Lord presided over the evening's entertainment, if one could call it that, dressed in his high-collared blues. He announced that the first bout was light welterweight and in the red corner for Dettingen was 'X', and in the blue corner for Waterloo was 'Y'. The bell would ring and the two contestants would give it their all, spurred on by their respective Company colleagues but perhaps more for the benefit of their officers who ultimately wrote their reports. I remember one huge mismatch when a comparatively small white boy took on a brawny Ghanaian – blood flowed, the eyes became puffy and his corner, knowing that he had tried his utmost, told him to stop. He would have none of it and finished the fight covered in glory – his Charlie George was secure, as well it should have been.

We were on the fourth or fifth bout of the night, when the RSM thundered that the next bout was between O/Cdt B. Robins of Blenheim Company in the blue corner and O/Cdt Clark of Inkerman Company, in the red. Brian Robins, as it happens, was known to me for we had completed our RCB together. He was my size, about 5ft 8in., with brown hair and a slim figure. The comparison ended there, for I am almost certain that he passed into Sandhurst top academically of 234 who took the examination – many or most failed it. It was only later that I discovered what a brilliant mind he had. At least I had someone to cheer for as the RSM vacated the ring and the APTC referee took over. Before the fight begins I should finally say that I had no idea why these young men were chosen to box so publicly. Was it because their officers thought that they were strong and the best candidate to show off their Company 's prowess … or the worst cadets who needed to have their courage tested … or perhaps it was purely random? In all events Brian Robins was there to box O/Cdt Clark and I could get involved in cheering him on.

The bell went and the two protagonists came out and touched gloves.

'Box on,' declared the referee but before a blow could be thrown O/Cdt Robins had lain down on the canvas, perfectly supine, almost at attention with his arms by his side, as if in death. What on earth had happened – had he had a fit? It certainly didn't look so – it seemed too pre-meditated, as he had placed himself so purposefully in the middle of the ring. The referee was clearly talking to him but nothing seemed to be happening, other than his opponent pacing the floor. Silence fell as the RSM, the premier RSM of the British Army, the man who had struck fear into hundreds of POWs, earned the respect of the Germans and whose very presence instilled us with terror, entered the ring and stood above the prostrate figure of this lonely cadet. The sparks would fly now.

'Get up Mr Robins,' he said. There was no response.

'Mr Robins, get up sir.' Just a silence.

'Mr Robins, I am ordering you to get to your feet immediately sir.' Nothing.

By now the stunned silence gave way to boos, feet stamping and jeers – but there was no response from O/Cdt Robins. The Commandant and officers sat immobile, for no one had ever disobeyed a direct and legal command given by such a man and backed by the authority of the Commandant, a veteran of Arnhem and a formidable figure himself. I was not privy to what took place in the ring that night for I was too far away and the riotous noise was climaxing into a crescendo. I only know that had we as a squad been ordered by Jacky Lord to throw ourselves over the cliffs of Dover onto the rocks below, like the Gadarene swine, we would have done so – but here was a diminutive figure, seemingly further diminished in his shorts and with torso bare, who had defied authority. It was only when the RSM raised his arms, cowed us into silence and declared O/Cdt Clark the winner that Mr Robins accepted the RSM's capitulation, got up and left the ring.

Imagine: the RSM beaten, the officers snubbed. The outcome was inevitable: surely Robins would be discharged, thrown out with ignominy, 'for cowardice' we proclaimed, as every man that night had only this subject on their lips. It was talked of for days, indeed, it has probably gone down in Sandhurst's history, 'the man who defied authority' and over fifty years later it is still resurrected by us when we meet. Obviously, Brian Robins would be before the Commandant before the night was out, the cells would be his abode until morning and by 0800 hrs he would be at Camberley station bound for home. We wondered if he would qualify for a rail warrant in the circumstances. Some suggested that he could be shot for cowardice as in the First World War, but that was the alcohol talking! Poor chap, what came over him? Were there such things as brainstorms or had he been genuinely terrified? Well-balanced people suddenly commit suicide without cause or reason, so had such a thing happened to him – his brain turned? All these conjectures tortured us as we made our way back to our rooms. I knew that he was down for the infantry, the Middlesex Regiment, which made the situation even more bizarre, for we thought of ourselves as being hardy. Still, tomorrow was another day and we all had our own little worries to contend with. *C'est la vie.*

Tomorrow came with breakfast as usual but there, as large as life, was Brian Robins. He was not actually in my Company, but he was pointed out. We went to luncheon the same day and dinner too and there was O/Cdt Robins, and as the days went by so was Brian rehabilitated as friends in his Company stood by him and the incident seemed to fade away. I don't know if anything happened discipline-wise; in fact, I have seen him since at reunions and talked to him at length but never on this subject. Indeed, having told the story and discussed it with my contemporaries, we have laid the charge of cowardice to rest and having reconsidered everything decided it was an act of unmitigated bravery and one certainly deserving of a medal. What guts it took to lie down, not only in the presence of RSM Lord and the Commandant but also in front of all your peers. I don't know the motives that led to such behaviour; someone said that he didn't agree with boxing and so strong were his convictions that he wasn't going to compromise … and do you know what? I think that the powers that ruled at Sandhurst weren't as blinkered as we thought and concurred with our revised opinion (but far ahead of us) that Brian Robins was an exceedingly brave man!

Postscript

My friend Robin Waters who was responsible for me seeing celestial lights did well. He commanded the Worcestershire Regiment and retired as a Colonel. The hero of our tale retired early as a Major and became an academic and an authority on Mandarin and Cantonese – interpreting at the highest level and for state visits. He has his own firm and still to my knowledge lives in Hong Kong. In fact, I haven't given his real name but I would like to as the more I re-live the incident the braver I think he was.

9

THE DORCHESTER

I was a young man in the summer of 1959. By today's standards I suppose I was somewhat to be pitied for my father was drowned and buried in a faraway land aged thirty-six and my mother was in her final three-year marathon with lung cancer. The story was that she had said to the cancer specialist that she must see her son graduate from the Royal Military Academy, Sandhurst.

'Oh good, that's a goal,' he had said, 'how long to go?'

'He's not there yet,' she replied.

The three months he had predicted extended to three years and she did see me graduate on 16 December 1960. The battle over, she finally succumbed a few months later in the cancer hospital at Shotley Bridge in the County of Durham. She was forty-seven, still beautiful of face with a cadaver's body and green eyes that stayed alight and inspiring till her last breath. She had been my guiding light; deprived, aged five, of the father I never knew (just three memories) she was my alpha and omega, the sun and the moon, my reason for living and a total inspiration. The warmth of her body, the reassurance of her arms about me and the sweet perfume of her body all remain with me. She had imparted to me the total supremacy of her gift for life. No one who met her ever forgot her.

She exuded charm, warmth and above all compassion. 'You are placed upon this earth to help others,' she had told me – a totally discredited affirmation now, but what she did give me in abundance was confidence in myself. 'People place upon you the value you place upon yourself,' she had said. She was right – in my journey through life most people are only too quick to see your faults and exaggerate them. If, through false modesty, you yourself record and highlight them you probably have only yourself to blame when the world unites to pillory you, however unjustly. This is not to say that one should go the other way, full of bombast and swagger – tread the middle road and try to be fair and honourable to all.

With this brief résumé of my upbringing I could have been intimidated by the world of wealth and privilege there was at Sandhurst; we were in those days almost exclusively from the public school sector. The two-year intensive course for regular officers was still a throwback to before the Second World War. True, the nomenclature had been changed – we were no longer 'gentlemen cadets' but 'officer-cadets'. I was lucky when I entered RMAS for we still had civilian servants, usually ex-servicemen, again a legacy dating back to before the Second World War. The more you paid them the better the service, and I remember there was one servant to every five or six officer-cadets. In any case, after paying towards Messing, breakages, frequent haircuts, items of uniform and other miscellaneous things some form of financial help from family or trust funds was a necessity. This brings me nicely to the point of the story.

My friend Charles Blakeney was a small but stocky blond boy. I used to think he had 'knitted hair', close to the scalp and tight. He was going into the famous Fighting Fifth, to you and me the Royal Northumberland Fusiliers, his father's Regiment. His parents were obviously not only doting but generous too. They had given him a Bentley as big as a bus, circa 1926, and the green brute was similar to the celebrated one that raced 'le train bleu' from Monte Carlo to London. It was by any standard exceptional. At today's prices it would be in the £200,000-plus bracket. Now it came to pass that Major and Mrs Blakeney would sojourn every year for two or three weeks at London's famous Dorchester Hotel to participate in the London season. It was Sunday mid-July after church parade when Charles dashed into my room and said, 'Well Stacey, fancy a trip to London for luncheon with my parents at the Dorchester?'

'Whose motor?' I said.

'Mine of course,' he retorted. I had never set foot in the Dorchester, only admiringly passed it on the way to my club. However, I knew of its formidable reputation and the fact that Charles was reputed to have a very pretty sister who could well be there.

Our journey was uneventful other than the fact that it was hot and windswept – there being no roof. The glances of others failed to impress me as I was preoccupied with hanging on for dear life – a Bentley 4½ litre isn't meant to be driven sedately. Indeed, when we arrived at the Dorchester and he applied the outside brake I noticed his side didn't even have a door – he was expert in vaulting over the side. My side had an apology for a door and I seem to remember being told not to go too near the exhaust. The Dorchester took all this in its stride; the green-liveried doorman resplendent in top hat came forward to greet Charles: 'Ah, Mr Blakeney sir, the Major's expecting you and your guest, he is in the American bar,' he said, not trying to disguise his Brigade of Guards background and ex-Sergeant-Major status.

'Oh thanks,' Charles nonchalantly said, throwing this tall and impressive man the keys to the motor. He may have said, 'please park it.' I can't remember. What I do remember vividly, however, was how incredibly impressed I was with this act of supreme insouciance. I hastily followed my friend as he strode into the hotel. Suddenly my perception of him had changed from fellow student to one of awe-struck admiration, a true man of the world, urbane and sophisticated, a nascent James Bond, except that I don't think he had made his mark then. I felt inadequate, my fine hair was windswept and tousled as I trailed in his wake, readjusting my waistcoat and fighting my wayward hair. Luncheon was fine and his parents charming, soon establishing an easy rapport, my only disappointment being that no sister turned up to add glamour to the occasion. My first but certainly not last visit to the Dorchester had proved impressionable, not to say invaluable as a modus operandi.

The following Wednesday afternoon I had arranged my first proper date with Jenny (Middleton-Steward), whose family hailed from Southern Rhodesia. She was nice, with a ready smile and an easy-going nature. However, she had not been used to the deprivations of diet that we had suffered during the war and well into the 1950s – the dreaded rationing. With this in mind I thought that the lovely Jenny should be taken somewhere really smart and special. Tea at my club was adequate for second dates or after one's first kiss. Someone of Jenny's background deserved something like, well, like tea at the Dorchester. Tea was good, it cost much less than dinner and it wasn't such a wasted investment if one failed to get the much-sought-after kiss. Tea it was then.

Charles's Bentley was impressive, nay, *magnificent*, but it didn't have a roof or the proper privacy of a back seat. My Hillman 10 had both and furthermore my motor car would preserve her hairstyle. In all it was adequate, I thought: it was twenty-six years old and the windows, as they did in those days, assumed an odd yellowish hue and the cracks in them, although illegal now, were well secured with gaffer tape. The black paint had totally faded, giving the bodywork a matt finish appearance, while both bumpers were well fixed to the bodywork by the aforementioned brown shiny tape, which also supported one of the headlights. Of course I cleaned it to the best of my ability and was quite proud of the cracked brown leather. The leather smell still lingered on but overriding it was a slight … well perhaps a little more than slight … mildew odour that came from the corroding floorboards and the damp carpets. The engine had been around the clock a few times and I suspect it had been badly abused during the war years, left un-garaged and neglected. Nevertheless, my first motor car had cost £5 while this 'modern one' was all of £15 – so I was gradually moving up the ladder.

I picked Jenny up outside Harrods and after she had settled in the motor car said in a nonchalant sort of way, 'What about tea at the Dorchester?'

I hoped it had been said casually enough to imply that I was a constant habitué at the hotel. She simply smiled and said, 'Yes, that would be nice.'

The drive from Knightsbridge was quick and I soon found myself parking in the very drive where I had been four days previously. Luckily a lovely Lagonda had just pulled away, facilitating my entrance. I had the standard Sandhurst walking-out gear on, a three-piece Prince of Wales check, highly-polished shoes and my Bond Street trilby, which I diligently placed on my head as I got out of the motor. No one could say that I didn't look the part – indeed, the pair of us would add grace to such an establishment.

I went around the Hillman and gallantly opened the passenger door. I felt very proud as the long-limbed Rhodesian, tanned and elegant, took my arm. The very same doorman looked on … did I detect a slight hint of admiration as we mounted the steps? I drew parallel to the towering green-clad figure, gave him the keys and politely said, 'If you don't mind parking it please.' There was a pause …

'FUCK OFF,' he said, and turned away.

Oh Lord, let the Earth swallow me up.

It's an unfair world.

10

THE REGIMENTAL
INTERVIEW

Whilst at RMA Sandhurst the officer-cadet was constantly assessed by his military instructors, particularly his commander and other Company instructors. There was also input from the civilian lecturers on his academic ability, and even the drill sergeants on his parade-ground bearing. However, it was a two-way system with the young cadet also looking for his own choice of arm – infantry, cavalry, artillery, engineers or other service corps. In many instances family tradition played a great part in one's choice. So often son followed father into his regiment and continued a proud family tradition going back generations. Some regiments were more popular than others and therefore competition was fierce and one did not always get into the regiment of one's choice. Regiments also chose young men who would fit the profile of the regiment; for instance, if you were an excellent rugby, hockey or cricket player you had a better chance of joining this or that regiment. This applied to any good sportsman for, after all, if one is to lead men one must be fit. This was particularly true of the infantry, for when I joined they still relied on marching and fighting their way to the objective. The cavalry had for many years been armoured and fought in tanks or armoured cars but they still retained a tradition of riding and playing polo and were therefore keen on those who aspired to such things. Of course, one must not forget the very fine mounted tradition of the Royal Artillery, still going strong with the King's Troop RA. Some regiments would be impressed by a title, others by a substantial private income (or preferably both), but all these observations are generalisations; there were many exceptions and anomalies. Many of us joined regiments with a territorial connection, for instance one's county regiment.

My regimental interview was, it must be stressed, not the norm. Indeed, by any standards it was notably bizarre. For a start, it was held after an Academy dinner or Mess night when the officers dined in a multitude of gold-braided Mess jackets, overalls and clicking spurs, while the officer-cadets were in their blues. The band played, the candles reflected the silver and I found myself sitting next to Father Cotton, Major, Royal Army Chaplains' Department. He was a popular and urbane cleric with a distinguished voice and the proud owner of a beautiful bay, in fact we sometimes rode out together. I think I was seated next to the padre, not only because of our interest in the saddle club, but because I was regarded as something of a goody goody. I didn't, at that stage, drink and I refrained – well, strongly disliked – the raucous singing of dirty songs which was the norm when travelling in the back of the ubiquitous four-ton lorries. It was probably this Mess night which changed my teetotal habit, for if one drank, the wine was included in the meal, but my orange juice (well, squash) cost another 6p and therefore added 2/- or 2/6 to my Mess bill; in effect I was subsidising the drinkers. The menu card gave one the evening's fare in French, no doubt to educate us in the ways of the sophisticate. This I read. The corresponding wine card did the same but this I did not read. The dinner also educated us in the

My school.

RMA Sandhurst.

The 'ugly' sisters

Patricia, five years older,
Ch. 4.

Cynthia, five years younger,
Chaps 4 & 40.

RCB, Westbury,
Wiltshire, 1959. The
author is wearing number
8. Many of the group
became comrades and
friends, Ch. 8.

The Two Georges

Major-General George Payne and King George VI, Ch. 39.

The Queen and Duke of Edinburgh. I was local ADC to the Duke on the occasion of the Nyasaland Independence Celebrations, Ch. 20.

HRH Princess Mary, The Princess Royal, Ch. 23.

Lt General Sir George Lea, KCB, DSO, MBE, Chaps 20, 26, 27.

On the Sultan of Brunei's yacht for a VIP visit up the Limbang River. General and Pam Lea facing (mid-ground); head of Shell Mr Coates (R); Brigadier (later General) and Mrs House (hidden). Ch. 26.

Above: The Sultan's Summer Palace: the great fire. All prompted by an early-morning call (Ch. 24). A sad sight.

Above: Baloo, our honey bear. What a character. Lord Head recommended that we part company for the children's safety, Ch. 37.

Left: A typical Borneo longhouse, as visited in Ch. 23. (Courtesy of the Borneo Literature Bureau.)

Rt Hon. Edward Heath MP, with the future Chancellor of the Exchequer, Anthony Barber MP. They were good company. In the doorway stands our governess, Miss Evans, Ch. 26.

Holiday snap of author with plastered right ankle, next to our Gurkha House Sergeant. Leeches out of sight. Bloody SAS holidays! Ch. 24.

A constant stream of visitors – a protocol nightmare for an ADC. Back: Brig. H. Tuzo; Major-Gen. W. Walker (then Dobops), very irascible. Front: High Commissioner Brunei; Lord Mountbatten; GIGS; Admiral Sir Varyl-Begg, C-in-C Far East. (Picture taken during my handover period.)

In training for leaving the Army. Totter and 'Thunderbolt', Byker,
Newcastle-upon-Tyne, Ch. 22.

A similar Bentley delivered me to the Dorchester Hotel, Ch. 9.

formalities of a Mess night, certainly a pre-requisite for when we were to join our own regiments. However, on this particular night Major P. E. Y. Dawson XX Foot, the regimental representative for the Fusilier Brigade and officer commanding Ypres Company, had decided to hold his regimental interviews. Consequently, as first to be called I found myself being marched into the Major's office by his Company Sergeant-Major.

'Left right, left right, Mr Stacey sir, halt,' he bawled.

The door was closed. I stood in silence for some time and reflected that the aroma of cigars was always better than the taste they left in your mouth. Finally, my interlocutor spoke. His question was straightforward and to the point but not the one that I was expecting.

'How many times have you had syphilis, boy?'

At this stage of my life I considered myself highly unfortunate, in that I had not even had the opportunity or the pleasure of acquiring it – but this is really hindsight. After all what would an old married man (he must have been forty or forty-five at least), a devout RC (was there a conspiracy here, I had just sat next to the RC padre?) and a Downside boy (you see I had done my homework) know of such an anti-social disease?

No, it was clear the Regiment must have great social standing, epicurean aspirations as well as expecting their young officers to be knowledgeable about good wines. The wine card had sat in front of me all evening … my mind was in turmoil … was it a Beaujolais that was served tonight or Syphilis '59?

My choice of Regiment lay on this crucial question and I had fallen at the first fence. Syphilis, Beaujolais, Beaujolais, Syphilis – a small bracket clock behind him only served to exacerbate my dilemma as it ticked away intolerably. The Company Commander, although inebriated, did show a little compassion at my discomfort, for I thought I detected the slightest flicker of a smile. Did I have it right after all – was it the Medical Officer's talk on venereal disease

– no, it couldn't be – yes, it was – no – yes. I took the plunge: it was that dreadful disease and this was a trick question.

'I can categorically say, sir, that I have never had syphilis.' I said this with military conviction, but tonight was not my night. The words had hardly left my lips when I heard, 'Well, f*** off then, you can't come to my Regiment until you've had it at least three times. Sergeant-Major, march out.'

'Mr Stacey, sir about turn, quick march, left right, left right,' as I disappeared down the long tiled corridor and so to bed.

11

A Lesson Well Learned or A Rollocking from my Batman

I joined my Regiment, the First Battalion XX The Lancashire Fusiliers, in Osnabruck early January 1961. In those days I travelled with a huge Saratoga, in plain terms a pirate's chest which required two porters to carry it. Over fifty years ago porters still existed, black trousers and waistcoats with a British Rail cap, but even then they were a dying breed. In all events travelling 'heavy' was not easy and required good planning, but things were better then, more personal and people took responsibility for their own actions and couldn't hide behind technology ... 'computer's down, mate' 'traffic congestion at...' Remember, the war had ended a mere sixteen years before and people, in my opinion, were more resilient and certainly more resourceful.

I was one of the last to travel on the boat train, which I found exciting – I love steam trains and ships. We arrived in the drizzling rain at Harwich Docks where the ship lay alongside the quay. The throb of engines, lights, hoots, bustling activity, evocative smell of bunkering oil and seagulls screeching overhead – wonderful. Even a cramped cabin to myself was a first for an impressionable twenty-year-old. Dawn broke depressingly grey over the Hook of Holland where we boarded a very slow train dropping servicemen at various garrison towns en route. The military train had been operating since the end of the war, so things seemed to work reasonably well. German staff served us breakfast in the officers' dining car and there seemed to be no shortage of staff; national service still existed, albeit in its death throes.

So many people ask me my opinion of this form of 'penalisation', and it is undoubtedly a complex problem but for every person who can legitimately say that National Service was detrimental to them, I can probably produce ten or more who can testify to its benefits. Over fifty years on and I am still in contact with my platoon, many of whom were national servicemen. So many young men were educated by the forces, introduced to a host of sports, taught to take pride in their regiments and give loyalty to their mates and some 'tough guys' found out there was always a bigger bully than them in the unit – often the Company Sergeant-Major (CSM) – 'round the back boy,' he would say and both parties would return bloodied but respectful. In short, I think that national service was bad for a professional, regular Army but jolly good for the country and the individuals who experienced it. I once had a conversation with Lord Howe, himself a national serviceman, who argued that the country couldn't afford it. However, can our welfare state afford the vast hand-outs we give, with its propensity to encourage idleness and crime? Isaac Watts summed it up nicely: 'For Satan finds some mischief still for idle hands to do.' We were pretty much on the go all the time, which negated a lot of today's problems, but not all. Absence without leave (AWOL) – one could write a book just on that!

Eventually, I was deposited at Osnabruck station where I was met by a very smart officer wearing a warm British overcoat, which meant that I couldn't see his rank. I saluted him smartly and punctiliously called him, 'sir,' only to find out on arriving in the Mess that he was like myself a humble Second Lieutenant (2/ Lt), the bottom of the pecking order. His name was Alan Dowd and he became a great friend of mine. He had a wicked sense of humour, an excellent brain, was fluent in German and French and would later leave us to become a Doctor of Medicine. He was also pompous but just to the right degree, for those who knew him would just laugh and soon a smile would appear which said, 'yes, I know, it's just an act.'

It was he who, having called for tea, stood in the entrance hall and said in his pompous mode (for I didn't know him yet), 'This is the bookcase that contains General Wolfe's orders to the officers of the XX Foot, as it was then.' The young General commanded the Regiment for some eight years and became the symbol of modernity, introducing new tactics, techniques and discipline which were all trialled by the Regiment. Hence, we became the most professional infantry unit in the Army at the time. This was all put down in this book which sat in its own display case in the hall of the Mess. Every day, the duty officer should at the appointed hour turn over a page of the book. The custom was that newly-appointed officers should read the freshly turned page on a daily basis and thus learn.

I remember my first Company Commander, a lovely man, saying to me, 'Lawrence, I want you to read what General Wolfe's advice is on young officers' haircuts.' That day at coffee I read the opened page of the book and continued to do so until such time as I arrived at the appropriate homily, 'That all ye officers should be smarte alertt and haf cleansed shorte hair'.

What a splendid way of teaching one. Major Tony Smith had shown great patience in allowing me to retain my unruly locks for so long. Major-General James Wolfe died, as every schoolboy used to know, in his hour of victory on the Heights of Abraham,

Quebec 1759, aged just thirty-two. However, to the XX Lancashire Fusiliers, he was always remembered and held in high esteem.

The day was Sunday and I was told that dinner that night was at 8 p.m. and we were allowed to dine informally in a three-piece suit. As I was unpacking there was a knock on the door and in marched a young Fusilier who was introduced by the Officers' Mess Corporal. Young Towle was to be my batman; yes, he had been a batman before and yes, he knew the ropes well. He was also a member of my platoon. Fusilier Michael Towle was a national serviceman and we became great friends. He was only eighteen and had a stutter; however, he was no fool, for he discovered that by playing the system he could avoid many unpleasant duties such as staying up all night on guard or perimeter patrols in the bleak mid-winter of North Rhine Westphalia. So often I would hear from the Company non-commissioned officers (NCOs) that Fusilier Towle couldn't do guard duty because Mr Stacey needed him to wait-on in the Officers' Mess. Clearly, I knew this to be untrue but I kept 'mum' – it was our little conspiracy, for if I kept faith with him he would in time-honoured fashion do the same for me, which proved to the be the case. I should also say that I admired him, for he wasn't intimidated by rank but rather refreshingly forthright and honest.

But back to dinner. I remember wearing my new and expensive suit, straight from the regimental tailor. Unfortunately, certain items of my uniform had not arrived, including the waistcoat of this suit; these things were to be dispatched in due course. I cautiously approached the ante-room where one congregated for pre-dinner drinks only to find that it was deserted. A Mess waiter informed me that the officers had already gone in for dinner and that I should follow. I could hear the hum of conversation coming from the dining room and biting the bullet opened the double door of the room. My eyes took in a pleasant sight of conviviality and warmth. Beautiful candelabra shed their light over a polished table with some twenty officers dining-in.

The Mess staff were engrossed in their duties and Sergeant McDonnell, the Officers' Mess Sergeant, stood smartly at ease dressed in his Mess kit on the other side of the room facing me. He sported a magnificent waxed moustache, the like of which I had never seen before. I was to learn that he ruled the staff with a rod of iron and ran a very effective Officers' Mess – but there again he had been in the job for many years. All this was an instantaneous impression, for as the door opened the senior subaltern looked up, his soup spoon poised between his lips.

'Good evening sir,' I said, as our eyes met.

'Get out,' was his immediate reply. 'We dine in a three-piece suit on Sunday; now leave.'

I actually hadn't crossed the threshold of the dining room but our brief altercation had disturbed the flow of conversation among the other officers. Those directly opposite me looked up and those with their backs to me turned around to see who had antagonised this bushy-eyebrowed officer, for that was my abiding memory of him. In all events, I was totally humiliated and quietly withdrew. I could have changed into another suit but the moment had been spoiled and the regimental brotherhood which I had expected to find on joining had been shattered, and I wondered how long one stayed a new boy for. It was a cruel baptism of fire but that was the way things were. Tomorrow was another day and perhaps I would be in more control once in uniform and with my platoon.

I was up early next morning as I was hungry from the previous evening, and anyway I would establish myself first in the dining room where some anonymity was afforded by the daily newspapers. I remember it was bitterly cold when I took my place on the Company parade ground, light sleet sporadically fell but the adrenalin was flowing too fast to be concerned with such trivialities. The platoons fell in.

'Fall in the officers,' commanded Major Tony Smith. I marched over to my platoon, where the man who would hold my hand and guide me skilfully over the year, the excellent Sergeant Lyons, saluted and said, 'Sir, number 2 Platoon correct and ready for your inspection sir.'

My inspection completed, he then asked if I would like to address the platoon. I replied in the affirmative and stood them at ease. Now, prior to this the CSM and platoon sergeants had fallen in the Company, inspected them and generally got the soldiers warmed up and up to the mark. This had taken about ten minutes or so, but what had struck me amidst all this shouting was the fact that I had heard very little of the Queen's English. Indeed, every swear word known to man was bellowed out on the parade ground that cold January day. Later, I was to discover that the Fusiliers could use the F word as a subject, verb and object. ('Sir, the flipping flipper flipped,' if you see what I mean.)

With this in mind I beheld my motley lot. I use the word advisedly for they looked at me with suspicion and resentment. 'Another bloody young officer to show us how clever he is,' they thought. They observed a young man, alien to everything that they had experienced in life, a young man of money (so they perceived), a youth who had been given all the advantages that they had been denied and whose position in life was not earned by merit but by the status of his family. A boy wet behind the ears and spoilt by family and society.

I looked afresh at them after my inspection. One, I had noticed, was old enough to be my father at forty-three years of age. Some were tall and thin, others short and spotty – a true hotchpotch. Some were to end up in prison on leaving the Army, one was a rapist and another was to be charged with murder (later reduced to manslaughter) I was informed. It was, as I said, a disparate crew – but I had been taught that one had to earn their respect and then one could rely on unbending loyalty. But how to do this? It would be a slow process, one of attrition, sometimes two steps forward and one step back – but for the time being I would show them how manly I was. I could swear as well as the best of them. I paused and began my address with some well-chosen expletives I had heard this morning. I pompously reminded them that they wouldn't get much past me – oh, no, I was after all quite an old soldier, for hadn't I already completed two years at Sandhurst! More swear words, more platitudes, together we would make the best platoon in the Battalion, nay the Army, more powerful swearing and bravado. I did put some good points across and I let them know that I would be there to help and always give them the benefit of doubt but that they should not mistake my kindness for softness, and so on. I finished with a salvo of vulgarity, keeping the best to the end just like the finale of a firework display.

They remained immobile, impassive and unimpressed. Clearly they had heard it all before. I had not changed their perception of me or of the officer class.

We then had thirty minutes to change into combat kit, rifles and small packs and then report to the assault course. This I led them over with consummate ease; in fact, I was first by a long way, but to be honest I would have been disappointed had that not been the case. Later, I was to understand why, for they all smoked heavily due to the fact that one of our privileges in the British Army of the Rhine was tax-free cigarettes and drink. Oh yes, I also received a boot in my face which gave me a manly nosebleed. We all finished in due course, but by now it was snowing hard and a cruel wind was enveloping us as I dismissed them and returned to the Mess for a shower.

I was dripping wet, bleeding bravely and covered in mud when I arrived at my room; nevertheless, I had reason to be happy with my performance so far. Fusilier Towle had evaded the assault course, 'to prepare your kit, sir.' I was pleased, for the radiators were on, the floor polished and I noticed that it must be coffee time as the batman for Towle had a soft drink and a chocolate bar by his side. About a year later I discovered that these had all been put on my

Mess bill – I told you he was clever! The inherited radio played British Forces Broadcasting Service (BFBS) tunes, and in all it was a scene of cosy domesticity. Fusilier Towle was bulling (highly polishing) my boots when I asked him, 'Well, Towle, how was my talk to the platoon?'

'Y, yo, you were F [flippin'] awful sir,' he stammered, spitting on the black toe cap and hardly sparing me a glance.

Nothing at Sandhurst had ever prepared me for this scenario, let alone the fact that he had sworn at me – so I asked again just to be sure I had heard him correctly.

'My talk to the platoon, was it all right?' I pressed the question.

'Y, yo, you were F [flippin'] awful sir,' he reiterated.

'Towle, you can't talk to me like that,' I said, half in jest.

'You asked s, si, sir,' he stuttered again.

I began to take him seriously, and paused from taking off my webbing. 'Why so?'

'We, well sir,' he put down my boot and turned to me, 'We expect our officers to be gentlemen, educated and able to set us an example,' he continued, still stammering.

'If you are going to swear like that, we may as well swap places, because you are behaving no better than me and besides I can swear far better than you – my swearing … well it's real.'

I was amazed: here was me, two years older, supposedly wiser, but learning from a boy who left school at fifteen years of age. His wisdom was indisputable and he had made his point succinctly and well. I had never sworn before, my vocabulary being sufficient to preclude it, and what is more, I don't like swearing: I regard it as vulgar and still do to this day. It definitely wasn't *me* – like tattoos. I think that both are horrible habits, so why did I swear, just to conform? He was right, and from then on I resolved to be myself – a fresh-faced youth, and slightly prim with it. I had learned a very good lesson from a very unexpected quarter. How humbling.

Postscript
Thank goodness I learned that lesson on my first proper day in the
Army and not on my last!

12

THE HERO

In those dark days of the Cold War, serving with the British Army of the Rhine, I was once afforded the opportunity for heroism. Already the mind is flicking back the pages of time. Checkpoint Charlie in Berlin, Harry Lime, midnight rendezvous in unsavoury street passages with flickering gas lamps, fleeting shadows elongated on dank walls, beautiful women moving swiftly through deserted, foggy streets, their upturned collars hiding anxious glances ... a cruising, sinister limousine. Alas no!

It was a sunny day in the countryside of North Rhine Westphalia, and the road led from the garrison town of Osnabruck, a Protestant stronghold in this military area, all flat farmland and with a few bends in the road. It led to the British Army camp of Quebec Barracks where my Regiment, the First Battalion the Lancashire Fusiliers, were stationed. The spring trees were in the first phase of blossom and my shopping trip had proved successful. My friend Ian Walker and I sat in my new motor car, a right-hand drive Peugeot 403, engaged in animated conversation on the merits of our obsession, our motor cars. He had just begun his eulogy on his passion, a delightfully shaped Renault Dauphin, when I rounded the corner to be confronted by a scene of sheer horror. Luckily I braked, but only just in time. My passenger side, where Ian sat, was in the middle of the road and I was to the pavement side (hence my mention of RHD). The motor shuddered to a stop as we quickly took in the scene of devastation. A motor car had crashed into a passenger van and bodies lay strewn all over the road; some were motionless, others were writhing, and blood was in profusion. It was a ghastly scene which shattered our senses on this morning of peaceful tranquillity. However, worse was to come. As we tried to readjust our composure and make sense of it all, an agonised face fell on Ian's window with a bang. The blood flowed copiously through his fingers which, somehow seemed to hold together bloody features, and it ran in rivulets down the window, but as his hand slipped away the flap of his forehead fell from his face. His mouth cavity opened and shut involuntarily, oozing blood and teeth. Between gasping breaths he pleaded for help. My reaction was instant as I took command of the situation. The bench seat allowed me to bring my right foot to bear on Ian's body, he already had the passenger door ajar, as I said, between bouts of deep-seated retching (my hand to my mouth to deter the nausea I felt), 'Get out and deal with it.'

He couldn't refuse, for in that instant a powerful right leg ejected him flat on his bottom and on the road amidst the carnage. Still retching loudly, I put the motor car in gear and with the passenger door still open I mounted the pavement and sped away ... or fled?

Ian had bravely followed my instructions, for as I disappeared I saw him in the rear mirror on his feet and in the process of removing his jacket. I continued retching before eventually coming to a stop half a mile away to be sick.

As I came up for air and took in the blue sky of spring I noticed a solitary telephone wire going into a terraced row of ten or so cottages. It was 1961 and telephones were not so prolific as they are now; I was lucky to find one in the countryside. I left the motor car still running as I ran to the door shouting and banging my hand against it. Luckily, it was lunchtime and it was answered. To this day I can't remember asking to enter – I just burst upon the scene and somehow in bad German telephoned for an ambulance. Drained and depressed I rationalised that it wasn't worth my while to return to this Dantean scene of hell; after all, I would only add to the list of casualties and walking wounded.

I did not attend luncheon in the Mess that day but I did await the return of Ian. He was carrying his jacket and I noticed that the sleeves of his shirt had been removed – apparently, they made adequate bandages. I even gave him a spare regimental tie that I had – which was nice of me; his had rather been misused as a tourniquet, a little sacrilegious as it represented service to our country since 1688. Still, it was for a good cause. Over the passing days I recovered, and in the fullness of time made a return to full health. So much so that when the adjutant, Captain Ian Cartwright, telephoned me and said, 'Stacey, report to Battalion HQ in an hour's time dressed in your service dress and Sam Browne, the press want an article and photograph of you,' I was happy to oblige.

Two days later it was official: 2/Lt Lawrence Stacey of the Lancashire Fusiliers was the 'hero of the moment' … 'prompt action' … 'undoubtedly saved lives' … 'quick thinking' … 'a young man to be proud of', all that sort of stuff. I had the photograph and half-page article for many years but somehow in my numerous moves and travels it has got lost. However, it is good to write about it so many years on and remind myself how brave I was. Who knows, perhaps it is something for my grandchildren to emulate and take note of … family pride and all that!

Oh yes, Ian Walker. We are still friends or were for many years until he stopped coming to the reunions. He had to buy himself a new suit of course – the blood and engine oil were just too ingrained.

It's a funny old world.

13

AMSTERDAM
– THE BEST JOB EVER

I had just turned twenty-one years of age and was on the great learning curve as a 2/Lt in Osnabruck. It was the Whitsun holiday so life in the camp was a little more relaxed than usual. True, duties still had to be done, inspections made and the welfare of one's platoon considered; with spare time on our hands it was always advisable to organise some form of activity to keep our young soldiers out of trouble. The week before I had been mildly censured by my commanding officer, Major Tony Smith, for it had been three of my soldiers who had disgraced themselves by getting into a particularly sordid sort of fight. The game was called 'homo-bashing' and it involved one of the three taking his trousers down in the area which attracted a certain sector of German society. When the young soldier was accosted he would plead innocence and say he was only relieving himself, shout for his mates who would then proceed to do the bashing. On this occasion the German police had been summoned and since I was Orderly Officer I had been called into town in order to apprehend the offenders. I remember pushing my way through the crowd in blues, crimson sash and silver sword and scabbard, and feeling rather important. Perhaps I looked imposing enough, for amidst the police cars with their blue flashing lights, they agreed to let the miscreants go under my auspices in the knowledge that they would suffer some sort of punishment, while they would do the same to those who had been lured into the trap. We locked the three in a cell for the night and I recall giving them a tongue-lashing, saying how they had not only disgraced the Lancashire Fusiliers but also their country.

'Why do you do it?' I ended up by asking them. Their response was quick.

'If it is good enough for Clint Eastwood, why is it wrong for us?'

Their point was simple: the surfeit of American films always featured some form of gratuitous violence. The answer to everything, even with the heroes of the film, seemed to be 'fist first'. As far as the three men were concerned, they were saving society from what they saw as an evil and illegal act. I understood their point of view. Our society peddles sex, brutality and all sorts of crime. Indeed, one can't seem to purchase a chocolate bar, dog food or whatever, unless sold under the distraction of a scantily-dressed young woman. Only recently a normal TV horror channel advertised a season of eight films featuring 'rape, murder and other juicy things'. Surely, we have lost our way and our youth will soon become inured to violence and killing. All I could do was to point out that justice was not ours to administer, especially in a foreign land.

‡

Major Gerry Evea, a great officer, who was still playing rugby at forty-three if I remember correctly, was field officer of the week and ultimately responsible for everything that happened in camp. As I was having tea and since I was the only subaltern available, the Major joined me and posed a question: 'Lawrence, have you ever been to Amsterdam?'

'No sir,' I replied.

'Well, here is a wonderful job for you and this is what you must do.' He briefed me thus: apparently, our old Battalion bus had taken a party of thirty-seven Fusiliers to Amsterdam and there breathed its last and died. The visit planned by C Company was in the spirit of what I said before, keeping the boys busy. The soldiers toured the Amstel Brewery where they were well looked after and then the highlight of the weekend was their time in a wonderful area, totally designed for licentious soldiers such as us.

'It is called Kanalstrasse, or the "red light area" and it's here you'll meet the boys. You are to give each of them so much money, order them to report to the Bahnhof [railway station] and tell them that they must all be home by first parade Tuesday morning,' he ordered. I was given rail warrants, money, written instructions, telephone numbers, consular addresses and a final instruction that I was to stay in the Grand Krasnapolsky Hotel in Dam, first because it was near Kanalstrasse and second the Battalion could easily contact me there.

I took a train to Amsterdam and duly reported to this rather nice hotel, which fifty-three years later is still there, I'm told.

'I am to stay here, in this hotel by order of the British Army,' I said with hubris.

'But we are full,' they politely replied.

'I don't care,' I said. 'The British Army has ordered me to stay here and that's that!' Perhaps I showed a little more charm, but the Dutch being the wonderful people they are would always go out of their way to help us. Anyway, they did find me a room of sorts: it belonged to the masseuse but unfortunately she wasn't there, so I slept in the bath! So, you now know why the first element of this chapter title is 'Amsterdam', for here I was. But the second part, 'the best job ever', was about to begin.

I was directed to Kanalstrasse by one of the hotel's pretty receptionists, who looked at me slightly askance. It wasn't far, but nothing had prepared me for what I thought was just to be another Soho, no doubt with tatty signs, unpainted doors, threadbare carpets with self-made signs and arrows pointing to the 'French Model' on the second floor. Kanalstrasse, as every young man knows who has attended a stag weekend there (something not done in my day), was a totally new experience. I remember thinking how beautiful it was, lights in every window, the bustle of the Dutch going about their daily lives, fruit and drink stalls, the barges on the busy canal and those quaint fairy-tale bridges arched high with a backcloth of higgledy-piggledy buildings, tall and narrow with many sporting the distinctive crenellated gables. The ubiquitous cyclists busy-legged and shooting in all directions, the cafés, the toy-town atmosphere were all intoxicating.

However, my delight was reinforced by scores of women of every possible shape, size, colour, denomination, nationality and hue, all basically naked and sitting in the windows of their cosy rooms. Was this what was meant by heaven? Surely not – this must be the other place. Hell, I decided, even with an inferno or two, would be my ambition, my goal – 'death, where is thy sting?' I would now go happily to my grave.

I had led a sheltered life: the swinging sixties had not as yet dawned, the pill was not prevalent and women's modesty in my part of England was puritanical. I remember seeing some nude plastic models in a women's dress shop in Newcastle but even these were hastily covered up. Of course, we all pretended to be men of the world, especially on Sunday morning at breakfast, when one's fellow cadets would ask, 'Well Stace, how did you get on last night, did you ... you know ... with Fiona?'

'Oh gosh, yes, super-twice, marvellous,' we all lied through our teeth – well I did anyway. In fact, one was lucky to get a kiss, and a little fumbling was a bonus seldom gained. But here I was then, in paradise or hell, this was the stuff of dreams, I had no idea that nature was so inventive: breasts in abundance, a harvest of boobs

(I don't know if that word was coined then), some pendulous, some pert, some perfect, some past their bloom, black, brown and pink. At first, I felt for their embarrassment, or was it my own, and glanced only surreptitiously at the goods on display. They seemed to have no such hang-ups and beckoned me gladly to have a chat. I was dry-mouthed and light-headed in a totally uncontrollable spin of carnal emotions. I took in the many different approaches, some simple – girlish smile as if to say, 'I am as new at this as you appear to be' – others challenging, slightly haughty and disdainful with a 'you can't afford' look, 'move on youngster.' Some, if you expressed a look of interest, would stand up and move to the recess of their boudoir with an alluring backward glance, as if to say 'come on in'. The tactic they employed was, of course, a shapely bottom, another of the weapons in this formidable armoury of female wiles.

If all thirty-seven Fusiliers had walked past me on that Saturday night I wouldn't have noticed them – how could I? I strolled down every side street, inspected every girl and smiled contentedly – or was it a leer of lust? Eventually, one young lady engaged me in conversation; she seemed caring and sympathetic. I probably said something to the effect that, yes, I would love to; she was lovely and so on but I was on duty. In all events it broke the ice and I had spoken to some super women by the end of the night, young and old who all spoke English quite well. I told them that if they did come across a 'young British Tommy' (their nomenclature) they should tell them that their officer was looking for them and he could be contacted at the Krasnapolsky Hotel.

My Sunday stroll among my new-found friends was pleasant but did involve one nasty and intimidating incident. Since people had seen me perambulating up and down with no sense of purpose over such a long period, they came to the conclusion that I was either a pervert, potential serial killer or some form of competition trying to muscle in on the act. Three rather unsavoury characters with strong accents but good English boxed me in and questioned me. I wondered if I was to end up in the canal; luckily, my jejune appearance, Army ID card and typed instructions convinced them that my improbable story was the truth. We parted friends with their cards given freely, 'blond bombshell' and 'Indonesian idol' … that type of card! By now I had or was becoming part of the scenery, drinking delicious Dutch coffee with a lot of the girls freely chatting to me. My eyes were still out on stalks and at times speech did not come too easily as I seemed to gulp and sometimes swallow my words, if distracted by too close a proximity to … you know. However, a plan was formulating in my fecund brain, perhaps put there by one of the girls.

'If you can produce, say, six of your soldiers on another visit, we can arrange it for six guilders, instead of the usual eight and of course for you, well next to nothing … a big bonus!' I thought that's fine, if I can only go first – but what a good idea! Monday dawned and I sadly resumed my last patrol of Kanalstrasse and bade farewell to those lovely girls I had made friends with. I thought what a wonderfully conscientious officer I was, how I had so characteristically thrown myself into the job with verve and enthusiasm. I had also become in the process something of an authority (artistically of course) on the female form, its abounding beauty, charm and the illogical effect it has on the opposite sex. If only women knew the dormant power they exercised over the male gender, I am certain that they could be twice as dominant as they are.

I had actually only met six of the Battalion prowling the street but those six had passed on to the others my instructions. Finally, we all met at the appointed time and I am happy to report that all thirty-seven Fusiliers were safely returned to camp in Osnabruck and made the Tuesday morning breakfast parade – something we thought quite improbable before – but as always there was a postscript, unhappily for me.

Postscript

The following September I was told to organise a long weekend for A Company. I had now been with the Battalion for nearly ten months and I was no longer the new boy but finding my way about. I knew exactly what we would do, not just free beer at the brewery, everyone did that, but who thought about the real needs for a real soldier? The saying goes, 'a soldier who doesn't fornicate doesn't fight' and we were fighting soldiers in A Coy. I prepared, with the aid of the clerical staff, a beautiful poster, gaudy, eye-catching and provocative. A Coy proudly presents 'Lulu, Sabrina and Fritsie, Kanalstrasse's voluptuous best – special offers and reduction for bulk bookings'. Here a busty female showed what to expect with a 'come up and see me' sort of smile. The posters appeared with great effect and unprecedented demand, 'Contact 2/Lt Stacey' the advert proudly proclaimed. I put the posters up in the Company lines, NAAFI and the Junior Ranks Club (JRC).

Now opposite the JRC lived a very decent middle-aged woman who belonged to the Women's Voluntary Service (WRVS). These super ladies performed wonderful work looking after the ordinary soldiers, their wives and families and dealt with problems outside the scope of the Battalion officers, a miscellany of tasks too many to go into now. Suffice to say that they were good, god-fearing women with Christian principles. The WRVS lady, naturally, on seeing such a poster with its blatant invitation of institutionalised immorality and leading the young astray, thought that it was the second coming of Sodom and Gomorrah. Furthermore, when she saw that it was a young officer who was offering such, she was incandescent with rage, bursting into the CO's office unannounced and bearing the offending 'artwork'. I was hastily called and saw the adjutant, the commanding officer and no doubt the Chaplain-General too, if he had been around. I was branded, pilloried, reviled by all in authority and obviously ended up with a few days of punishment in the form of extra orderly officer. This, I should explain, was a twenty-four-hour duty done in uniform, which had to be immaculate at all times, and involved dressing in blues in the evening, swords and Sam Browne and calling out the guard in the middle of the night. Girlfriends were therefore out of the question and life was miserable, especially when it lasted for so long and involved major incidents, all requiring paperwork in triplicate.

Later, as I inspected the cook-house for the umpteenth time, I was pulled through these days of disgrace by my platoon. 'Flippin' Mr Stacey, always in flippin' trouble sir. It was the poster that dunnit sir, didn't include the WRVS lady on it with Lulu, Sabrina and Fritsie – jealous that's what she was,' they laughed. Nevertheless we still went to you-know-where in September – but sshh, it's still a secret and it was still the 'best job ever'.

14

The Camel

Drunkenness is an occupational hazard in the armed services, a sort of hobby and badge of manliness. It was more prolific fifty years ago as many soldiers found themselves in an alien country, with little money and no form of personal transport to get out of camp and explore. Indeed, I cannot recall one Fusilier who owned a motor car then. Corporals' and Sergeants' Mess, yes, but no others. Furthermore, the modern fad of gyms and keeping oneself fit was not in vogue. We had fitness on a 'corporate' scale, e.g. Platoon, Company, Battalion and all forms of sporting activity in the afternoons – but not many soldiers would go off to the gymnasium under their own steam and bodybuild. What they did love was the opening of the Navy, Army and Air Force Institute (NAAFI) and pursuing the noble art of beer-drinking. Often they would spend all their weekly pay in the first three nights and the remainder of the week was fallow until the next pay day. Remember, there was no TV and the local German girls were not that keen on going out with an impoverished young soldier who could hardly afford a bus fare.

The four Fusiliers whose story I now recount had ventured forth into town and had drunk their fill in the local hostelry where beer was more expensive than in the camp, which meant that they had no bus fare for the sparse service that operated on the long road back to barracks. No doubt they walked in the centre of the road in the hope that a motor car might come to the rescue. Certainly, as they weaved their path home they sang and swore at each other in the usual jocular manner. Fusilier Fish recalled that they kept on looking behind them in case any military transport came along and he was in the process of completing this manoeuvre when he saw a camel in the fading summer light. It was 100 yards or so behind when he belched and thought, 'Flip, oh gawd I really drunk much more than I thought, I'm seeing things now.'

He didn't share what he had seen with his comrades, fearful they would brand him a bigger idiot than he was. Later Fusilier O'Leary let on that he too thought he'd glimpsed the animal, but had also kept mum, probably for the same reason as Fish. In the end all four of them could not deny the fact that a camel's head had indeed appeared among them, scattering them in the process. Slowly, they recovered their senses and, since the camel seemed to like their company, they warmed to it.

'Flipping hell, flippin' camel,' they drunkenly shouted. When later they found themselves the target of ridicule, they would defend themselves: 'Well, how would you like a bloody great camel pushing you around?'

'Bloody great man-eater,' they said. When told that camels weren't carnivorous they replied, 'We didn't know that at the time, did we?' Luckily, Karl the camel, as we shall name him, had a halter on and could therefore be led, albeit gingerly at first. As they gathered confidence, and sobered by the shock, the irrepressible Lancashire humour came to the fore. 'If your mum could see you now Fishie Boy, you look like flippin' Lawrence of Arabia.'

The arduous march to barracks thus shortened by the novelty of a camel in their midst, the intrepid Camel Corps eventually reached the gates of the camp.

The white-painted stones hedging the smartly painted guardroom, the big brass bell of our affiliated ship HMS *Eurylus* and the silent de-flagged pole presented a formidable problem; for the custodians of the guardroom represented authority. The regimental police were one's first point of contact with the Regiment, so smartness was paramount and smart they were with their shiny brasses, white belt and anklets contrasting with bulled black boots and razor-sharp trouser creases. The sleeping guard (four hours on, two hours off) comprised soldiers from the infantry companies; they were lucky tonight for their mates were on duty and would help them through the 'gates of wrath'. They slowly led a rather shy camel through the gate and the least drunk of the four (one faced arrest for being belligerently drunk) said to his mate on duty, 'Tell the Guard Sergeant we've got a camel here, Nick.' This was duly reported to the ever-alert and eagle-eyed Sergeant Coulter, inside the guardroom.

'Tell them to get to bed or they will be banged up in the cells, if they're not careful.'

'Yar, Sarge, but what should they do with the camel?' he shouted.

The Guard Sergeant, not looking up but continuing to write his log, humoured them: 'Take it to flippin' transport.' Later he owned that he thought they were just a little happy and it was all a joke.

That was good enough for the incipient Camel Corps lads; they had their orders and off they went. Those coming out late from the NAAFI and probably worse for wear rubbed their eyes and thought that they were seeing things. The four, now imbued with a sense of importance, pressed on to fulfil their mission to rid themselves of Karl; as they sobered up they noticed that there was a distinct odour to him (I don't think the gender was actually established) which wasn't too pleasant. They entered the MT compound where the duty NCO was deep in slumber.

'Here, Scouse, we've got another addition to the fleet, where do you want it mate?' they announced.

'What is it?' he sleepily replied.

'A camel, mate, where do you want it?'

'Just leave it here,' he yawned and rolled over – and that's just what they did, but not before they quipped to each other, 'Should we get him to sign for it?'

The story becomes a little confused from hereon as we have no primary witness. Allegedly Scouse, thinking that his chums were drunk (and here he wasn't short of the mark) curled up and played dumb just to get rid of them. However, when a rather bored camel started slavering in showers over him, he allegedly jumped out of the window in sheer terror.

The last part of the story was well documented, for my chum Charlie Carmichael was the duty officer and he ordered that the camel was now part of the newly formed L F Camel Corps and was therefore eligible to be held on the unit's ration strength. At 0700 hours Karl was fed a soldier's breakfast in the cook-house and his photograph was duly taken with his rescuers; they smiled and Karl looked haughty. Later, the police were contacted and it transpired that he belonged to a travelling circus, who had travelled but somehow forgotten Karl the Camel.

Postscript

A week or so later the very blond debonair ex-Rugby schoolboy Charles appeared at coffee time, nonchalantly, smoking his cigarette. He was opening his mail when a broad smile spread across his face.

'Isn't it marvellous?' he laughed, '£12 from the *Daily Express* for the camel story – which will be published today.'

He didn't miss a trick did Charlie boy!

PPS

Years later, truth would out. The old tale of the runaway camel was gradually replaced in the telling by the facts: our lads had liberated, stolen, borrowed (whatever you will) Karl from the circus. But I don't think the *Express* will ever get their money back.

15

KAPE

Keep the Army in the Public Eye, or KAPE as we called it, was a way of doing just that, letting the country know that we still had a Navy, Army and Air Force around. The armed services have a high profile now because of our involvement in Iraq and Afghanistan. However, I am certain that most right-minded people saw our presence there as a step too far and meddling in other people's affairs, while at the same time putting at risk the well-being of our country's youth. They, therefore, divorced the culpability of our politicians from the actions of the fighting services and once the casualties came streaming home there followed a massive vote of sympathy for us which still exists today.

This was not the case in 1960. The Second World War had been over for just fifteen years and people remembered the terrible deprivation of it all. This was kept fresh in our minds with the ongoing Cold War and the fact that we had national service which required all able-bodied men to give two years of their young lives to their country's defence. This commitment was a burden to many and gave everyone a great excuse to grumble at what they saw as wasted, unproductive time. It is only now perhaps, some fifty years on, that our generation looks back with nostalgia on these halcyon days when young men forged friendships for life, discovered sports that had been denied them at school, while being introduced to something called loyalty, both to their unit and more importantly to each other. For many it was their first introduction to foreign climes, such places as Cyprus, Malta, Libya, Aden, Bahrain, Norway for winter warfare, and British Army of the Rhine, Germany. Some were to wear exotic badges, like the Somaliland Scouts, Gold Coast Regiment, and be seconded to the far-flung King's African Rifles and sent to a host of other lands too numerous to mention. In my own great Regiment I should think that many of our branches are kept alive by those national servicemen who have this great pride in gentle hindsight.

The story I relate now refers to some of these young soldiers who were national service and, even though they would have refused to admit it then, already had an incipient loyalty to the Yellow Hackle and the red flash on our shoulders which proclaimed us to be infantry, but, more than that, Lancashire Fusiliers.

KAPE took place every year about May or June time when thirty hand-picked soldiers were selected to represent the Regiment in our traditional recruiting area of Lancashire, as our corps d'elite. It was a coveted job for it meant that the lads could travel home and see girlfriends and families at the Army's expense. We therefore picked the smartest men in the Battalion, with an emphasis on youth. The 1960s was a time of resurgence, Carnaby Street, the Beatles, hot pants and fun; there was also full employment and this spelt doom in the world of Army recruiting. For who wanted to submit to military discipline while receiving half the wages of one's contemporaries in 'civvy street'? KAPE therefore had to show the populous that not only were our soldiers bright and smart, but happy too.

Furthermore, the XX recruited throughout Lancashire, and with their remarkable fighting tradition were well thought of in the area. Bury and the First and Fifth Battalions were closely allied with their 'six VCs'; it was a matter of great pride that the Regiment won a total of eighteen Victoria Crosses in the 1914–1918 war, more than any other Regiment in the British Army, prompting the military historian Sir John Fortescue to give us the title 'the VC Regiment'. Even so, such pride was not a guarantee of good recruiting and I remember it being an uphill struggle.

Manchester airport had just been refurbished for I remember being impressed by the teardrops or large plastic 'thingies' that hung from the ceiling. I was then a 2/Lt I think, with ideas far above my station, for I remember proudly leading the contingent in, best uniforms and all displaying our Hackle. I was in service dress, Sam Browne with my British overcoat casually (well to be honest effetely) draped over my shoulders. I carried a new twenty-first-birthday present, a leather briefcase, and had my silver-topped swagger cane clenched under my left armpit. I was playing the part, and I suppose just showing off, but I jolly well did look smart, for every item of clothing was pretty much brand new and shoes and Sam Browne would have been immaculately polished by my batman. Young Fusilier Michael Towle was always two paces behind me, somewhat akin to Blackadder and Baldrick, not in looks but being 'put upon'. He struggled not only with his baggage but also mine, resembling a pack mule weighed down and weary.

We were led into the customs room where there were about half a dozen customs men. I hesitate to ascribe to them the word 'officers' as they always seem to behave abominably to the soldiers. I have noticed this so many times since, when they confiscate, penalise or just generally obstruct some impoverished squaddie who may have saved up to buy his mother or girlfriend a gift, only to charge him a whacking duty which he cannot pay. In short, they were bullies, considering the status of the soldiers they dealt with … but now it was my turn for public humiliation, before they started on the boys. My case was placed upon the counter by Towle. I knew the form. They would first ask me the questions and then prove me a liar by opening my case to find the illicit contraband.

'Have you anything to declare?' No 'sir' was added here, just an inimical attitude.

'No, nothing,' I said.

'No alcohol?' said he.

'None,' said I.

'No cigarettes?' he continued.

'No, none at all,' I replied.

'Any perfume?' he persisted.

All eyes were upon me now, both customs and Fusiliers as his interrogation continued towards his hoped-for coup de grace.

'No perfume,' I continued.

'So, nothing at all?' He leered distrustingly.

'No, nothing,' I insisted.

'So you are trying to tell me that you have come from the land of milk and honey where cigarettes and booze are tax-free and you haven't brought any with you?' he hectored.

'I don't smoke,' I retorted.

'You're telling me you haven't got a girlfriend or relative who you haven't brought cigarettes or perfume home for?'

'That is exactly right. I haven't brought any home for anyone,' I replied forcibly.

Perhaps this customs man had done his national service? Perhaps he didn't like officers, but he was certainly enjoying his moment of glory, or perhaps he thought that he was pleasing the Fusiliers and undermining my authority? Who knows, for he continued, 'And are you trying to tell me that your girlfriend isn't going to be the recipient of some exotic gift?'

He didn't have time to finish his question for out stepped Cpl John O'Grady, straight as a ramrod, immaculate as ever and intimidating with bright ginger hair, all of which added to his effectiveness as a fearsome competitor on the rugby field.

'Excuse me sir,' to the nasty customs man. 'Are you doubting the word of our officer?' he said, not belligerently but firmly. Still the customs man did not see the trap he was walking into, for he had alienated his audience and must have been a bad judge of the collective psyche: no smile was seen on the Fusiliers' faces, no side-long glances of pleasure admiring the custom man's pluck and my discomfort. Indeed, just the opposite as Cpl O'Grady reiterated his question.

'Are you doubting our officer's word?'

'Well, I suppose I am,' came the reply while a smile of pleasure spread across his face, for he would now reveal me as a cheat, scoundrel and liar – but it was not to be. Cpl O'Grady had had enough.

'That's it lads,' he shouted, 'get the bastards.'

It was all very quick, the six customs men backed right up against the wall unprepared for the onslaught to come. Most of the Fusiliers still had cases and other impedimenta in their hands which gave me just sufficient time to stop them going 'over the top', although about six were already on or over the counter. To this day I remember the scene vividly, but I cannot for the life of me remember what it was that I shouted to recall my happy Fusiliers, all ready and itching for a punch-up.

Suffice to say I never did open my suitcase, and before you ask, had I done so no cigarettes, alcohol or perfume would have been found there. It was a moment of great revelation, for in that moment I realised that we, the soldiers and I, were one. I may have tried to give the world the impression of an arrogant young man but the lads had seen through the façade and knew better. 'F*****g Mr Stacey sir, always in trouble,' were the words they would say in their cook-house when they saw me doing extra orderly officer's duties. So I suppose I well and truly identified with them now. What loyalty.

‡

Michael Towle was not really 'put upon'. In actual fact, quite the reverse, for when I said to him that my shoes were not as well 'bulled' as usual, he had replied that the chambermaid (in the Royal Hotel in Bury) 'hadn't quite got the hang of spit and polish yet!'

He didn't see as much of his family as he should have done, for he was staying in the same hotel as myself and not in the drill hall, because he had moved into the chambermaid's bedroom, who during those three weeks really did learn how to clean my Sam Browne every bit as well as young Michael! He told me later it was the best time he ever had in the Army, all play and no work!

We travelled to Rochdale, Oldham, Bolton, Shaw Middleton, Ramsbottom and lots of other venues within our territory. One day found us on a bombsite in Eccles where our anti-tank gun, 3-inch mortars, light machine guns (LMGs) and a miscellany of small arms and grenades were all on display to good effect. Suddenly a smart Humber Hawk motor car stopped and out stepped a well-dressed lady, rather too soigné for a bombsite. There was no doubt that she had a certain presence about her: imperious, striking, and with a strong aquiline nose. She asked who was in charge and was directed to me. She produced an impressive visiting card bearing the German title 'Von' and a hyphenated German-English name, and haughtily said in excellent English, flavoured with a distinctive Teutonic accent, 'I love the British officer class but have little time for the rest. However, my son wishes to join the British Army. Here is my address for tea at 4:30 p.m. today.'

I had no time to say other than, 'Hello, thank you and goodbye,' but since this is what we were here for I duly turned up with my driver, L/Cpl Riley who was driving a tough-looking Champ (a forerunner of the ubiquitous and reliable Land Rover), which I thought would impress the boy. Tea was nicely served, albeit in a very old rambling Victorian residence. Afterwards, I was plied with Benedictine of all things, although I had posed the question,

'Don't you think I should see your son now, time is getting on?'

'Well, he is only twelve and at prep school – but come and have a look at his bedroom you will see how interested he is in all things military.' It was indeed, festooned with flags, pennants, models of all kind and a wonderful variety of militaria which I would have loved to have played with ... well, examine, but I was urged on my tour to see next door ... 'so different,' she enthused, 'as it is maintained in the Biedermeier style, my favourite décor.' It was an impressive bedroom; at my age I had never heard of Biedermeier but I had to show a little zeal about an obviously unusual boudoir. It was a salutary experience being in the hands of an older woman as I didn't wish to appear too gauche and unworldly, for she was after all twice my age. Later, it was to remind me of a film which did the rounds in the 1970s called *The Graduate*, although I would have preferred Mrs Robinson (Anne Bancroft) to my enforced choice. At some stage I asked if there was a Mr Himmler von Brown only to be told that he was upstairs. Like so many times in my life when I have wanted to be brave and urbane I have found myself to be lacking a certain moral fibre, a loss of resolve. I guess it is a character flaw, for I had lost interest after the event. I was pursued down the path and was still being passionately kissed as I climbed embarrassed into the safety of the Champ to face the disbelieving, quizzical looks of L/Cpl Riley.

'Bloody hell, sir,' was all he could say.

'Shut up and don't say a word,' I said, half-imploring, as we sped off – but he did, for next day in Bolton the boys solicitously asked me how grandmother was? But who was I to complain when such loyalty had been so instinctively given. For afterwards I was told by my OC just how lucky we had been when we threatened the customs men. The Fusiliers' action in 1961 would not have found public approval in the climate of those days, for we, as I said, were looked on as licentious soldiers and little better than thieves, villains and vagabonds – but a happy band of men!

Postscript

L/Cpl Riley later became my full-time driver in Bury. Totally reliable, honest and hardworking. I wonder what happened to him? Cpl John O'Grady reached the top as Regimental Sergeant-Major before retiring as a Captain. To this day he is still a bulwark of the Regiment, tirelessly working for the XX in reunions and welfare. Recently, he donated a large amount of money for the XX the Lancashire Fusiliers memorial at the Arboretum in Staffordshire.

16

THE STORY OF TRUST

The summer of 1963 was an exciting period for a young man. The swinging sixties burst on the scene like a great tidal wave, sweeping away the grim austerity of what had come before. Suddenly, money was freer, restaurants blossomed in hitherto unknown places. The girls changed overnight, losing their coyness and suddenly being imbued with dazzling confidence … mini-skirts and hot pants liberated them from their mother's fashion sense and Biba, Mary Quant and others encouraged this permissiveness with cheap, fashionable clothes. The contraceptive pill was either *à la mode* or about to be so, and this was to change the nation's morals, or certainly those of the young. Soon Supermac, our Prime Minister, was to tell us that, 'We had never had it so good' – and he was right. Was it because we were young and everything a novelty? Was it because we were gaining in confidence with a little more money in our pockets? Probably a combination of all these things, though my generation's nostalgia for the 1960s is no doubt paralleled by our children now, when they too look back on a comparable time from their own past.

I remember foreign holidays were becoming increasingly popular. Spain in particular needed our foreign currency and we needed their glorious sunshine, cheap food and hotel rooms. Their dictator General Franco was ageing and becoming more pragmatic and in doing so allowed the building of hotels along the Mediterranean coast in the unspoilt fishing villages, still in a 1930 time warp. So it was that John Steeds and I decided to motor to the sun in my Peugeot 403. We started from Cuerden Hall, Bamber Bridge in Lancashire, our excitement somewhat contained by being asked to drop off two people unknown to us, but friends of a friend. They were twice our age and a rather successful man and wife team in journalism. John and I took it in turns to drive through the night and to share the petrol before finally dropping off our acquaintances in Barcelona some 1,000 miles away. They thanked us and gave us a bar of chocolate each for our trouble. Well that is how rich people become rich I guess! From then on we were able to relax and take the tortuous coast road which ambled along Costa Dorado, Costa del Agahar, through the historic city of Valencia until we reached the Costa Blanca and came upon a village which enthralled us. The hotel was the only modern building there, with an enchanting alfresco dining terrace and an inviting azure pool. It was everything we were looking for, a fishing village of some five hundred people, still friendly and eager to please. The sun shone all day and the small secluded beach was heaven. Its name was Benidorm ... now a metropolis of over one million souls. I returned to show my children this tiny village some years back, only to be overcome by the sheer terror of thousands of tourists, the infrastructure of a huge city with its noisy traffic and half-clad tourists in a miscellany of bars, restaurants and clubs all strangely replicating a sort of Blackpool in the sun. We didn't stay long enough to savour its night-life, which I am told is even more extreme.

Here we spent our time as young men do: swimming, snorkelling, drinking and chasing unattended bikini-clad girls. John was particularly successful ... Noella I think. An attractive young Detective Inspector's wife and I became friends; she was very encouraging with a great sense of fun.

'My husband wouldn't suspect or detect anything,' she said, 'not when he can drink beer all day.' Just as well the sea was there to cool me off! Unfortunately, I got a bad case of sunburn, unaware that prolonged periods in the sea did not negate the rays of the sun. We were reluctant to go but shaking the sand off our feet was imperative as our leave drew to an end.

Unfortunately, our journey home was not trouble-free, as we discovered to our chagrin that the water pump on the engine had broken, thus causing a serious overheating problem. Luckily, we limped over the border where a small one-man garage, besporting a 1920 petrol pump and other vintage artefacts (modern for this part of France), fitted a vintage 1920 water pump to a 1961 motor car. Needless to say, having charged us the earth for working 'overtime' ... well, the sacrosanct lunch hour ... and fitting a 'brand new pump', a further 150 miles on in the beautiful area of Languedoc the same problem manifested itself. The poor old engine spluttered and coughed with another serious bout of heartburn. The garage explained that some old duffer had fitted an old and inappropriate pump, hence our predicament and an even greater bill than before. Some things never change over the years! Now there are breakdown services included in your foreign travel package – perhaps there was then but we didn't avail ourselves of it. Now there are plastic credit and debit cards and ubiquitous 'holes in the wall'; then, there were only travellers' cheques and these were all but depleted. What were we to do? Our children would have resorted to their sophisticated mobiles and other such things but we could only just manage to use a French pay phone and that got us nowhere.

Nothing daunted, we noticed that we were in the environs of a place called Carcassonne. Our eager – well, desperate – eyes had seen that it possessed a military garrison and it was to here that we now repaired – just like Tweedledee and Tweedledum. For more formal dining and crossing back into the UK we both had brought our regimental blazers complete with XX buttons and our identical rose and primrose regimental ties. Now Carcassonne, I should explain, is a superb walled medieval city on the banks of the River Aude, now noted for its vineyards. In the thirteenth century, however, its past was not so peaceful as the Albigensian Crusade swept down the Rhone valley and besieged the Cathars, a religious sect of south-west France, which the Pope had vowed to stamp out. Over the centuries this magnificent fortress fell into disrepair until some far-sighted archaeologist persuaded Paris to restore it to its former glory, circa 1850. It is now a World Heritage site and a great tourist attraction.

It was here that we marched up the ramparts of the castle to the military camp that the fortress had originally been built for. With our bad French we briefly explained our plight until we were eventually shown into the office where the adjutant sat, magnificent in his blues and unmistakeable kepi. We were even more impressed with his brilliant English and his immediate grasp that two young men (looking like twins), whom he had never met before, wanted a considerable amount of money to repair a motor car (albeit French) which was to disappear over the channel into perfidious Albion never to be seen again. We would of course repay the money immediately on our return to UK shores. A likely story indeed. Well-dressed con men … more likely!

He showed us every courtesy and disappeared next door, presumably to brief the Commandant. The latter was equally impressive, both fit and smart, as were all the troops befitting their infantry/parachute role. The Commandant without a murmur or even asking us our unit authorised full cash payment. We were overcome with such kindness and their boundless faith and trust in us. Indeed, when John stepped forward, 'And this sir, is my address,' proffering his visiting card, there was a quick riposte.

'And why would I need that,' said the Commandant, 'I am not planning on visiting you.'

To this day we both laugh at this little story – I say little but in truth it is far from that, for it was largesse on a monumental scale. At no stage did they ask to see our passports or our military identity cards, although to hand. I suppose the very act of doing so would have implied that they disbelieved we were what we said we were, young Army officers; after all that would never do for the brotherhood of arms.

Postscript

The money was returned within an hour of us arriving in Dover. When we returned to RHQ Bury we sent these wonderfully trusting French officers a XX Regimental Shield. Could it be that fifty years on it still adorns the bar in some French Officers' Mess? It would be nice to think so. As for John Steeds ... still what we used to describe as 'smooth'. An excellent sportsman, both real/royal and even 'unreal' tennis, still possessing endless energy and enthusiasm for life with a great knowledge of art – but we won't be going to Benidorm again!

17

A NAUGHTY STORY

And not to be read by my daughters,
Or even granddaughters

When I was doing recruiting in Bury, Lancashire, I fell for a lovely young woman who was bright, nubile, beautiful and quite a senior grade civil servant. I kept bumping into her in the shared offices of the MOD (Army) recruiting centre and a tax department of the civil service. I say bumping into her but it was really observing her shapely figure disappearing down the long corridors of this Manchester building, while the vagrants drank methylated spirits on a bombsite outside, all under the shadow of HM Strangeways prison, perched on the hill.

Eventually, Sgt Harvie, RAOC, introduced me and I was to take her out regularly during my year-long stay. She was already divorced and had a charming little girl aged four. She also managed to model for a catalogue magazine and I still possess lots of her photographs over fifty years on. We had wonderful weekends in rural hotels – the Bells of Peover in Cheshire, the Spa Hotel in Buxton and other hideaways in the Trough of Bowland and Cumberland. The great thing about the British Army is that however impetuous and romantic one is, cold water in torrents is poured down like a waterfall, extinguishing any flames of romance … and by this I mean far-away postings.

So it was that the death-knell tolled for the end of the relationship, but not without a little fight. I had just been promoted Captain and was soon to fly out to Rhodesia; however, like all youth, we wished to squeeze every minute of the day into a lingering farewell. As always I had a 'cunning plan'. We would spend out last weekend together in the Army & Navy Club in Pall Mall, London. Now this establishment, as it still is today, is a very bastion of middle-class conservatism. It had, however, shown remarkable prescience by being the first club to admit females. In 1962 this was indeed a bold innovation which other London clubs were to follow.

Marjorie and I arrived on Friday afternoon, having previously booked in as Captain and Mrs Stacey, which sounded very respectable and grown up. In those days it was still a 'crime' to carry one's immorality into such an institution and if I had been caught I would not only have forfeited my club membership but may have been thrown out onto the street without compunction. It was therefore essential that the correct jewellery was worn – an engagement and wedding ring – and that we behaved with propriety. Now it so happened that I always entertained my girlfriends in the Ladies Suite for afternoon tea and dinner and was therefore known to all the female staff. Furthermore, my favoured sofa was right under the bewitching portrait of naughty Nell Gwynn, favourite mistress of Charles II, which seemed more than appropriate for an illicit weekend.

It was here that we ordered tea and, as bad luck would have it, my favourite young waitress was on duty. Since everything was put on the bill, she knew that we were staying there. I therefore had to shyly admit that we had just got married. This prompted a quick flight to the kitchen and a cohort of other young things all coming to see us and offer their congratulations. I suppose the average age of the club was fifty-plus and mostly made up of retired officers, so any young man caught their eye and there was some communion between us. By the same token young decorative women did rather stand out. Our weekend was further complicated when my friend telephoned to say the Commanding Officer of the First Battalion the Lancashire Fusiliers, one Lt Col Jim Wilson, was staying at the club the following night. This meant that we were conveniently confined to our bedroom and any movement became surreptitious. It was on Monday morning that we bade our sad farewells, Marjorie returned to Manchester and I took flight to Africa. It was all rather sad, but at least I had a continent to explore.

My first stopover was in the then lovely city of Salisbury (Harare) in Southern Rhodesia, probably some 24 hours later. From there I flew on the next day to my final destination of Lusaka, in Northern Rhodesia, so perhaps two or more days had elapsed since I had left my true love behind and distance had already stretched my loyalty, or so it would appear. I was met at the airport by a handsome young staff officer Captain, Alistair McKenzie, obviously in a Scottish Regiment for he sported a kilt and wore what we called 'mutton chops'. The airport was nondescript and my first glimpse of the local women was a couple of cleaners, old and bent with toil. As we shook hands, he later declared that my first question was, 'What does one do for women here?' Now, I don't deny that at some stage I did indeed ask this question but I maintain that it was my second or third enquiry.

'You go black dear boy, you go black,' he smiled. Looking at the little old lady in her brown overall and facial hair sweeping up in the transit lounge I heard myself saying, 'You have my word that I will never go black.'

We departed the airport and that evening I had a very pleasant dinner pool-side in the Ridgeway Hotel with my General and Pam, his very attractive wife. I even remember that we had chicken-in-a-basket, circa 23 April 1964. I remember that but I have forgotten what I did a week ago!

I soon settled in the job and loved the constant sunshine but something was missing in this paradise and I found myself ringing Alistair three days later.

'Alistair, how did you say one goes black, dear boy?' I quietly whispered; he was only three doors down the corridor but the telephone was more secure and I hastily took the details of what was to be an exciting night-rendezvous. I still thought of the lovely Marjorie with her jet-black hair ... I think ... but she was half a world away and here was I celibate and lonely. That night after dinner and still besuited I motored into town and along the dual carriageway until the road came to an end and only darkness extended into a void. Underneath the wash of the last street lamp I beheld some ladies of the night who flashed brilliant white smiles in the semi-darkness. One young thing said, 'Yes, you come home with me for 7/6' (or about 37p). One could hardly call this prostitution ... it was just a little honorarium. I opened my motor car door for her and nervously said, 'Take a seat,' or words to that effect.

'No, no,' she emphatically declared, 'follow my reflector man.' It appeared that these women were rather high-class for they took pride in being independent and owning a brand new Raleigh bicycle. Apparently, the girls in Frankfurt am Main employed a similar technique but in smart open sports cars and wearing beautiful hats! I had no option but to do as she pleased, so I followed her reflector and observed her ample buttocks working hard as she progressed through the gears. To my mortification she suddenly did a U-turn and I found myself in the glare of the town lighting as I proceeded at about 6 mph in first gear. Then, horror of horrors, I saw three officers with their wives coming out of a popular restaurant and walking towards me and their parked roadside motors.

'Goodnight, Elizabeth, see you in the morning Peter,' I could clearly hear them say as they continued towards me. By this stage I was already underneath the dashboard ... well, almost, the tiniest aperture of vision was afforded as I peered through the steering-wheel spokes. It must have looked like the *Mary Celeste*, as it not too majestically proceeded driverless on its way. My other worry was would they recognise the motor car, which I had taken over from the previous ADC, my lifelong friend John Steeds. Somehow I negotiated this hazard and proceeded at this lumbering pace … until suddenly the reflector turned left and we bumped along a dirt track into a black world of shadows and roundels. At this time my beacon was her teeth which shone like pearls. I waited to get some sort of night vision and perceived the silhouette of round-shaped huts with quaint half-doors to which I was led bent double. It was an earthen floor and I could detect the faint breathing of children. I think there was a sort of mattress or material as we laid on the floor. I was still fully dressed and totally disorientated in a room of darkness. Suddenly, she kissed me with a passion and I swear to this day that I saw her tonsils. Her kiss reminded me of my childhood experience with Mr Parker the dentist, when he placed a wadding of chloroform over my face in order to put me asleep. I could not breathe and began to panic, for her wet kiss had completely enveloped my face. Somehow, I pushed her away gasping for air and said that I must undress. In that instant I was up and away and making for the strip of moonlight that had shown itself through the entrance. I quickly gained my motor car and negotiated my escape along the little track and to home.

I never did go black and I didn't feel too bad for my erstwhile amour as I had given her a handsome bounty which would adequately feed her sleeping family. Looking back on the experience it was like swimming out of one's depth for one needs the reassurance of one's own little world. Marjorie was still alive.

My next love, some two weeks later, was an attractive green-eyed woman with a bubbling personality and a good sense of humour. She was married with two small children and a husband. She invited me to dinner which was very pleasant but when I noticed the table set for two I asked the whereabouts of her husband. He apparently lived in the bush for about six weeks out of every eight; she was very much available and needed a passionate affair to bring some zest into a marriage which had been in the doldrums for some time. Over the following weeks I discovered that the husband was a geologist – a big, rather taciturn Scot who had two Rhodesian Ridgebacks to look after him in the bush. These she thought were his first love. He diligently practised knife-throwing and was something of a celebrity in throwing these with accuracy and speed at barbecues and parties. Lastly, in his home and on his belt was ample evidence of his profession in the form of geological picks. They lived in a company compound of eight identical bungalows, all in a neat row. At the windows were mosquito meshes and the back door was locked every night from the outside by the houseboy who lived in the garden and let himself in every morning at 6 a.m. to prepare breakfast.

I have been told many times what a cad I am but I have always rationalised my behaviour by the fact that all the women I have met have been free agents and I have never made the first move. Indeed, Anne in this instance had told me that she had been dreaming about me ... now, how silly was that? Furthermore, as a man I knew that the very husbands who pointed a finger of infidelity at their wives were the greatest hypocrites of all in doing the self-same thing on a regular basis. On the other hand, I simply do not understand people who cannot give up smoking, have a drink problem or gamble for I have the will to terminate these in the same way as turning on or off a water tap. I can go without food for a good five days and have done so at least twice, I can go without water for excessive periods and have the strength to run marathons or perform long feats of endurance but I am unhealthily lusty. However, this is a thin veil to part-justify my behaviour.

Anne and I spent many happy evenings together. I never met the children for they were always in bed. I never saw the houseboy for he had always long since departed, nor did I bump into the company neighbours for darkness descends quite early in this part of Africa. We had dined well and were in bed blissfully happy and now asleep. Suddenly, there was a loud, imperative banging on the bedroom window and I awoke to Anne hiding her screams.

'Oh my god, it's my husband, he has come back early. Oh my god, he will kill you. Oh my god, HE WILL KILL YOU. He'll be done for murder. Oh god, Oh god.' I was out of bed and like a shot had my underpants on, still the same to this day, like swimming trunks; unfortunately in my haste, the waist and two leg holes were mixed up and I was already in terrible pain as they succeeded in castrating me. I was already disadvantaged if there was to be a fight – but now I repeated my mistake but this time it was my braces, instead of going over my shoulders, they trussed up in between my legs ... now a double castration. My hair was probably damp from the heat anyway but now it was wet and sticking to my perspiring forehead and sweating, florid face. My kneecaps were like tappets, jumping involuntarily up and down and my legs wanted to bend and give way, all this while nauseous groans erupted from the bottom of my stomach as I retched to be sick.

At this point I have to say that I don't think I am a coward but when you are plainly in the wrong – then you probably deserve to die. I just hoped it would be quick; throwing knives or dogs would be slow and painful. I could not escape through the windows. I could not leave through the back door. I could not hide in the baby's cot and the small divan of the other child was floor-bound and anyway, he was bound to go there in time. My only escape was to lie under the marital bed...

'But the dogs will sniff you out,' said Anne, distraught and keeping up her chants.

'Don't let them in here, say they smell or something,' I replied. I had not put on my Chelsea boots but in those seconds, deemed it prudent to wear them like gloves – in this way as I lay under the bed

I could punch the dogs as they growled and tried to scratch me out of my lair. All these thoughts went through my head but what was worse by far were the headlines in the *Northern Rhodesian Times*.

'ADC Murdered By Irate Husband'.

I would bring disgrace on my Regiment and the General more so, as he was on the spot and would probably have to make a statement. Never again, if I were spared, would I endure such humiliation. I would willingly embrace celibacy forever … perhaps a monastic life would be better with no temptations … but don't they sometimes mix with nuns? No, probably not. One more thing was to go wrong, as Anne lifted the bed and I crawled under I realised that, as thin as my 11 stones were, the stubby legs of the bed did not quite reach the floor, short by about half an inch. If Iain, whom I had still not met, was longing for his wife's affections, I realised that my brains would be pounded to death by any exertions from above. I lay there in a pool of cold sweat surrounded by an aura of fear. The banging returned impatiently and Anne began shouting.

'I am coming, I am coming … just wait.' I heard the door open … I could hear exasperated voices … I heard the door close, was he going to unload his Land Rover? I heard Anne running down the corridor and open the door to the bedroom. She struggled this time to half-lift the bed as I began to crawl out, as tear-stained she said, 'It's all right darling, come back to bed – it's that drunken sot from next door, he is so drunk, he has got the wrong house … let's get back to bed.'

I didn't, I was so appalled by my cowardice and behaviour that I was chastened … I was off sex forever … in fact I was, for a whole four days! Africa was not easy, but my next girlfriend was everything proper. White, single, attractive, but when I suggested a long weekend at the Victoria Falls Hotel, she insisted we travel separately.

'Why so?' I asked.

'What if the Foreign Office got to know I was on a dirty weekend?' she groaned.

Life has really progressed since then. We were looked on as depraved youngsters, especially if caught. Now young people go on weekends without such derogatory remarks as 'dirty' being directed at them. What's wrong with a ski-weekend, a sailing weekend or in my case a sightseeing weekend to the falls. Why should the FO object ... it was our weekend and not theirs ... but that's how things were, not so long ago.

Postscript

When my lovely Marjorie and I were Captain and Mrs Stacey at the Rag (Army & Navy Club), the female staff had laundered something and packed my case, or perhaps opened it in the foyer, prior to my departure. When I eventually reached my destination and I opened it, out shot shoals of rice and a lovely card congratulating me on my marriage. Rice I think was an old tradition representing fertility. However, there was one more near-scrape for me to survive, and once again appropriately underneath the Nell Gwynn portrait. It was almost a year later, February 1965, and I had met a girl in Durban with whom I had spent some leave. Jenny, a lovely blonde, had followed me over to the UK, indeed, she was to spend some months here, but a posting to Borneo ... well you know the scene. I ordered tea as I introduced her to *Country Life*, and who was to bring it but my favourite waitress.

'Captain Stacey, how wonderful to see you,' she said enthusiastically. I smiled. 'And how is your beautiful wife?' she added.

Jenny looked daggers at me ... a look that said, 'You bastard I have come all this way and you are married.' My smile faded but my brain was quick.

'Oh, how sweet of you to ask ... but didn't you know ... well, how could you ... oh, it was dreadful, she was killed in a car crash only two months after the wedding.'

I didn't want a free tea for two. I really did try to pay, but when they all came to commiserate with my loss what could I do? Dreadful business, but I said it with such conviction that I even believed it myself.

PPS
If ever read by my daughters or granddaughters by mistake: this is all made up. I didn't do it. Honest.

18

AFRICAN IGNORANCE

When I was in Central Africa some of my friends would write to me and say, 'Dear Lawrence, I hear that you're stationed in Lusaka now. How fascinating – just a line to say my sister's moved to Lagos so why don't you pop up and see her – she would love to meet up again.'

I would write back and say words to the effect:

'Remember Clarissa Wristwatch? Well she has just been posted to Boston, USA. Why don't you pop over – she will give you a good time for your money. Oh yes, and you're a thousand miles nearer.' The joke isn't original, I purloined it from Kenneth Horne, I think, but the ignorance about Africa and other parts of the globe is genuine. We all have views and opinions but so few of us actually know the facts and understand the local problems of so many things we comment on – including myself. However, I was lucky enough to see something of the vast continent and, if not totally comprehend its many complexities, have at least some knowledge of its immense diversity and multifarious cultures. However, on returning to the UK my knowledge was to land me in deep trouble for I was invited (well actually ordered) to give six lectures to teachers' training colleges and other institutions.

We were all highly critical of apartheid in South Africa while at the same time the civil rights movement in the USA was about to take off. The Americans of course condemned South Africa but couldn't see the terrible intolerance and injustices operating right under their own noses. In Britain all the black officer-cadets and undergraduates were well-educated, generally well-turned-out with stiff white collars and from good families and this was the perception held by most people in the UK – that the Africans they had met were educated and should be in charge of their own destiny. However, as my African chums freely admitted, they were probably less than 1 per cent of the population. Africa was a brooding, boiling maelstrom just ripe to burst.

Northern Rhodesia was a case in point. Alice Lenshina was a self-proclaimed prophetess who led a religious party against the elected President Dr Kaunda. It broke into open rebellion and she was able to convince her followers that they would be immune from the black soldiers' bullets if they spread excretion over their bodies. The tribal women also placed their babies on the backs and proceeded in front of their menfolk who wielded the traditional assegai as they marched into battle and the fire of their own country's troops. The British were only responsible for foreign policy in the lead-up to independence, so this was in no way a confrontation of our doing. People back in England listening to my lecture resented the fact that about three people a month were hanged in the Congo for infanticide cannibalism. Indeed, later I was to learn that a super Nigerian officer of my intake at Sandhurst had been wounded whilst serving with the United Nations Forces in the very same theatre; his ambulance was ambushed by the rebels and he was butchered and eaten on the spot.

However, what seemed to upset my audience most of all was when someone asked me, 'Well, why don't their mothers' blow their noses with handkerchiefs or even paper tissues?' and I tried to explain that the poverty of so many of these people was indescribable and that luxuries such as toiletries, sanitary towels and even handkerchiefs were unheard of.

'Well, what do they do?' they inimically hounded me.

'What everyone does, they place their mouths over the children's noses, inhale the mucous and spit it out.'

The truth was too much to bear and certainly three if not more young women walked out, branding me a liar as well as 'disgusting'. I was carpeted for this and censured for trying to explain that our worlds were poles apart and therefore it was wrong to try and judge them by our own standards. I haven't been back to Zambia or the beautiful 'highlands' of Malawi, but I am told on good authority that the town I once thought of as Harrogate (without the spa) or Tunbridge Wells, the town of Harare (formerly Salisbury), is no longer the idyllic place it was. The country of Zimbabwe is under a far worse master than colonialism, and justice and human rights are non-existent, well and truly buried.

The poor Africans simply swapped one yoke of oppression for a far worse one – but wasn't it ever thus?

19

THE STITCH UP

When I was serving in Africa in 1963 I was lucky to see the last days of colonialism. I don't think there was much 'Raj' about it – by which I mean the majesty of Empire as associated with India – but by and large I observed that most of the civil servants and expatriates were hard-working and conscientious.

Our role was to break up the federal armies of Northern Rhodesia, Southern Rhodesia and Nyasaland and reconstitute the national armies of Zambia and Malawi. To me Africa was seen as a puppy must view the world in its first few days of life – a mixture of bewilderment and sheer excitement. I met every head of state and was present in the Royal Box on two occasions when we witnessed what we called rather shamefully the 'flag trampling ceremony', when the Queen's representative came to see the British flag lowered for the last time and bid good luck to the newly independent country. To those cynics who thought our role as Empire builders was wrong, I would argue the opposite: that is not to say everything in the garden was rosy, but thank goodness it was Britain and not other major powers who filled the vacuum. Here is one little story that demonstrates my point.

Any of our local staff who became ill would as often as not

come to see me and ask if, we, the Headquarters, would pay for them to see the white doctor. This we always did. The white doctor was not only on our social list for drinks and dinner parties but as a resident and working doctor in Lusaka for some thirty-five years, he was undoubtedly a pillar of society, a mentor to those of us who were ignorant of the ways and practices of the Dark Continent. In short he was wiser than Solomon – who I never actually met! He was also the epitome of a gentleman, gracious to all, black and white, young and old. His height, his looks and unconscious urbanity commanded everyone's respect. His wife also ran a lovely home with manicured gardens providing a haven for those lucky enough to know such a couple. It was to this man that our staff went and invariably he would put their minds at rest, give them the necessary tablets and say emphatically, 'Now Joseph, I want you to go to the witch doctor in the market so he can confirm my diagnosis.'

This of course he was happy to do, not only because he knew that the witch doctor's magic would cure him but by the time he had hitched a lift to town and queued to see the witch doctor the morning or afternoon was gone.

I had actually been to the witch doctor quite unwittingly when I was taken around the market. A place so alien to my idea of a market and so full of foul smells and evil skeletal fish all hanging in various states of decomposition and liberally covered in thousands, if not millions, of flies. The witch doctor's hut and his display of dried bits of animals, penis, testicles and other unmentionable things did not fill me with confidence – but there again I didn't see myself getting my prescription from him. To continue, Joseph would indeed attend the witch doctor, who would ask him if he had seen the white doctor. 'Yes, Bwana,' Joseph would reply.

'And what did he give you to take?' the witch doctor enquired.

'These tablets Bwana,' was Joseph's reply.

'Well Joseph, I want you to take the white doctor's tablets, but what you really need to get better, and must take, is this alligator's claw. Now you must promise to suck it three times a day.'

There was a small charge for the witch doctor's service but, before you complain, the British taxpayer was in no way involved.

I saw the doctor, the white doctor that is, quite regularly at the many social functions held in the city and he and his wife would always say, 'Lawrence, do pop in for a sundowner when passing. We would love to see you anytime.' I suspect that, since I was a bachelor in a largely married community, they felt sorry for me. One day when passing I heard the ping of tennis balls and thought that I would take them up on their invitation. I was invited in and asked what I would like to drink by a member of the staff, who also informed me that the doctor was outside. I made my way to the garden and saw a very plush garden-lounger with tasselled canopy gently swinging. I recognised the white hair of the doctor as his head turned and he got up to greet me ... 'Ah young Lawrence, what a pleasure, have you got a drink? Come and meet my friend Kwazi.'

As I walked to the other side of the swaying seat I saw a fly whisk agitating the air, an oldish black lined face under a traditional African hat and a voluminous and gaily coloured kaftan. The man was probably in his sixties, with tired rather bloodshot eyes, but nevertheless he gave me a warm smile as he continued rocking.

'But you're the witch doctor, sir,' I said, astonished.

'Yes, that's right,' he smiled even more.

'But you're the opposition,' I protested.

'Oh no dear boy,' the white doctor interjected. 'We've been friends, how long now Kwazi? Thirty years is it, yes, thirty years.'

He kept on laughing and answering himself. 'We have our sundowner every week, always on a Thursday ... isn't it Kwazi, yes every Thursday. How do you think we keep Lusaka healthy?' They both laughed conspiratorially, like schoolboys, as they took another gulp of their whisky and soda.

Now that's diplomacy.

20

THE NYASALAND
INDEPENDENCE
CELEBRATIONS

Nyasaland, now Malawi, is a small landlocked country in east Africa, squeezed in between Tanzania to the north, Mozambique to the south and east, and Zambia to the west, all considerably larger neighbours. When I set foot there it had a population of around 4 million. It gained its independence on 6 July 1964, and I was twenty-four years of age at the time and wondering what I was doing in the Royal Box on this, my second independence celebration.

I suppose that I should have been honoured and privileged to see history in the making, but there was an ambivalence to it all, a certain niggle and queasiness with which I couldn't entirely come to terms. It hadn't been that long ago that I had sat in a classroom and proudly gazed at a map of the world painted pink for 'Britishness'. It was even less time since I had graduated from RMA Sandhurst, when we studied our military history, and there realised that it was British arms that had been responsible for our hegemonic world presence. Indeed, as a boy, we still had an Empire, now in the process of metamorphosis into a Commonwealth.

Now, I think that independence is all well and good but then as a partisan young Englishman I didn't entirely agree that everything we British did was bad. I know that this is a terrible thing to say and that we should as a nation be wearing sackcloth and ashes while simultaneously writing cheques to the rest of the world for our atrocious behaviour and bloodthirsty deeds. Wouldn't it have been much better if Russia, China, Turkey, the Nazis, the Boers or those benign Japanese had enlightened them, or better still one of the Arab nations, who would of course extended to them their religious tolerance? I am inordinately proud of our Victorian forebears and what those cerebral and industrious people did for us and the world, but there again I have always been out of step.

I was then what was called an aide-de-camp (ADC) to Major-General George Lea, an officer in the Lancashire Fusiliers. As such it was his prerogative to choose an ADC. This was usually done within the Regiment, hence my appointment. I considered it a great honour, as it allowed me to see the political machinations that took place during the independence of Zambia and now Malawi (Nyasaland).

HRH Prince Philip, Duke of Edinburgh, was representing Her Majesty the Queen and General George Lea had as General Officer Commanding (GOC) Northern Rhodesia and Nyasaland, appointed me to be the Prince's local ADC. The duties were not that onerous but since I was the man on the spot I was there to help his equerry. Prince Philip was in his prime, just forty-three years old and with his easy charm captivated all those with whom he came into contact. I remember all the good and the great lining up to meet him as he disembarked in his naval whites. I think that I was last in line to shake his hand as number ten or eleven. Consequently, he was probably running out of original witticisms by the time I was introduced, which produced a temporary lull in the conversation. I therefore helped him out by saying that, 'I was pretty unpopular today for my new uniform had not arrived (together with George Lea's) from England and I was therefore wearing a pretty shabby one,' or words to that effect. He promptly took a half-pace back, re-examined me and said as he brought his elbow pretty hard into my sternum, 'I don't blame them, dear boy,' which of course produced a light-hearted moment and a laugh at my expense. In fact, I was far less in awe of the Duke than I was of my own General, for I found him very easy-going. The following year in Borneo was a revelation for he was much more brittle, but then we were on a war footing, whereas Malawi was projected as a celebration with a carnival type atmosphere.

Royal visits are not all smiles and play time, especially behind the scenes. I remember thinking that it was just like being at Sandhurst again – one big rush. One event followed another and all required a quick change of uniform. For the royals, it was obviously a little easier as all our plans revolved around them and their convenience was therefore paramount. Besides, they had professional valets and dressers with them who were experts at their job. For the rest of us it was much more difficult, often in temporary accommodation, perhaps without a batman and with so many bits and pieces to cope with, swords and sword belts, boots and spurs, a miscellany of epaulettes, gold or blue to wear with screw-in buttons and tiny holes, silver scabbard for this, leather one for something else. Mess kit, whites for this event but not for that one, cummerbunds, dinner jackets, white gloves, leather gloves and different hats for different occasions. I think in one day we had five changes of uniform and as ADC I had other concurrent duties, for instance, checking up on the drivers, making certain that they knew the routes, inspecting their vehicles to ensure that they were polished, that the correct pennants were flown and the correct rank plates displayed. Consequently, I had less time to change than anyone but had to be ahead of all in order to receive everyone and brief them as to their duties, seating plan and any differing protocol which may from time to time take place.

General George and I sat behind Prince Philip, and in that way he was able to communicate with us. In the front row together with the Duke of Edinburgh was the outgoing Governor and his wife, who sat on either side of the President, Dr Hastings Kamuzu Banda (born 1905). His official biography stated that the British had come to the area in 1889 and the Shire areas were to be administered by the British government, while the British South Africa Company held sway elsewhere. It went on to say that a Presbyterian or Church of Scotland missionary school had opened, in about 1908 I think, and this is where Hastings Banda's education had begun. What I found distasteful was the fact that it stated, 'denied a university education in his own country he was forced to seek it in South Africa.' My question to the General was that as we, the British, had just arrived, why hadn't the Bantu tribes built their own university in the preceding 1,000 years. This produced a *sotto voce* request from the Prince to shut up as he smilingly said to us something like, 'you'll get us all locked up.' So it was a very easy-going and friendly atmosphere but alas, it was not to continue. I should add that the remarkable Hastings Banda did indeed walk some 1,500 miles to attend a university in South Africa, but more of him later.

I found myself sitting next to Mr Iain Macleod and his wife. They had been personally invited to the celebration by Dr Banda for the loyal support and help Mr Macleod had given the President when he had been Foreign Secretary. He was a lovely man and we got on rather too well. This always surprised me, for I wondered how an ex-Cabinet minister who was well over twice my age could have anything in common with myself, still ignorant about most matters in life. Anyway, we had an animated conversation as we witnessed the events at the stadium in Zomba. Some two hours later when we got up to go, Mr Macleod produced from the other side of his chair a pair of crutches which I had been unable to see until then. I felt honour-bound to help him and his wife negotiate his way from the top tiers to the very bottom, where the VIP car park was. I should explain that the stadium was not purpose-built and although probably red-carpeted it had certain pitfalls in its scaffolding, especially for someone disabled. Indeed, they could not have done without me. I helped them all the way but was very conscious of the fact that I was going to be very late and had already noticed that there were only two motor cars left and looking very lonely. The Rover 110 was the Macleods' – the other a large American motor was literally bouncing on its springs (I was really ashamed of this vehicle, all bulbous and fin-like). The driver beckoned, holding open my door, as I hitched my sword up and ran bidding the Macleods a hasty farewell. Once in the motor car I was subjected to a torrent of acerbic abuse, delivered in terms of stentorian hysteria, a side of General George I had never seen before. I recalled later his experiences when commanding Eleventh Battalion Para at Arnhem and his time in captivity which could, I surmised, affect his equilibrium under stress. Lady Lea for once had no restraining influence on him, nor did she try.

'You are my bloody ADC – not his,' he snorted. Now all this might seem totally trivial to the reader – protocol is bad enough now but fifty years ago it was even more so. One could not be late – lateness was not an excuse but a crime. It meant that we would arrive after the great dignitaries and this would upset the strict precedence of the occasion. In between the blows of invective I was just able to say to him that I knew the back streets of Zomba well and could make up time and thus regain our correct position in the motor cavalcade – and this is just what I did.

'Go left down here,' I shouted to the driver.

'Now right, straight on, left here and…' I continued, as we negotiated our way down the deserted streets. The tyres squealed, the motor car bucked and bounced as the General shouted, 'Faster.'

Suddenly, we were where we were meant to be, as I gained

the side street which led to the main thoroughfare. I breathed a sigh of relief for my timing seemed impeccable. I saw the hordes of schoolchildren all dressed beautifully in clean clothes for the occasion, their parents and extended families all patiently lining the route. We had made it! The squealing tyres of the vehicle alerted the policemen that a large motor car was bearing down on them, its pennant flying and its intimidating chromium grille grimacing, as if to devour them if they dared not move. They sprang with alacrity to their duties, quickly clearing a path for our entrance onto the main road, a diffident hand indicating 'stop'. 'Slow down' was proffered but this was only temporary as I saw the reason for their caution – the police outriders in wonderful precision had passed by. The 'stop' hand signal now urgently beckoned us on. The motor car rolled and lurched to one side and the tyres again complained as we completed our right-hand manoeuvre onto the main drag. Lady Lea was thrown towards her husband, for we had no seat belts then – but still we had made the parade. Our sighs of relief were palpable but short-lived, indeed, about to turn to terror as we realised our faux pas. Suddenly, from the banks of eager spectators lining the road, there came ecstatic cheers, accompanied by thousands of Malawi and British flags which appeared from behind their backs. They were carrying out their well-drilled instructions.

'Once the motor cycle outriders go by the first motor car is the King's,' as someone told us later. We were therefore subjected to a thunderous welcome, the like of which only a friendly African crowd can give. I noticed a thousand faces smiling, shouting and looking at us, inclining their heads to see us better and all awhile the noise of welcome 'King' or some such thing. I waved back to them, initially rather bemused, but then with more confidence as I saw their adulation. Alas, the General had been better placed when we negotiated our tight 90-degree turn onto the crowded street, for fifty yards behind us loomed the Rolls-Royce containing the royal party … and we were stealing their thunder! If I had thought that I had been subjected to a venomous attack in the VIP car park nothing had prepared me for the next onslaught. There was a veritable stream of blasphemy as the General shouted at his long-suffering wife, whose beautiful hat was about to take a battering, while all the time berating me and shouting, 'get down you f***ing fool, get down.'

I may have been too preoccupied with the warmth of our reception to acknowledge his advice immediately, as I still continued to wave. I was now to be subjected to my second physical assault in two days, but whereas the punch in the chest from the Prince was playful, the General's was not for he had removed his hat and this became his weapon as he continued to swear at me. It came crashing down on my head not once but two or three times as he continued to exhort me to 'Get down you f***ing fool, get down.' I did have the presence of mind to be dignified as I slowly sank down into the well of the motor car for my left hand was still waving like a metronome as I disappeared beneath the dashboard – sunk without trace! If my demise had been relatively neat, I dreaded to think what was taking place in the back seat, for Pam was in all her lovely finery and the General at 6ft 4in. encumbered by his sword and medals had little place to go. They must have been like sardines and in all the heat too! However, as the ghost staff car glided on its way, apparently bereft of its passengers, there still continued a muffled but thunderous tirade which left me in no doubt who would be on the first VC10 flight back to London. The rest of the journey is a forgotten nightmare for I had sullied my General's good name and my report to my Regiment on being RTU – returned to unit – would tell them how I had let him down and therefore the Regiment too.

I can't remember much after that but my memory returned for the dinner given by the Governor and his wife Lady Jones, that night. I can't remember anything more being said, other than that the Leas had met the Macleods and they had got on so well together as they shared mutual friends or came from the same locality but this may have been sometime after the event, I think. I remember that Government House was rather quaint, like a pseudo fort, being castellated. Twenty-four of us sat down for dinner and for once the pressure was taken off me by the Governor's ADC, Peter Bicknall. In essence, he was a civilian and had been recruited as aide-de-camp through the civil service. I remember asking him 'but how did you come by your very smart uniform?' He explained that he was told he must be 'uniformed' for the appointment and had therefore been given a TA commission in the Westminster Yeomanry Dragoons. I had never heard of such a thing, nor, indeed, of the Regiment but that is what gave him such a refreshing personality; he was totally unencumbered by any form of rank or militarism. It was during one of those unfortunate lulls in conversation, when everyone is being on their best behaviour, that I heard a tapping on the table. I was near enough to be rather conscious of it, and thought that we were about to be called to order for some toast or other. Suddenly, the imperious voice of the portly Lady Jones said, 'Captain Bicknall, what on earth are you doing?'

The eyes of all were directed towards him as silence fell on the diners. He continued his tapping totally unfazed and simply said, 'It is all right Lady Jones, I was just showing the lady-in-waiting how to get the weevils out of the cheese biscuits.' Something no hostess wanted her guest to hear – least of all Prince Philip! There again, being a naval man and having served in HMS *Valiant* and HMS *Whelp* during the war, he must have eaten his fair share of weevils I guess! I also remember having to dance with Lady Jones, quite an authoritative figure but she softened once she had ascertained that the evening was going well. Someone told me that she had at some stage been her husband's nurse when he had been ill and she ran a tight and efficient ship. I think that I was as ingratiating as I could be, bearing in mind my misdemeanour earlier in the day – but I heard nothing more about it as I said, just a little bruise on my pate caused by George Lea's peaked cap. I wonder how it ever survived but it did for he wore it thereafter!

The official festivities lasted some four or five days and I remember standing with Peter when we were approached by a group of very attractive women, all young, probably married or daughters of expatriates. It was a drinks party, so they may have been acting under a little alcoholic haze as they came in a swarm towards us. Life had been hectic and sixteen-hour-days were the norm; we needed some light relief and this was to be it.

'You're so handsome in your splendid uniforms – we would like to get to know you better,' would be the chat-up line – but not a bit of it.

'You are the ADCs aren't you?' they chorused.

'Well, yes,' I replied, while Peter smilingly stood by my side.

'Please can you introduce us to your Generals?' they fawned – silly, empty-headed women, but I had no option. The Generals they referred to were General Sir Charles Henry Pepys Harington, who was at the time Commander-in-Chief, Middle East Command, and formerly of the 22nd Foot, the Cheshire Regiment, and my own General. They were both very handsome men. The former, with his fine proportional features finished with a smart military moustache and George Lea with his expansive and all-embracing smile which said 'just for you.' Peter and I sought solace with Lady Harington, recounting the hurtful experience of being trampled on in the rush to meet two 55-year-olds – well, let us be honest, they were old men! She was very philosophical about it and she explained that she thought women aged earlier than men, generally speaking, for the very obvious reason of child-bearing duties, but she also said that soldiers, especially infanteers, were naturally fit by nature of the job. It didn't help really, it had been humiliating and nothing could change that. She mused that she was constantly aware that Charles was still her Adonis, but ruefully declared that she was 'matronly'. She may well have been matronly to us at about 24 and 26 years of age but she was engaging and wise and it was in meeting people like her that we matured and were able to formulate our own values in life.

I only wish in hindsight that I had taken more note of my surroundings and the influential people I met. I hardly ever took a photograph or ever asked for an autograph. I think that we would have considered that intrusive; true, life was very busy but there again I suspect that I thought life would always be this way. Looking back over my seventy-four years, I now say to my wife and children that I started life at the top of the pole and have been sliding down it ever since! At prep and public school one was treated with deference by the domestic staff. At Sandhurst one was always a 'sir' and later in the Regiment one had batmen and drivers, while being stationed abroad just continued the act, and all so young. The fact is that I never wanted anyone to dress me, and I certainly never wanted anyone to drive me – all I wanted was to get behind the wheel of anything, be it Land Rover, 4-tonner or family saloon, and drive it fast! Then, there were some wonderful Officers' Messes and the exclusive clubs and balls but life has been eroded. When I joined the Army, its strength was about 279,000. We had fine traditions and wonderful regiments going back 300 years but since the day I joined it has been a depreciating asset, in regiments, barracks and influence generally.

Life is totally topsy-turvy: now I would love it if someone could help me dress, bend down and tie my shoe laces; sometimes my waist band is just too tight and I now revert to 'slip-on' shoes, something I regarded as rather suspect before. As for driving, wouldn't it be lovely never to have to park the motor car, fumble for money, feed the meter and run the gauntlet of traffic wardens? I need staff now, someone to bring me tea in the morning, as they did in the Mess. I invariably left it as I was always in a rush, and as for young marrieds wanting to meet me aged fifty-five – well that passed me by too!

Well, the ordeal of the independence celebrations came to an end. Prince Philip flew home and was to do many more similar duties. The redoubtable Dr Hastings Banda, as he had always done, ploughed his own furrow and did things his way. For instance, he was opposed to the Central African Federation, which threw him into the arms of the Portuguese countries and the pariah state of South Africa with their policy of apartheid. However, this pragmatic approach was purely to sustain his precarious finances, for Malawi was small with no natural resources. There was no doubt that he was a clever man and a brave one too as he defied the other black leaders of the area. As I said, he studied in South Africa at the start of the twentieth century while graduating in philosophy and medicine in the USA. He was finally to complete his medical training at Edinburgh University, becoming a Licentiate of the Royal College of Physicians in 1941. Indeed, he ran a successful practice in London until 1955, eventually returning to Nyasaland in 1958. He even did thirteen months in prison, courtesy of perfidious Albion. I found him deep-thinking and quite serious, but it is my belief that his life presidency in 1971 gave him an unhealthy say in Malawi politics; rather like Robert Mugabe he became reluctant to concede power and in the end regarded the lovely country of Malawi, with its beautiful 'highlands', as his personal fiefdom. But in 1964 all this was far into the future.

21

THE TOSS OF A COIN

I said farewell to Lusaka, capital of the newly independent country of Zambia, in November 1964. I could have steamed home on one of the Union Castle ships, or the Italian line of Lloyd Triestino, but I had agreed to stop-offs in Dar-es-Salaam, Nairobi, Cairo and various other places to see friends and old flames, one in particular in Frankfurt. Again, fifty years ago when things in theory were meant to be much more difficult with no computers or modern communications, I found life much simpler, especially travel. The travel agents arranged all your tickets and airlines were positively charming, no penalties for missed flights, just smiles and catch the next one. Now we have people trained to be officious, impolite and ugly.

My second stop was Nairobi in the newly-named Ken-Ya, as opposed to pre-independence day pronunciation of Keen-Ya. Nairobi had a reputation as a swinging city. Indeed, high and immoral living had been a hallmark there since the 1930s when British aristocrats bought land in Happy Valley and lived it up, with bored wives having cheap domestic labour in the house and too many gin and tonics at lunchtime, leading to wonderfully romantic, amorous nights … usually with someone other than their husbands, hence the name 'Happy Valley'. It was just the type of place a young man needed after such an arduous tour in a city which was relatively unknown, small and very suburban. My hotel was probably the best in Nairobi then, the Norfolk I think, which for a few nights wasn't too expensive with my savings from Zambia. I was somewhat surprised to see the newly-liberated ladies of the city coming to take tea in the hotel. The reason soon became obvious as they bared their breasts to the perfectly fitting sugar bowls in which they rubbed their nipples to encourage the babies to take their milk. I believe later the hotel introduced sugar-shakers. It didn't bother me, I must say – but there again I didn't take sugar in my tea.

I think my Sandhurst chum came to the hotel and our first night's dinner was respectable. The rear party of the Staffordshire Regiment was commanded by him and he rather savoured the fact that he would be the last British officer to leave our ex-colony. We had our second evening with the 'lads', swilling beer in the heat of their tented camp, before I was taken off to a nightclub called the 'Starlight'. This was a huge revelation to me, for all the black girls looked so different from the young women of Lusaka. They were positively beautiful in the raunchy sense of the word but this was only to be expected in a sophisticated city such as Nairobi. Nevertheless, it was a very changed scenario from the one that I was used to and I found myself intrigued by a young black woman who looked like Diana Ross, a popular American singer of the time. I can't vouch for her singing but her erotic dancing in a scanty outfit (mind, it was hot) and her voluptuous figure would have put the dancers at the Moulin Rouge or Raymond's Revue Bar in Soho (not that I have been to either ... in the shade. The dancing seemed to get wilder and the girls more attractive in proportion to the alcohol consumed and I couldn't help thinking of the great Fats Waller 'and the joint is jumping'. I remarked that the females were more glamorous in this part of the world than others I had seen, only to be told that their hair had been straightened, thus giving them modern hair styles, while the use of wigs was also *à la mode*. This was totally new to me.

It so happened that my preoccupation with, let's call her Diana, had not gone unnoticed by Fergus who remarked that as it was his last night here, he was going to take her home.

'But I am your guest and therefore have precedence,' I complained.

'No, not tonight and anyway I have been wanting to take her home for ages,' he said. We agreed as muckers that we wouldn't fight over a girl, so instead of pistols at dawn we took the cowards' way out and decided to toss a coin. We did. I lost. He won and had all the fun ... as vouched for by previous ... let us be kind and say 'boyfriends'. I didn't find out as the Staffords departed and I went to the game park the very next day.

My journey home was educational but good, especially in Cairo where the Dutch Ambassador took me under his wing and organised pyramid trips and things. I really wanted to see a belly-dancer or even lots of belly-dancers, and missed one romantic opportunity which still galls me. It was a pleasant Air Italia flight, a Caravelle three-engined jet if I am right, where I found myself sitting next to a most lovely Italian cabaret singer. Over our gin and tonics at luncheon, she invited me to stay with her in Rome where she would show me the sights. She was just a little older than me (five to ten years) and in my haste to get to Frankfurt I turned down this wonderful proposition. Who knows, I could be speaking Italian now, have half a dozen bambinos, no doubt be divorced and selling ice-cream in the via wherever.

It was about two months later when I was motoring north that I suddenly thought I would pop into Lichfield where the Staffordshires were based and see Fergus. A call to the adjutant's office as etiquette decreed resulted in me being given the brush-off. I suppose that since I was in civilian clothes I could have been anyone, so I tried again by insisting that I was a great friend of Fergus, in fact in the same term at Sandhurst.

'Oh well,' he declared, 'that's different. Just close the door a second and have a seat ... poor old Fergus is in hospital.'

'Oh, not again,' I interrupted, 'not another motor crash?' I should point out that Fergus, although a skilled and enthusiastic driver, had a propensity for driving too fast and not always negotiating some of the bends – although most of them he did – I have got to be fair.

'Oh no, not this time,' he smiled but grew serious again, 'no, it's not that ... well, it is difficult to say, but no doubt he will tell you himself anyway – no, he has had a terrible time poor chap, apparently, well so he says, on his very last night in Nairobi he threw a coin with some dubious character to see who would bed one of the girls in this shady night club. Yes, he has got the most terrible dose of ... in fact it's quite a rare and difficult dose of the CLAP. Well, I ask you, it serves him right really – an officer shouldn't do that sort of thing – should one, well, not with a black girl with that sort of reputation don't you agree?'

'Oh yes, quite so,' I said reflectively.

'Well why don't you visit him in hospital, I am sure he will be pleased to see you,' he urged.

'I don't think I will have time. I think I'd better go or I will be late in Bury,' I said determinedly.

I vacated his office and into the corridor, with the de rigueur highly polished floor of a Regimental HQ.

I felt nauseous.

There but for the grace of a penny coin ...

Postscript
There is none ... I still panic when I think about it. Why did I even remind myself and write this? I've gone hot and cold again.

22

'Eney Auld 'ags and Bownes?'

I was on home leave, having just left Africa and being about to go off to what was called the Borneo Confrontation. The island of Borneo is the third largest in the world and is divided between two factions. The larger part, the old Dutch East Indies, is Indonesian, while the remainder, the old British domains, are Malaysian. Indonesia, although incapable of running what it had, over 13,000 islands and a huge population approaching the 200 million mark, wanted to do for Malaysia what it was doing so well for itself – namely, reduce its neighbours to the poverty and chaos it experienced. It always amazes me how dictatorships pursue such aims – wouldn't you think that they would like to put their own house in order first, before coveting other nations who have expressed no desire for change anyway? However, I am not there yet but still enjoying my leave in Newcastle-upon-Tyne.

Now it so happened that my ex-school friend was a journalist in the North East and, in common with all journalists, loved stories. In fact, he loved them so much that if he couldn't find one then he and his chums would make them up. His friend and work colleague, also a David, one rainy February day hitched a lift with him from Whitley Bay to Newcastle. As he climbed into my David's motor car he had to pick up his mail before he could sit down in the passenger's seat.

'Good heavens, a sunny ski resort … what a change from here, Alpbach … Austria … oh is it your friend … that chap I met in the Army?' He chuntered but continued to read the postcard that I had written. In it I had said that I had twisted my ankle and missed a day's skiing because of it. By the time that he had got to Newcastle, he had formulated, perhaps fabricated would be a better word, a ski story of pathos and drama, in the blizzards and snow-swept mountains of the Alps. Apparently, his editor had told him that if he didn't come up with a good story soon he would be on his bicycle. It was given headline treatment on page 3, which is, I am told, a good position newspaper-wise.

'Young officer in ski-drama,' it screamed. 'Saved by mountain rescue team,' 'plucked from jaws of death,' 'appalling conditions,' 'pennies saved for holiday of a lifetime,' 'now confined to wheelchair and crutches for his après-ski parties.' It did actually get my name, rank and age right but nothing else. Two million people read the *Journal* … or so they claimed. Unfairly, people blamed me for this publicity stunt; indeed, one aunt and uncle would not talk to me for ages for being so brash. A visit to the *Journal*'s office produced no remorse, no apology, just the journalistic shibboleth of 'we stand by our story.' What, from 1,000 miles away? I was therefore blamed for something that I had certainly not encouraged, indeed, had absolutely no knowledge of – perhaps I thought that this justified David's suggestion of appearing in the national press and being paid for it.

'How so?' I said.

'Simple,' he replied, 'the *Daily Express* runs the William Hickey column and this deals with social chit chat, who has been seen with whom. Lord So and So's mésalliance with a bus conductress, debutantes coming out, wild parties at nightclubs, general goings on, anything involving the upper class, chinless wonders and the young royals.'

We therefore had to think of a story which would be both appealing but unusual and where better to think than over a pint in one of David's favourite pubs? Now all journalists have at least fifty favourite pubs. It is here, often in an alcoholic haze, that their work is done and inspiration hits them. In fairness I had to admit that David had an immense rapport with everyone in his taverns. He could chat with cloth-capped workers, coax stories (with liquid inducements) out of almost anyone, chat up the barmaids and generally be at home with all classes. Something of a chameleon ... obviously not in looks for he was handsome but changing colours in order that he could talk to all. A veritable attribute!

Perhaps it was one of the drinking fraternity that came up with the idea of being a totter for the day ... a Steptoe and Son. For they knew our propensity for breaking into the dialect, especially when the pub minstrels broke into 'Blaydon Races', 'Cushy Butterfield' or the 'Lambton Worm.' The problem was solved and on our way home, our tongues and vocal cords loosened by the famous 'Newcastle Brown hinny', we practiced our battle-cry ... 'eney auld 'ags and bownes? It is a plaintive call but by no stretch of the imagination could even a Novocastrian decipher it ... it seems to be unique to totters, the 'r' is swallowed deep in the throat and may be followed by a well-aimed mouthful of saliva by some of the fraternity. It is in any case not just plaintive but a wonderful blood-curdling cry which carries 'doon the back lanes man' of our North Eastern towns. It should in theory, like a Viking war cry, drive the 'canny little housewives' scuttling for safety but in fact it is an inducement for them to congregate outside with 'the bairns', perhaps bringing a sugar lump or an odd bit or carrot for the nag and sometimes the totters may even be persuaded to part with a few coppers. David with his customary vigour got us a horse and cart and on the appointed day (luckily dry) and with a winter's sun we turned up appropriately dressed in dirty, despicable clothes. We even prowled around the back streets of Byker and got some old pram frames, bits of rusty bicycles and the odd broken mangle – but no bones. Still it was fun and we loved the charade of pretending to be one of the lads with our raucous calls. We then decided to go further afield and shock the more genteel areas of Jesmond and Gosforth.

Now it so happened that I was dating a lovely girl called Joan Morton whose parents lived in a delightfully large and comfortable house in Gosforth. I remember Joan for her beautifully modulated voice and the fact that, even at her young age, her well-groomed mother insisted on her attending the Queen's dressmaker. Mr Morton, an impressive man, ran if not owned the famous Clarke Chapman's shipbuilding and engineering firm on the River Tyne, when we still had an industry there … at that time it must have been entering its death throes, I guess. Their life was privileged and they still had staff in the 1960s – driver, gardener, cook and cleaner.

Indeed, I still remember the cook, her name was Jesse and I got on very well with her. The Mortons were wonderful and if they were attending some function or other, they would invariably say to me, 'save your money Lawrence, we are out tonight so why not let Jesse cook for you and have an evening at home?' We were indeed lucky and Jesse would answer the door, take my hat and coat, pour our drinks and serve us a delicious dinner and pamper us far better than the smartest, most expensive restaurant would. I probably took all this for granted then but would certainly not do so now. Jesse was a Geordie lass but acculturation at the hands of her employers over many years had produced a tolerably decent accent. Now with all these memories flooding back I recall that Joan's sister was one of the first newsreaders on BBC TV, hence the family's great diction. If only I had met Joan later … she could have done the voice-overs and things and I could have stayed at home enjoying Jesse's cooking. Alas!

Anyway, there we were on our cart, almost breaking into a canter on the Great North Road just about the time that the shop girls, typists and secretaries were queuing for the lunchtime buses. I can remember feeling most upset when we stopped and offered them a lift. I can understand why they wouldn't want to climb aboard a dirty old cart with a manure bag dangling from it but what amazed us was that we didn't even get a smile, a laugh, not so much as a vulgar oath. We were totally ignored and I remember thinking that I had never experienced what the humbler, more ordinary workers in their dirty overalls felt like. It was like being one of the untouchables in the Indian caste system – with the populace regarding us as non-persons. The early 1960s was still a deferential age – although things were changing fast, we still looked up to 'our betters' – but even so I didn't like being on the receiving end of a cold shoulder … and these were just ordinary folk.

Things would change when we got to the Mortons. We could have one of Jesse's ground coffees and scones and Thunderbolt, our game little mare, could crop the lawn. We were just going up the drive at a decent trot shouting our slogan of 'eney auld 'ags and bownes?' in our best Geordie accents, when, like a whippet released from its racing gate, came a wild creature – knotted headscarf, a pinafore covered in flour and wielding a large, lethal rolling pin. As this diminutive but pugnacious figure came bearing down on us like a Dervish warrior of old, there came a scream with a far better command of the vernacular than ours.

'Haddaway, yer dirty ald buggers … haddaway, yer filth,' she roared.

Faced with such a foe … even Thunderbolt capitulated and came to an abrupt halt.

'Why Jesse, I didn't know you had it in you,' I declared, raising my moth-eaten cap.

'Ee, Captain Stacey, it's you, what are you doing rag and bone collecting?' as her voice assumed a more dignified tone.

Well, we did have a laugh and a pleasant coffee break, outside the kitchen door mind you, before saying our genteel farewells. We arrived at our satanic journey's end in the depths of Byker (not noted as being a garden suburb) where we unloaded what little we had, paid our money for our horse and cart hire ... which of course we would recoup when David had sold the story. A photographer friend of David's was on hand and took some very authentic shots and armed with these, William Hickey (who wasn't, I am told, William Hickey at all but a conglomerate of journalists) accepted the storyline. It read something like:

'Captain Lawrence Stacey, of the Lancashire Fusiliers and ADC to a General seen here practising for his civilian occupation when sacked ... or subsidising his Army pay ... or having found his dream job.'

This was great and we were actually going to make a profit on it all until things turned sour when the *Daily Express* telephoned me. 'What is your General's name, decorations and present job and is it true that he commanded the Special Air Service in Malaya?' they asked.

'Well, I can't give you that, if, he sees his name in print in a frivolous column like yours he will go mad,' I said anxiously. 'After all, isn't this about me?'

'Good grief no ... the story and photograph may be concerning you but you're not news. You see, we need a peg to hang the story on and that's got to be a name which the public can identify with ... someone famous you see, so his name and as much as you can tell us about him please,' they insisted.

I am ashamed to say that I shrank at divulging such things, judging that even if he didn't read the *Express* (which he didn't) someone would draw his attention to the prank and in those days of propriety no one would laugh. It seems strange now but I suspect that such an upstanding man as George Lea may not have been amused. Now, of course, we are all publicity-mad and seek celebrity status. In those days it had to be the right kind of publicity, in a word *respectable*. So as usual I lost out, but I do possess the photographs, they hang in the loo and one can be seen in the picture section of this tome, a reminder of my wayward youth.

23

GENERAL FOR A DAY

As ADC I quite enjoyed standing in for my General on important occasions, usually for dress rehearsal parades. It was rather like the Queen's corgis, for however yappy and troublesome they may be, few people take a kick at them, I suspect – they just smile benignly and accord to them the rank of the Sovereign. In the same way no one was ever tiresome or rude to me as they obviously knew that whatever was said would be reported back to the boss … probably hugely exaggerated!

A large dress rehearsal in Africa was usually fun and generally easy-going. Lovely blue skies and a warm breeze would waft over the parade ground, which always put people in a good humour. The General's motor car only flew a pennant when the commander himself was in the vehicle but this was waived for the dress rehearsal so that the motor wasn't held up and could therefore drive directly to the saluting dais. I waited for the door to be opened, General Salute Present Arms would be given and the band strike up appropriately. I would of course wait for the parade commander to salute me but always naturally responded, as my rank demanded, politely. Even the Brigadier would be word-perfect in all that he said, in order that everything was the same on the day. Key words, for instance, would alert others as to what was coming and therefore played a vital part in the whole panoply of events. Timing was especially important and to the second, especially in Brunei when we had HRH The Duke of Edinburgh, HRH The Sultan of Brunei, Lord Louis Mountbatten, High Commissioners, Ambassadors, Ministers from far and wide of other nations, to say nothing of five-star Generals from Navy, Army and Air Force of many different countries. These were not pleasant occasions, however, as everyone was on tenterhooks in case others whom we had little or no control over were early or late or brought along an entourage not catered for on the seating plan. Tempers were frayed, pride hurt and people slighted if their feelings were upset by other people's precedence, incorrect anthems or a host of other reasons, thankfully now forgotten, but they could be the stuff of nightmares for an ADC. My role was not that of a puppet and although I attended in full uniform, as on the day, I carried a clipboard on which times, names and every small detail which might present a snare was noted; in that way I could brief the General step by step on what was expected of him. All would not be lost were he to have a lapse of memory as to procedure or the personalities he was to meet, for I was the young officer just a few paces behind who could say *sotto voce* what was what.

On reflection there was one incident involving the Royal Family in Lusaka, Northern Rhodesia (now Zambia), which at the time I thought would land me in the Tower of London, but I am still here to tell the tale. HRH Princess Mary had come out to represent the Queen for the independence celebrations. I had met her at the airport, or rather the General had, with me in attendance. All seemed well, especially as BOAC's wonderful new VC10 was able to land on the restricted airport runway. We were able to marvel as the four-engined aeroplane, with its Rolls-Royce engines all on the tail, simply soared into the sky. The following morning an early call from a lady-in-waiting was put through to me as I shaved.

'Captain Stacey,' she said, 'can you please inform me what depth are the steps up to the saluting dais?'

'I beg your pardon,' I replied, thinking I had the wrong end of the stick. At twenty-three years old I thought that a step was a step: a rise or drop in level. Indeed, if anyone asked me to this day what thickness is a slice of bread, I would not have a clue and wasn't this exactly the same thing? She persisted, 'Captain Stacey, I need to know the precise depth HRH will be required to raise her feet in order that she will not trip up the steps.'

'Lady Margaret,' I said, 'I have not an idea what depth the step is … all I know is that we had difficulty getting them done in time – in fact, a final coat of paint is being completed after one of the rehearsals.' It transpired that Kensington Palace, or whoever was responsible for the visit, had written to the government or me, to say that the steps should be no bigger than say 6 ¼ inches and that I would be in for a severe ticking off, reprimand or custodial sentence when the royal party returned to civilisation. It mattered little that we were in darkest Africa and things moved exceedingly slowly, added to this the new African minister in post must have had a host of more important things on his mind than passing such trivia onto me. Certainly, no instructions had ever reached me. HRH Princess Mary, the Queen's aunt, was quite old, then about sixty-six. At my age I now appreciate that she would have liked to have known whether the steps were mountains or molehills; clearly doing a Humpty Dumpty so publicly would be an acute embarrassment for an elderly lady.

The ordeal was not over: even earlier than the previous morning another call from Lady Margaret was put through.

'Captain Stacey,' she began, 'I need to know the wind pressure for today's parade please.'

Here we go again, I thought. 'Lady Margaret, today we have blue skies, tomorrow the sky will be equally as blue and thereafter for a good few weeks…'

'And the wind pressure?' she urged.

'There is no wind, Lady Margaret, I promise,' I replied, conciliatory. There then followed a heated discussion on why these questions were not answered by me before the visit, my ineptitude and probable demotion to dungeon warder at the Tower of London or even an inmate of the same. Apparently, the lady-in-waiting's job was to see that, if, let us say there was a force 6 gale, then HRH's skirt would have 6oz of lead distributed around its hem. If a force of gale 2 wind was prevalent then let us say 2oz of lead would be inserted. The figures are mine and purely arbitrary – but meant, very sensibly, that the respected aunt's skirt would not perform the indecorous act that befell Marilyn Monroe when walking over a New York subterranean air vent. In short, her skirt regally stayed put. In truth, it was the same principle employed by us: in the days of battle dress, trousers and anklets, lead weights kept the overhang in perfect control. HRH therefore displayed the discreet amount of leg at all times and quite right too. It didn't stop me living in fear and trepidation for a few days ... what would happen if she told her niece? The visit went well and Princess Mary came and went and I sat near my rival in the Royal Box but no darts were shot in my direction, unless they missed and hit someone else of course!

‡

We were in Kuching, Sarawak the following year and here was an entirely new scenario. We were fighting a war and jungle greens, side arms and military Land Rovers replaced the smart staff cars and sand-coloured barathea of our previous theatre. Meetings were not held in beautiful colonial government buildings but as likely as not in some hot, stifling basha in the Sarawak jungle, or a military airport with the sound of helicopters coming and going and the heady, omnipresent smell of AVGAS (aviation fuel) filling one's lungs and nostrils. Here, pallets of supplies lay everywhere, ammunition boxes, countless jerry cans and 'compo' ration boxes. Soldiers were stripped to the waist, with rivulets of sweat running down their backs, revealing mosquito-bitten white bodes as they toiled at their back-breaking work. In hastily established camps, surrounded by rolled barbed wire and laid with the ubiquitous pierced steel plank, soldiers laden with equipment and bearing Armalite rifles and machetes waited to board the choppers and face the hazards of jungle life with its sunless canopy and overpowering humidity. Life was fast and febrile in such conditions as we fulfilled our treaty rights to defend Malaysia after its independence. We therefore kept in close contact with the rulers and politicians of the Malaysian federation, one of the reasons for our visit to Kuching today. We returned hot and weary to the Kuching hotel, probably the only hotel at the time where one could spend a reasonably comfortable night; we were the lucky ones, for we could have a shower, a sandwich and a cold lager before retiring to bed in an air-conditioned room. My room was adjoining the General's in case there was an emergency such as happened tonight.

We had hardly got to sleep when my bedside telephone rang at about 0200 hours and the brigade duty officer said, 'Lawrence, the brigade commander needs a word.' The Brigadier quickly briefed me as I hastily took notes and marked my map. There had been a serious incursion of Indonesian troops at what was thought to be about brigade strength in his sector and he needed to meet the General at his field HQ urgently. I knocked on George Lea's door and woke him up by turning on the lights and saying, 'Sir, there has been a big attack over the border.' The General was a big man, well over 6ft, and as he climbed out of bed securing his sarong, which he always slept in, he quickly appreciated the situation.

'Right, Lawrence, you will need to contact the Prime Minister's office [it was a federal system] and the chief of police and cancel our meetings, together with letting the Chief of Staff know in Labuan. What else were we to do today?' he concluded.

'We have a longhouse meeting with an influential local headman, in an area which has so far been hostile to us … pro-Indonesian … and allegedly they have never seen a white man,' I said breathlessly.

'This must go ahead,' he said urgently, 'for reasons that I shall explain later.'

'But General,' I said, 'there is no way you will be back in time to fly to the longhouse. I shall obviously need to cancel the visit or put it back to another day.'

'No, you will have to stand in for me,' he barked, scratching his chest.

'But General, I am not a General,' I pointed out forcefully.

'Don't be bloody stupid,' he shouted. 'They have never seen a General, they don't know what a General is and they have never seen a white man for that matter … so put your number 1 dress hat on [best red-banded peaked cap] and be a bloody General for a day.'

Well, that's that, an order is an order and that's exactly what I would do, but not before I had solicitously said, ticking my notebook, 'I will phone the Brigadier now.' I turned on my heels to go, when suddenly there was a roar, 'Lawrence!' I quickly spun round expecting to be congratulated on a good briefing or getting things moving quickly, perhaps an MBE or something?

'I chose you to be my ADC because you are from a good family and here you are using such common terms … the word is "telephone". I compromise with "ring", but never "phone", it's slang.'

All I could say was, 'Yes, of course,' or some such platitude and reflect that someone really had got out of bed on the wrong side this morning. Still, one always had to watch one's 'p's' and 'q's' even at such times as 0200 hours. One never said, 'car' but 'motor car', perfume was 'scent' and if one ever said 'kids' one should certainly be shot, quite rightly so, and just to show that I have prejudices too, I would add that torture would be even better. So we all have our pet hates but my education began quite early in the day. What did it matter now, at least I was a General, promoted in the field so young!

The visit to the longhouse had already been arranged for some time and only necessitated me getting to the airport after I had cancelled all that morning's appointments. I duly arrived to find my team of guides, translators, pressmen and photographers (both civil and military), a local Iban policeman and miscellaneous officers all waiting to interview and click the General only to be told of the deception that must take place that afternoon. There were other officers around more senior than myself, those that had fought in the sector and had some knowledge of this vast area and those responsible for the journalists and I let it be known that since it was now a low-key affair, they were free to go if they so wished. No one did. The atmosphere became carnival with me the centre and butt of their jokes.

'Now, remember dear boy you may be asked to sleep with one of the headman's wives tonight ... in which case we will all need to stay the night,' said a Major of Royal Engineers who was in charge of the press boys. There followed the usual ribaldry which always accompanies such banter, with a photographer asking if I wanted this event recorded and did I have a particular angle for a preferred shot? Someone else who had stayed in a longhouse said that the living was totally communal so I had better lay on a good show to prove the prowess and superiority of the British if we really wanted them on our side. We departed in two Wessex helicopters, flying over the dense tree canopy of the jungle, with the occasional glimpse of a silver thread of a lazy, meandering river on its vital trip from the interior. I say vital for that is what the rivers represented, not only did they provide water for the longhouses but also food from fishing and roads through the jungle and contact with other communities. Our journey there was much quicker than the return one for reasons which will become obvious. The longhouse we visited was for the sole purpose of psychological operations, commonly known as 'psyc-ops' or better still, 'hearts and minds', to win over the population by being seen as fair and trustworthy; hopefully it would become a symbiotic union. They would become our eyes and ears if the enemy infiltrated our territory, for it was amazing how fast news travelled through the jungle. The other role was equally beneficial – giving succour to any of our patrols in the area.

This longhouse or house on stilts was what was known as a thirty door longhouse, quite large and near the Indonesian border, hence it being regarded as unfriendly. Contact with the outside world was minimal and perhaps with some updated news of our successes the time had come for a more pragmatic approach. Our reception, for such an insular society, was wonderfully warm. We climbed up notched tree planks to gain access to the house, quite a feat in itself for older people I thought, especially in darkness – no handrails here. Some of the women were initially shy but soon the ice was broken and smiles and laughter were the order of the day. I noticed that many of them had goitres neck – a deep swelling of the throat, a thyroid deficiency brought about by lack of iodine in the diet. Also, they seemed to chew incessantly the betel-nut which produced a red saliva which I thought was very bad bleeding gums. The reason for this was the filed teeth which must have been extremely painful, revealing as they did the nerve endings. The betel-nut juice with its chemical properties reduced the pain to some degree.

Tattoos were universal in both the land and sea dyaks: these Ibans had the painful throat tattoo which was a test of manliness; just enduring the 'operation' must have been horrendous. Others had total body coverage, a task only done by the menfolk; the pattern being covered by pig fat and soot, sharp needles were then driven into the flesh by taps with a small wooden instrument. We were told that their women had no tattoos but I certainly had seen some Iban women sporting them elsewhere. Lastly, we were told that only men who had tattoos on their hands and fingers had in the past cut off and shrunk a head; we were shown no old men that claimed this prize.

I remember the mixture of smells that assailed my nose as we were led around the longhouse, mostly comforting, wood and thatch and the raffia palm. The women were highly skilled at weaving blankets, coats, matting and basket-work. It was their job to carry the water gourds, a fleshy fruit which doubled up as a water bottle once the fruit had been eaten, to winnow the hill padi-rice and generally grow the produce for the longhouse needs. To the men went the hunting and the fishing in the rivers, although meat-eating did not feature heavily in their diets, the pigs being kept for feast days … they believed in many spirits. I remember eating some glutinous rice wrapped in leaves and puffing their local cigarettes which used palm or banana leaves for paper. It was considered a great luxury to have European cigarettes and these were included in our gift list which I officiated over, since I had the red hat! I know that we took some medical supplies including iodine salt or something similar to alleviate the goitre. The beads were still much appreciated by the young women who made them into large, attractive necklaces. I thought that the women were striking in their youth not only for their unblemished skin and lack of clothes (they all wore long skirts) but in their patient faces resided a certain empathy. They made wonderful mothers, I was told later, and their role in the longhouse was not purely subservient. They would choose their lovers in a sort of free love way and it was their prerogative to name the father of their child, who then became responsible for that offspring. Nevertheless, the ageing process was not kind to many of the longhouse people for their life was busy, hard but overall happy. On reflection I wonder now with deforestation, if any genuine longhouse people survive.

I remember being shown the fecund illipenut trees with their rich harvest of nuts, the terrible sickening smell of the durian fruit and the peculiar-looking jack fruit collected from the trees that line the river bank. The pigs with their piglets grunted underneath us and squealed as they competed for the scraps thrown to them. The headman proudly showed me two hornbill birds, the feathers being used for ceremonial dress, his cock-fighting birds and some old word-work which recorded some famous past events – similar to our history books but in wood form.

I had been told that the longhouses were the repositories of the head-hunters' art and their prowess in decapitating their enemies, and it was by my gentle persuasion that I was eventually taken to a corner where hung a collection of seven heads. They were insistent (through my interpreter) in telling me that this tribal act was no longer practised, since it had been banned by the government. I don't know if I believed them. The heads that I saw were, if my memory serves me correctly, small and almost doll-like – obviously through the shrinking process – but the hair was luxuriant, long and black. The skin was preserved like parchment and the mouth set in a grimace. The teeth could not be contained within the smallness of the mouth cavity and these I think constituted the necklace, bits of bone replacing them in the mouth for a true effect. I know that I pressed my host for the latest addition to the collection and he wisely told me that two of these were Japanese soldiers. They were fascinating but I am not good with things like this, so total memory recall is difficult. I have since learned that Ibans did indeed perpetrate this macabre form of warfare but perhaps are a little disingenuous, inasmuch as it didn't really have to be a fellow combatant. In fact, if the girl you wanted to marry (a simple ceremony) demanded a head as a token of love, you were quite within your rights to creep up and kill any man, woman or child of any unfriendly tribe. Perhaps there was as much skill in the shrinking as there was in the hunting? I feel certain that some bone removal took place to produce the doll-like heads that I saw, but don't take my word for that – perhaps I should consult the British Museum?

Our trip was cemented in goodwill by the early introduction of the famous Iban drink of rice beer or rice wine. I remember it as 'tuak'. It was fed to us liberally and although I did not find it pleasant, I partook of it in the spirit it was given ... generously. The things that I have done for Queen and Country! So far though I had not been invited to perform an act or ceremony to bind our nations together (like days of old) in the marital bed. It was just as well, for the headman and his wife were old and obviously past such things and I couldn't remember the attractive girl who was his elder daughter under the influence of tuak. Anyway, perhaps they had been joking about us, with the shoe being on the other foot. Imagine, 'you may have to sleep with their headman, their tribal chief' ... and afterwards saying 'oh thank you spirit of the bed chamber for sparing me from that sweaty, round-faced man whose ridiculous red hat matched his stupid red face.' You never know!

What I do remember vividly, even with my consumption of tuak, is being observed by a sinister man from beginning to end of our visit. He was about twenty-five to thirty years old, totally bronzed with tattoos and Iban-type hair, bobbed slightly at the back but with a front fringe curled over as was the fashion. He wore a loincloth and carried a wooden spear. He was absolutely impassive and never moved far from me. It was most disconcerting and I half-expected him to suddenly lunge at me and sport my head in the latest addition to the longhouse's museum of fame. Or perhaps the Indonesian intelligence branch had got wind of our visit and decided that they could assassinate our top man with this subterfuge of an alien Iban. It was creepy but I had to have faith in my hosts.

By the time we left we were inseparable mates and I knew that any unofficial treaty made that day would be kept ... for the longhouse men were honest, kind and generous but not stupid. They finished with the men performing a dance, perhaps a war dance out of respect for their guests … again, the women as I understand never danced, it being purely a male prerogative.

Our flight back was hilarious, our New Zealand Flt Lt was as intoxicated as we all were. I know I ended up in the front of the helicopter with a BP road map.

'What good is this?' I asked Ian, the pilot, 'a road map in the air?' It was finally agreed that if I could identify a certain river we would fly along it until we came to the coast and then turn left or right as the case may be. I do remember that our undercarriage sported a great deal of jungle canopy, making a landing difficult until we had removed it as best we could, suffering an intolerable down thrust as we completed the task. Later, I was able to intervene with a letter from the 'General' to say what sterling service he had given … in the most difficult conditions and although he didn't get a Mention in Dispatches he was spared a Board of Enquiry.

So ended my day as a General. I could look back with pride and satisfaction on an unsigned treaty of friendly intent towards one another. I pondered: if only everything was given to junior chaps like me, with a propensity to party and to soften up the opposition with beads and participate in drink, we wouldn't need reams of paper, high-paid diplomats, deeds of intent, weeks of negotiations, in fact the whole of the United Nations could be disestablished and go home, saving us millions of pounds. The old phrase, 'make love not war', seemed so apt.

Postscript

It was about four years after this incident and I was dining with Lt General Sir George and Lady Lea (you see how well he did with my help) at their home in Kensington, London. We had both left the Army at this stage and we were laughing at all the outrageous things I had done in my time with him and the family and I mentioned the above story and the sinister-looking Iban who I thought was there to assassinate me or something.

'Oh, Lawrence, I feel bad about that but I couldn't tell you at the time, other than say that the visit had to go ahead, remember? – You didn't mention it again so I let the matter rest. He was an SAS soldier and he had been undercover for nearly two years,' he said. Here was a young man who had become part of a longhouse some miles away. He had canoed for two days so as to see us but had under intense self-control given me no indication as to who he was or even shown any surprise when he saw me instead of General George. He asked for nothing ... goodness knows how he would have appreciated a chat in his mother tongue, a cigarette perhaps, a look at a paper we had brought along? He had had no mail, no Saturday nights out with the family or girlfriends. He had just lived as an Iban in some crucial nodal centre where rivers meet and in a part of the jungle in which we operated. His dedication was unlimited, his devotion to duty total and his loyalty unsurpassed; yet in all probability his work was secret, unsung and unrewarded. Someone in my party may have passed on fresh orders or new signal codes or something of that nature, but he departed as he came, unnoticed, to continue his silent vigil and do what he knew best: dissemination of information and passing it back to us. What I did know was that he had a powerful radio with which to work and that made his solitary life worthwhile. Now, his is a story that I would love to read, but I suspect it is hidden, if not forgotten, in some dusty archive. Our loss.

24

THE JUNGLE – SAS STYLE

A spectacular red sun bade farewell to the day as it hung low over the sea, as if Neptune himself was slowly extinguishing it. From out of this firmament the noise of a helicopter could be heard until, bursting out of the sky at tree level, it landed on Muara Lodge lawn. Almost caught unawares, I sprinted to the figure emerging from the machine and took the confidential bag. General George and I gave a perfunctory wave to the crew as the downwind blew us towards our waiting whisky and sodas. Tonight though was different, for I felt an avuncular arm fall on my shoulder – was an apology coming for some forgotten slight?

'Lawrence, dear boy, Tony Farrar-Hockley tells me that you are the only one in the theatre that hasn't been on rest and recuperation [RR – normally given after six months]. It won't be easy without you but I will get some staff officer from HQ to help out.'

My heart missed a beat as I imagined the Susie Wongs of Hong Kong and the saronged beauties of Singapore. I would lie watching the ceiling fan lazily revolving above me in between bouts of lascivious passion and ice-cold Tiger beers. What bliss!

'Now dear boy, I have spoken to Major John Slim (SAS) about you doing a spell with them, so how long would you like to go for?'

'Hang on,' I thought, 'but what has the Special Air Service got to do with my RR?' My heart began to sink and my stomach churn – leave spent with the SAS, was the man mad? I tentatively proffered a suggestion which somehow I knew was not going to be accepted.

'A week, General,' I unconvincingly whimpered.

'No, no dear boy, take at least three months, go out and enjoy yourself.' There was no turning back for with that he gave me two hearty slaps on the back to signify that the matter was closed.

'Now let's have our sundowner,' he said. So it was that the most reluctant recruit in the entire history of the Special Air Service entered its ranks.

About a week later my Gurkha driver drove me to one of the many deserted beaches, saluted smartly, stepped forward and nervelessly shook my hand. Was this the kiss of death? Perhaps he thought he would never see me again? I don't know but I went along with the charade. With perfect timing I heard the hovercraft skimming the gentle waves and I watched the troopers perform an unopposed beach landing. John Slim (later Viscount, assuming his father General W. Slim's title) was a fairly frequent visitor to Muara Lodge but my friendship with him would have no bearing on my time with the squadron – for a start he was about important matters, whereas I was, in reality, a 'holiday trooper'. Regimental Sergeant-Major (RSM) Ross was a totally dedicated soldier and it was with him that I learned what this special type of soldiering was all about – but first there were games to play. My webbing I had and that was fine, but the troopers all had Bergens, which were not normal issue, but fitted for them and which in time moulded into their bodies with a tolerable amount of comfort. Mine was a virgin prototype and the steel frame dug into the flesh around my waist. It didn't help that I was carrying a horse in it, and the first day's march to base-camp soon saw me bleeding like a piggy.

On forward movements the steel stuck perfectly into what was becoming a neat hole and plugged the bleeding, but as I progressed on the alternative leg, the frame moved from its socket, releasing yet another gush of my precious blood. Obviously, I could not complain, for not only was I an infanteer but also an officer and the boys were just waiting to see me crack. That night I made running repairs and when one of the troopers who had been behind me remarked on my bloody shirt and trousers, I replied with great *sang-froid*, that it was of no consequence. However, what I found to my chagrin on arriving at base camp two days later and unpacking, were tins of 5lb potatoes and a miscellany of other heavy 'compo' rations – the boys just laughed and said, 'Just dump those, sir, where we are going you won't be needing them.' I had passed my first test of being a pack mule and having carried about twice as much weight as anyone else in the Sqn. It was no wonder that later my Bergen leather straps snapped.

Base camp, if, I remember correctly, was non-tactical, indeed, I found a clear water stream which I was able to take full advantage of, washing off the congealed blood which seemed to have got as far as my foot. On emerging from my bath, I found to my horror that all my clothes had disappeared and I was forced to retrace my steps back to camp ... totally naked. The troopers were too polite to take any notice but I did see a rather guilty-looking RSM with an unusually amiable smile on his face.

'Oh someone found these sir, I thought that they might be yours.' I was reunited with my belongings but not until, *sotto voce*, he had told me that it was best to blend into the jungle, smells and all. Apparently, even the everyday soap that I had brought along could be compromising. It was not used again, being considered superfluous when we went out on patrol – space simply precluded the carrying of anything as luxurious. The logic being that when wildlife passes you by, you know that you are part of the scene. I never subscribed to this as any wild animal is attracted to odour and we became pretty smelly as the unwashed days went by.

It was that evening after our last proper meal that the RSM dished out the condoms. We were given two each and the troopers took them without comment. How ungrateful I thought; I, of course was delighted, fancy the Regiment thinking of such a morale-boosting exercise to look after such details as our manly bodily needs! Bloody marvellous, I thought, some Iban women in one of the longhouses, perchance?

'Well RSM, this is a turn-up for the books,' I remarked.

'What's that sir?' he replied.

'Well condoms, when do we get to use them?' I said hopefully.

'Oh, those sir, well now I suggest...' Apparently, the first was for the barrel of our Armalite rifles – placed over the muzzle it prevented the damp and detritus of the jungle entering the barrel and fouling it up ... and the second?

'Well, sir, that's for your escape map and that tiny compass you have [something you get in your Christmas cracker]. Place that in the second condom and insert it anally.' This holiday just kept on getting better and better, so full of surprises. Our escape maps were nothing more than a postage-stamp-size or flannalette with two or three local rivers drawn in the direction they flowed. The diet, it was true, contained very few solids, so the maps lodged pretty safely in the place suggested.

We were also given blood money and this was simply sewn into some part of our uniform, perhaps our jungle hats or the double seam of our shirts. If we were caught by indigenous tribesmen or even an enemy patrol a single note of 50 Malay dollars may well secure our freedom. We travelled light, just four pouches and two water bottles attached to our webbing, a light Armalite rifle and our floppy jungle hat. At night we simply rolled down our shirt sleeves, perhaps unbuckled our belts, while our hats became a simple pillow. Our jungle boots were rubber, supple and comfortable and these as I remember were never removed at night. In fact, with our finger through the trigger guard, we could break camp in a matter of seconds: turn over, arm over one's head to collect the rolled-up floppy hat, buckle belt and away.

On these patrols we seldom carried machetes, for a trail of devastated jungle was a death trap. Here, I should reiterate that while the SAS are masters of the surprise attack, going in silently and striking like a hammer, most of their work is performed in a much more subtle manner, being the eyes and ears of our Army. Our patrol was just that, the tedious, gentle pushing away of the foliage but with devastating consequences, as the thorns stretched our skin before its elasticity snapped. Our bodies were therefore perforated and punctured to an alarming degree. We spoke in whispers, when at all, and soon became adept at understanding each other, although a word may not have passed between us for hours. We had been led to believe that we would be operating in virgin jungle but on one patrol we suddenly came to clearing, probably done by a fighting patrol of the enemy, for circular cleared areas like corn-field-art just don't appear so immediately. We were glad to get the sun for a short while, as life in the jungle makes one as white and gaunt as a cadaver. It was here that a most bizarre scene was witnessed, for attached to a tree there appeared a notice. It was in black and white, crudely executed but therein was its impact. A female sat on a bed; her lover was partially hidden but one of his arms embraced the naked figure cupping her breasts – tantalisingly so. Its message was simple: 'British Soldiers, where is your wife now?'

At the bottom of the poster were the words: 'GO HOME'. Here we were in territory that until weeks ago was, as we thought, unseen by the world, untrodden by any feet until suddenly contended for by opposing nations. Later, back at camp, it was soberly discussed and had obviously hit home – for so many soldiers had not seen wives, children, family and loved ones for many months and mobile telephones had thankfully not been thought of then.

Cooking on
an Arab dhow,
Ch. 29.

Abu Dhabi
c.1970.
Now it's all
skyscrapers,
Ch. 29.

My guide's
tent, the Empty
Quarter of
Arabia. With
NCOs of the
Sqn and the
saved son,
Ch. 29.

The Singing
Sands.

The oasis area by
our camp, trees out
of shot. The donkey
was tethered here,
Ch. 29.

Abu Dhabi, a typical house, c.1970. The tower is to catch the breeze and give downward draught. Been there recently? (Ch. 29.)

The intrepid traveller – eight days alone! All he wanted was a cigarette, Ch. 29.

Our camp in the Empty Quarter, scene of the scorpion attack, Ch. 29.

An occupational hazard.

On the front line in the Borneo Confrontation, Ch. 23.

This Dakota may look old now – it was old then – but it was quite luxurious inside. This one belonged to C-in-C Far East Singapore, Air Chief Marshal Sir John Grandy. He and his family were frequent and welcome visitors.

My Jersey Lily, or Jungle Rose in this case, Ch. 25.

These tattooed Ibans provided labour in forward areas, but came into their own when acting as jungle guides. One was my interpreter in the longhouse, December 1965, Ch. 23.

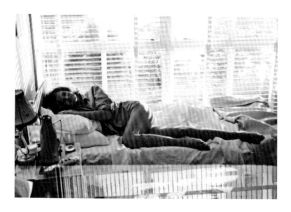

Brunei, Muara Lodge. We entertained the good and the great: Royalty, Cabinet ministers, a future Prime Minister and many others.

The serene Limbang River, as it was in 1965, Ch. 26.

ADC's garden. It was never used – time precluded any leisure.

Front lawn, and the daily transport to work at Labuan Island. Beats the train!

F-M Sir Richard Hull (L) and General George (R). The Field Marshal was rather taken by my palatial office ... June 1965, Ch. 21.

Lord Head, High Commissioner (Malaysia), with Pam Lea, Georgina and Annabel, October 1965, Ch. 40.

Flag Trampling

The 'Royal' Dais became the 'President's' Dais once the ceremony was completed and the President installed, Ch. 23.

Unfortunately, my invitation for Nyasaland's Royal Dais seems to have vanished. Probably withdrawn in the light of what happened, Ch. 20.

Visit of HRH the Princess Royal.

Water was always a problem and if denied a jungle stream we resorted to animal drinking holes; these might be a mere stinking puddle, the type a child on a Sunday walk would take delight in jumping into. To us it was life – on one occasion it did prove to be a lifesaver for our bottles were depleted and had been for some time, our mouths parched dry. Perhaps another twelve hours would have seen us in a state of collapse, humidity and sweat having taken its toll. I remember our tablets, one which purified and the second which made the festering water just palatable. They were added to the water bottle with a recommendation that they needed four to twelve hours to work, obviously the longer the better. In this instance I remember the trooper chewing the tablets for expediency's sake but with insufficient saliva to be able to expel them, I dislodged the crushed product from the white coagulated spittle into the water bottle. This done we shook the water bottle and drank from it immediately. We all survived without any ill effects although the stinking stagnant water hole defied description.

Life did have one silver lining – towards dusk we would, if we thought it safe, pull out a crude tin or hexane 'cooker'. The word is a misnomer for in essence it was (and probably still is) a flimsy folding container 4-5 inches long and an inch deep containing two blocks of white fuel, probably methane. Four of us would share a cup of tea brewed in one water bottle cup. It was like a witches' coven sitting in silence, passing a deliciously hot, sweet, milk-powdered tea. I am never certain if this was strictly legal but who was I going to tell? I remember the advertisement 'Happiness is an egg'. If, any of us could have been granted a wish in these circumstances we all agreed that it would be a mug of this elixir in preference to anything else. It sounds silly now but at the time it assumed a status of great magnitude. So simple had our tastes become, so far away from reality, so removed from our past lives. Life is truly transitory – especially a soldier's. Up until now all the years of training had been just that – learning our art and honing our skills. Now it was different: the next bullet we heard would not be a blank but for real … to kill. It does rather bring you down to reality.

On another patrol we were on the Indonesian border, just a recce patrol of four men. In this instance we were lucky (debatable) to have a radio; so often, though, they failed to receive or transmit or both. They were in some ways a double-edged weapon for their crackle, aerials and urgent pleas of the operator could compromise your position. As a recce patrol, we were vulnerable in being so easily outnumbered but fortunately we were warned that the enemy was in the vicinity. The jungle was dense and we could have lain low and hoped to avoid detection. However, we had machetes (not to be used unless in an emergency) and with these we hastily cut away a small clearing wherein a Wessex helicopter could winch us up. The chopper found us and our upward journey began. As last man I realised that we must have attracted a considerable amount of attention. If I could have appreciated the thickness of the jungle canopy I would have felt more secure, for it probably totally hid us (other than the noise of course) but to be honest I felt like a sitting duck dangling on a line just waiting to be popped off. My insecurity was palpable and the winch seemed to take minutes instead of the seconds that was reality. Anyway, the feeling of relief was almost worth it as the majestic machine swooped like a bird of prey having clawed us up and sped us on our way.

My time with my silent friends was coming to an end (thank goodness) but was hastened by an unfortunate accident. On patrol in strength (my Bergen somewhat lightened) I was traversing a fallen tree when the whole rotten moss-covered infrastructure of it gave way, causing me to keel over, trapping and breaking my right ankle in the process. As it happened we had a medic with us and he quickly assessed the situation and applied a plaster of Paris. The downside to this cure was everyone being invited to urinate in it, on it, whatever, in order to constitute the plaster to its optimum strength – water as always being as precious as gold. The smell over the next few days became ferocious as I limped my way back with the medic and a small escort. Somehow, the doctor was alerted and together we moved towards each other and miraculously met in some jungle rendezvous, still some way from home. My ankle had been causing concern, for it was thought to be going gangrenous as my upper leg and veins had become infected. It was then that the doctor and medic discussed my plight. Could I make it home or would the ankle need to be amputated? I was aghast, when I asked the Royal Army Medical Corps (RAMC) Captain how he intended to do so in the jungle – just remove my ankle – so cavalierly?

'Oh, I shan't do it,' he confirmed forcefully.

'What do you mean, you won't do it, you're a bloody doctor aren't you?' I complained equally as forcefully.

'Yes of course, I am and don't worry I shall be on hand … well ankle, in this case,' he quipped to put me at ease, 'but Cpl Thompson's your man,' he said complacently. Apparently he, together with another SAS chap, had spent two years in Los Angeles, as something called 'paramedics'. Now you and I know all about paramedics but fifty years ago we didn't have a clue … we probably thought it was an aspirin! These remarkable young men had crawled into crashed and concertinaed motor cars, down crevices and other miscellaneous death traps, happily depriving unconscious … or otherwise … victims of arms, legs, hands or fingers … I make light of the situation but in the process, they were credited with saving many lives.

When I eventually met young Cpl Thompson, he boldly declared that he had 'never amputated an ankle yet,' but he seemed positively enthusiastic at the thought of removing mine … with his army issue clasp knife, the type we were issued with. I now felt like one of Sweeney Todd's victims, with my travelling companions just itching to get at me and claim another first … an ADC's right ankle – perhaps they won't stop there and will claim a double first, a right and left ankle, just to exercise their professional skills!

Over our painful journey home I got to know my 'captors' well. The young RAMC doctor had always wanted to join the Army but apparently one arm was shorter than the other by an inch. This obviously precluded him, so he took himself off to medical school, qualified and read a newspaper advertisement for the TA or Territorial Army. In those days there was a thriving TA centre at the Duke of York's Barracks in Chelsea. He ended up becoming doctor to the TA SAS Sqn stationed there. Having proved himself it was a hop, skip and a jump to join the regulars – although technically still medically unfit. To him and Cpl Thompson I suppose I should be grateful, for happily I can report that I eventually made it to Brunei, where my foul-smelling plaster, now very yellow, was removed, thus depriving many flies and other 'crawlies' of a home. My stinking clothes were probably burned and I recollect an orderly offering to burn off some blood-gorged leeches which had found a home on my testicles. This I found distasteful, the thought of these slug-like parasites living off me, so comfortably in five-star accommodation … and worse still a male offering to remove them. I remember asking very politely if there was a nursing sister around, but alas there were no volunteers. I quickly learned to smoke and gratifyingly saw them drop off immediately.

We know that absence makes the heart grow fonder and so it was with the Leas. I was treated as the prodigal son that night and even given a dinner party in which I was expected to do nothing. To be back in civilisation was wonderful and General George had said that if I ever wanted to do a secondment with … well, you know who … I think it was at this stage that I pondered on the wisdom of keeping my right ankle! As it was I had a plaster on for some time which gave me lots of time to plan excuses.

Dear old General George and Pam could not have been kinder, so concerned for my health and welfare. 'I just want you to relax and get better Lawrence, light duties as it were ... bed rest dear boy,' he insisted. This bonhomie lasted all evening and most of the night ... but at 0500 hrs my bedside telephone rang.

'Lawrence, I've been thinking, have you a pencil and paper to hand ... well, here it is...' he began.

Postscript

The project in hand was major work on the Sultan's summer palace. During this extensive renovation, involving many people, the Malay electrical contractors managed to cross crucial wires. I was involved in a terrifying fire which burned down the building on what should have been a peaceful afternoon. Still with my leg in plaster I suddenly found myself playing a fire chief ... yet that is another story and rather a sad one.

25

JERSEY LILY

An equerry is in effect an ADC, but to a member of the Royal Family. They must suffer even greater consequences for any misdemeanour, although in one instance I suspect that the equerry to King Edward VII, 'Bertie', must have been somewhat better placed to withstand royal disfavour. You may remember that as Prince of Wales he was the bane of his mother's life. Queen Victoria held him responsible for the death of her beloved Albert. The Prince Consort, we are told, went to Cambridge to chastise his son verbally for having an affair with an actress but during his journey he contracted typhoid fever and died, whereupon Bertie's mother confided to her diary that, 'much as I pity him, I never can or shall look at him without a shudder.' Plainly, his austere upbringing allied to a rebellious nature manifested itself in his desire to upset his mother at every turn. He was in modern day parlance a playboy, but in spite of his immorality he was adored by his people. A man of gargantuan appetite, many meals a day, some of ten courses, we are told, mistresses by the dozen (well, in the region of thirteen regulars) and how many more servants, chambermaids and others along the wayside.

His brief reign of nine years, though, gave us the Edwardian era, where British values and the monarch's popularity at home and within the rest of Europe gave Britain a certain panache after Victoria's highly successful reign but dour approach to life.

One of his equerries was from the newly formed Irish Guards, 1900/01, who happened to live in Pont Street, at the point where it intersects with Sloane Street. This was most commodious for Lily Langtry, born Emilie Charlotte Le Breton and daughter of the dean of Jersey. She married Edward Langtry in 1874 and was pursuing her acting career when she met the Prince of Wales. A famous beauty, she was painted by Sir John Everett Millais, himself from a Jersey family, hence her nickname, the Jersey Lily. Her house was on Sloane Street, back-to-back to the equerry's house with only a small street, Pavilion Road, dividing the two.

This was the ideal situation, for the King would say to his Queen (probably after a good dinner), the ever-patient Alexandra of Denmark, 'Well, my dear, I must go to be briefed on tomorrow's parade by my equerry,' and off he would go to Pont Street. From there in the old lift it was seconds to the basement, where a small door revealed a hidden passageway under Pavilion Road and like a mole he would surface in Sloane Street into his lover's arms ... all in about two minutes.

What Queen Alexandra of course should have asked was, 'But darling, shouldn't it be the other way around, your equerry visiting you?' Perhaps she knew the form, for it is said that, as Edward VII lay dying, she was forgiving enough to let another famous mistress, Mrs Keppel, pay her deathbed respects. The small room that had the blocked-up passageway is to this day where I keep my suitcases and other impedimenta. So there!

The equerry must have had a pretty free hand with this kind of intimate knowledge of his superior's behaviour at his fingertips. For me, no such intent of bribery or innuendo did I possess but I did have one little trick up my sleeve to preserve my independence and privacy.

George Lea was a large man and when he sat in my room or office I noticed that his bulk destroyed my cushions. As he sat in one of my chairs, an idea would come to him, and a period of meditation followed, whereupon he would then raise himself and pace the room before evincing his argument and sitting excitedly on yet another chair and destroying my second and third cushions in quick succession. To my neat and tidy mind such vandalism was incomprehensible and provoked an instant response. I knew deep down that any running repairs to my carefully plumped-up cushions had to be fairly surreptitious. I would therefore half-follow in his steps, either agreeing with a point he had made or proffering a suggestion, all the time carrying out my real mission of cushion restoration and rescue. This I overdid on one occasion when he was on his second or even third circuit of pancaking my perfect cushions.

'Damn it Lawrence, I am meant to be the General here and you the ADC, yet why is it that you make me feel insecure and not the other way round?'

It did mean, though, that he was a rare visitor in my private place ... which was just as well, as my Lily Langtry came and went with almost as much subterfuge as old King Edward VII.

26

A Letter from my Foot

I have mentioned our very hectic life during the Borneo campaign where one had to balance operational duties with those of a social nature. These probably gave us bigger headaches than the enemy. Government ministers were quite often benign, as in the instance of Fred Mulley, Labour Minister of Defence, who gave us no trouble at all and was grateful in a quiet way for everything we did for him. I remember he came down for dinner dressed exactly as we did at prep school. A white flannel shirt and blazer with the shirt collar neatly pressed down over the blazer collar. I thought him very avuncular and was touched by his total lack of self-importance.

We had so many VIPs that I became punch drunk, even blasé. Often Pam, the General's wife, would be back in England and menus, indeed everything down to dinner parties, guest lists, seating plan, wines and daytime social programmes, fell to me. We usually tried to give our guests a morning or a few hours to take in the sights, decidedly not tourism but more anthropological, trips down the Limbang River to see the local tribes, to Mount Kinabalu in Sabah to see a rare orchid bloom, to the cave at Niah where one of the biggest bat colonies in the world existed. Others wished to see the Shell Petroleum plant in Seria, or the Brunei woven kain.

One visit of monumental significance was from the doyenne of foreign correspondents, from a famous newspaper. It was widely announced that this person would write five major articles on the Borneo crisis over a period of a week. We entertained the small press party at Muara Lodge over half a day. I briefed them on certain aspects for an hour or so, Colonel Anthony Farrar-Hockley (later General Sir Anthony Farrar-Hockley) for a period, ending up with an operational brief by my General, the Director of Borneo Operations (DOBOPS). We flew them to Labuan HQs, jungle bases and gave them free rein to do and see as they pleased. The outcome was a diatribe of lies and subjective opinions, which bore no relation to the facts, all gained over a two-night stopover and covering about seventy-two hours in the theatre. The result was that I have never read that particular paper since and I have little faith in what most journalists report. I am always amazed by their arrogance: fly in, fly out and hey presto … I know it all. The consequences were epic in this instance: the recall of the High Commissioner, Max Webber, to London, the flight to Singapore and Kuala Lumpur of DOBOPS to repair the many broken fences and the genuinely hurt feelings of the Sultan of Brunei. He was amazed at the principal charge of the articles, which implied that our presence there was for his financial benefit, when in effect it was totally the opposite. The journalist had hinted that our soldiers were lured there for the rest and recuperation, known as R & R leave, so they could part with their hard-earned money on the riotous living in the town and its reputation for prostitution. The truth was that the then Sultan of Brunei, Sir Omar Ali Safuddien, paid for all of Twelve Brigade who were stationed in the country and built them a splendid camp, Bolkiah, into the bargain. He was a constant visitor to Muara Lodge and when we had drinks parties and invited his ministers they always made a point of arriving early, which puzzled me. It soon became apparent that they did so in order to have a quick gin and tonic, a whisky sour or a glass of Pimm's. When the Sultan did arrive he would wickedly approach them and say to the Mentri Besar or Prime Minister: 'What a nice tie you have on,' gently feeling the fabric and smelling his alcoholic breath simultaneously. I remember he was always smiling and seemed to be a popular and kindly man. He was later to abdicate in favour of his eldest son in 1967; he was then a nice young man of about seventeen or eighteen who was about to go to RMA Sandhurst. I doubt if my shadow would be allowed to touch his now ... anyway, my only criticism was that it was a highly celibate and very oily state, in spite of the authoritative articles written maligning the country.

Now Singapore was a different story!

One visit I remember with nostalgia and tiredness was that of the future Prime Minister, then Leader of the Opposition, Edward Heath, the shadow Chancellor of the Exchequer, Anthony Barber, and Christopher Chataway MP. All very charming in their different ways. As soon as it became known that this high-profile party would be spending five days with us, I was plagued by telephone calls, mostly from women or wives of the 'top people'. Some had a strange way of putting things: 'Lawrence, just to let you know that we would decline an invitation to meet Edward Heath.' This General George quite rightly interpreted to mean, 'Lawrence, don't leave us off the invitation list when Mr Heath arrives.'

The main problem was that they thought him full of hubris and unable to relate to people, especially women. In truth he was the opposite, very engaging, interested in everything other than small talk, for which he had no aptitude. If, on briefing him as to whom he would be meeting, I mentioned that she was the local gossip, his eyes glazed over and he would bring up a topic relevant to the area and our reason for being here, and was there anyone he could meet who would be *au fait* with this subject? He quickly separated the wheat from the chaff and was not only highly intelligent but charming with it. He was also capable of a good laugh. He insisted that I meet him at the House of Commons, where he would look after me or us, if the family wished to come, in the same way as he had been so well looked after at Muara Lodge. I didn't take him up on his offer until twenty-seven years later and he was still true to his word. I thought he was rather maligned. The shadow Chancellor of the Exchequer was a warm-hearted man, who as I remember was liked by all and perhaps provided what Edward Heath was lacking in the common touch, while Christopher Chataway was probably only ten years older than me, so therefore young enough to be looked on as a friend and confidant. Later he was to marry a very nice friend of ours, but I never actually saw him again, more was the pity.

I do recall my tiredness, though, on looking after such guests. A drinks party of fifty would be followed by a more intimate dinner party and when these guests left we would finally relax in the comfort of our majestic balcony. Here with a whisky and soda we would discuss the evening while marvelling at the millions of stars which lit the night sky. The warmth of the day squeezed from the flora aromas of scented bliss which all added to this unreal existence ... while the effervescence of the waves lapping the shore gave us somnambulant background music from below. So often the time clock of our guests was at variance with ours, or, like many ambitious or driven people, sleep was of secondary importance. It was then that this gentle dream was broken with the General's bulk rising in silhouette and saying,

'Well, gentlemen, I have a war to fight and an early start tomorrow, young Lawrence will do the honours.' It was then that the guests, after lingering for a little while, would retire, leaving me to do my rounds briefing the staff on early morning calls, breakfast timings, driving schedules and final liaison with air movements for the next day – well actually that day. I would be abed at about 0200 hours with the promise that I would take them for an early morning swim at 0500 hours. I lost about two stone and at one stage fell asleep with my head in the soup.

It was after one such session when all our guests had left that I ventured down to the ADC's beach on a peaceful Sunday evening for a swim. The children were watching me from our balcony as I threw myself down into the foam pretending that I had been shot and performing other contortions for their benefit. One became very realistic, for I was hit by a bolt of pain so frightening in its power that it literally folded me in half. I was bitten, stung probably, by a sea snake in the fleshy arch of my left foot, which was so powerful that it brought my left knee up to my head, hitting my eye with such force that it momentarily knocked me out for a minute or two ... I think the sea probably revived me. The spectators above, as they explained later, were immensely impressed by this hitherto unseen display of gymnastics. When I recovered there was a pool of diluted blood ebbing with the tide from my foot. I remember dripping blood all the way up the eighty-seven steps of the cliffs and back to the lodge. For half an hour Pam administered to me, but to no avail. I finally climbed into a Land Rover (it had no carpets to despoil) and drove through the jungle to our nearest hospital an hour away. By driving myself I was detracting from my agony, and there was also the consideration that I didn't wish my Gurkha driver, or my Chinese naval steward (batman), to see that we suffered pain; it was important to show that we could be every bit as stoical as they were. I was still in my swimming trunks, flip flops and a polo shirt when I arrived at the hospital. They had been forewarned and had a hefty injection of a drug called pethardine ready for me. This magic panacea was a wonderful revelation in what palliative medicine could do, for within minutes the excruciating pain had subsided. The young Army doctor, a Captain who I knew, cheered me up no end.

'Gosh, Lawrence, it was a good job it hit you – an infanteer. If it had been anyone else more sensitive, it could have killed them with shock,' he observed. The implication being that a 'thicky' infantry officer could take it ... his remark went unchallenged, I was just so grateful to be in heaven.

When I awoke next morning I had the biggest and best black eye one had ever seen. A total closure which gave me the look of some prize fighter. It also gave some wit a new name for me. Alistair Cooke broadcast every Sunday morning on Home Service and later Radio 4 in a programme called 'Letter from America', for some fifty years I believe. He began at point A, worked his way full circle, and in the last minute of the programme made his unexpected point. So it was with me and went something like this:

'Bloody hell Lawrence ... what a shiner ... you look awful, how did you get a bruiser like that dear boy?'

'Well, I was bit in the foot by a sea snake while about to swim at Muara ... on Sunday night ...'

'No, I am not interested in your swim, haven't got time dear boy ... how did you get such a black eye?'

'Well, my foot was ...' I would begin to justify myself.

'I don't want to hear about your wretched foot,' he or they would unanimously say and so it went on.

'You're just like Alistair Cooke going around in circles, just get to the point.'

The fact was that no one thought I was athletic enough to knock myself out with my knee ... but I was ... unknowingly.

Anyway, don't be bitten by a sea snake, or two mating scorpions for that matter, but that's a story for another day.

Postscript

I don't know whether the forces ever hit back at the press, other than a military photographer from *Soldier Magazine*. He produced a lovely shot of 'the girls', or flying camp followers, going from

Kuching to Jesselton (now Kota Bharu I think) in preparation for a Battalion taking its R & R there. The Fokker Friendship stopped in Brunei for half an hour to pick up new passengers, and the prostitutes from Kuching were only allowed to get off onto the tarmac, lest they contaminate the Transit Lounge. The chap got a smiling troupe of girls, some in their sarongs, the Chinese in their Susie Wong slit skirts, with flowers in their hair, smiling and waving at the soldiers through the high security wire. So seriously did the Sultan take his obligations. Spoilsport.

Postscript to the postscript
Jackie ... endlessly typing:

'So Kuching sounds exotic, what was it like?' she said.

'Alive, well far livelier than Brunei – I liked it,' I replied, 'but I had a near scrape there.'

'Go on,' she said.

'Well, I can't really, I certainly can't write about it as it really is a bit too near the knuckle,' I tailed off.

'Go on,' she urged again, 'you've never been shy.'

'Well it was one of those things that wouldn't have happened had our aeroplane not been recalled, but something important took place, perhaps another incursion over the border; do you know I can't remember, other than we turned about and landed back at the airport we had just left an hour earlier. Anyway, as we got back to the Kuching Hotel the poor old manager was beside himself with embarrassment,' I confided.

'Well, I can, at a push let the General have my spare room. I am certain my wife wouldn't mind, if he doesn't, that is. It is full of my daughter's things but she's not here. I can't see what else we can do, we are bulging at the seams,' he said regretfully.

'No, that's fine – very kind of you,' I said sincerely.

'But where can I put you?' he chided himself. 'I can put a camp-bed up in reception, behind the desk with a screen, it's cramped but there are the lounge loos where you can shave, if that is amenable?'

'Perfect,' I said. 'At least it will get me away from the General, I won't be so easily contactable through the night,' I mused with satisfaction.

'Remember there is the reception telephone and the night manager is on hand although he does have other duties,' the manager compromisingly said, but already an evil plan was hatching in my head.

Now on our very first visit to Kuching I had been briefed by the Royal Military Police (RMP) Captain, an obliging young man of about twenty-eight or so. He had said that if we ever needed guides, escorts and the like, his young RMPs were always there to help – just let him know our requirements.

'Actually,' he explained, 'we have quite a high profile around the hotel as not 200 yards away there is a 'house of pleasure' which we occasionally raid and generally keep an eye on.' This was pointed out to me so that I could guide the General away, if he ever witnessed a few inebriated soldiers going there when on their RR.

Now it happened that we ate out with the brigade commander, a working dinner as it were, so General George was tucked up and asleep at about 2300 hrs. However, my own attempt to rest behind the reception desk proved more difficult. Telephone calls were constant, guest queries never-ending, late-night bar drinkers came and went, while the Chinese restaurant seemed to have a stream of diners. I would get no sleep tonight so I took myself off for a walk, only to find that my path lead to the 'soldiers' hotel' or the 'house of pleasure'. In fact it was far cheaper than I thought but the cubicles were, it has to be said, very modest. A crude wooden slatted bed devoid of everything else except for a fan which worked busily, moving from side to side in the corner of the room. There was not even a door but a simple curtain which didn't guarantee a lot of privacy. I think there was a communal light which helped to hide the dark goings-on of the occupants but it had a certain atmosphere and I always like the woody smell of floorboards and the raffia and bamboo which served for partitions, etc. As I said the price was, indeed, less than a breakfast at the hotel but one had the added advantage of a delightful bed companion (a change from mosquitoes) and all thrown in for nothing really, and to think that I was on a General's allowance! What luck and how comparatively quiet compared to the bustle of the hotel foyer.

This Iban girl was attractive and sported a lovely figure, her filed teeth when she smiled, though, did warn me that I could not be too avant-garde in lovemaking unless I wanted to end up in the Jewish faith!

I had a most contented sleep, after I had put aside any thoughts of the General trying to contact me with some brainwave he had had in the night. It was a calculated risk but without immediate access to telephones one that I was prepared to take. It was during this innocent slumber that I was rudely awakened by a familiar sound of rude oaths, shouted commands and the scraping of steel studs on wooden stairs. My mind was in a total turmoil as I tried to take in my strange surroundings and to work out where I was. I turned over and saw the clear reassuring eyes of my sleeping partner, and at the same time I realised the enormity of what was taking place. I had seen it in Second World War movies but never thought I, as an officer, would experience it – a Redcaps raid! The Military Police were on the rampage and their prize a naked ADC. I had done it again. I had walked into the jaws, if not of death, then certainly of ignominy and shame, for I realised that if they charged the ordinary soldiers then they were honour-bound to charge me. Could I plead civilian status, for I was not in uniform? Such an excuse was denied me, for my new-found lover, clearly cleverer than I, silently arose with her finger to her lips, and deftly kicked all my clothes under the bed. At the same time she lifted the bed, if one could call it such, and pushing her free arm to her breasts indicated that I could hide beneath, clutching onto the frame. I needed no induction, for there I was as quick as a whippet, while she resumed her supine position in deep sleep. She was only just in time. I heard the oaths of soldiers as they complained vociferously and the footsteps approached our space. I saw the skirt of the curtain violently pulled back. The Iban maiden responded magnificently with sublime insouciance and surprise as she swung her feet to the floor (giving me some protection) while at the same time letting the sheet fall, thus revealing her shapely breasts. In poor English she whimpered: 'I alone.'

Was it her acting which gave the lie such truth, or the disarming act of being suddenly woken and dropping the sheet? Certainly, the young Lance Corporal would have appreciated a naked figure and taken it as a bonus for his night shift. In all events he shouted, 'Nothing here Sarge,' before taking one last look I presume, for the curtain closed with only half the velocity with which it had opened.

I emerged from under the bed as I seem to have done on countless other occasions, chaste but grateful to my lover for her Sarah Bernhardt thespian skills, or perhaps due to the distraction of her alluring body. Whatever, she had saved my reputation and probably my commission. She deserved to be rewarded for her alacrity of action and such incipient loyalty. Luckily, I was her captive and thankfully couldn't move until all the commotion had evaporated another two hours later or so. We spent our time profitably.

What an evening of love, excitement and drama I had experienced. I returned to the hotel with a light step of relief before breakfasting with himself.

'Poor Lawrence, so you had a bad night, old chap?' as he ordered breakfast with gusto, ready for another day's slog.

'Awful sir, quite dreadful, not a wink of sleep, the noise … quieter in the jungle' … pause for cornflakes … 'WHAT A NIGHT!' I added but this time said with feeling.

'You dirty creature,' Jackie scowled. 'You are quite incorrigible with your louche behaviour. No you certainly can't let people know about that … disgusting, be off with you – oh see you tomorrow, goodbye.'

'No we can't include that,' she said to her typewriter – 'but I will just for the devilry.'

… And so it was …

27

'What?'

We were serving in Borneo, Brunei to be precise, and I was still aide-de-camp to Major-General George Lea, now the Director of Borneo Operations. But this was now an entirely new experience – we were on a wartime footing against Indonesia. Lea commanded Commonwealth forces in a tripartite Headquarters of Navy, Army and Air Force. Strangely enough, being an ADC was one of the few jobs that a young officer could refuse, but I regarded myself as lucky as I learned a great deal from my mentor, whom I was later to come to see as a father figure.

It was not, though, a job that suited everyone, for in reality you were literally the General's dogsbody, not only did you 'live in', hence a twenty-four-hour day, but you were also at the beck and call of the General's wife, with responsibility for the children and governess too. So many people would object to such a situation but it was quite inevitable, for the General and his wife were a team, indeed I reckoned that the Ministry of Defence (MOD) or the government got them on the cheap. The wives worked extremely hard: not only did they help run the house, organise menus, entertain the VIPs, sometimes to the detriment of their own children, but it was quite essential to have a charming hostess to preside over things and Pam Lea was everything one needed, charm and beauty in abundance.

The Sultan of Brunei's summer palace stood on a magnificent promontory, overlooking the South China Sea. My own air-conditioned office had a window of some 25ft looking down on an idyllic, deserted beach with an ever-inviting tide, lazily lapping on the shoreline. It had a palm-fronted hut, and it became known as the ADC's beach, but the times I used it I could count on one hand, so busy were we. It was surrounded by a host of bougainvillea in its many varieties, rosy bracts exuding a heady perfume, aided by the stifling heat and humidity. The grounds were exquisite and surrounded by thick jungle; this contained a formidable protective fence, constantly patrolled by a Company of unseen Gurkhas. By British standards, 'palace' was probably something of a stretch – it certainly wasn't Buckingham or Windsor, and some of the properties in leafy Bagshot and Ascot would be in the same bracket. However, to the average indigenous Brunei/Malay it certainly represented palatial living. I remember Field Marshal Sir Richard Hull, seeing my set-up, exclaiming, 'Young Lawrence, I have been a General seventeen years and never had such a luxurious office.'

However, my accommodation did not always make up for the difficulty of my work, for life was not easy. Sewage was removed once a day, the water bowser came twice a day and electricity, if it failed, was backed up by generators. On the almost daily entertaining roster, somewhat similar to a small hotel, I ordered my salmon from Singapore (1,000 miles away), my fresh tomatoes, vegetables and salad from Jesselton, in Sabah (since renamed something else, 250 miles away ... roughly) and after-dinner chocolates and other delicacies for our pampered guests from the old Shell Petroleum base at Seria, about fifty miles away. Every day we flew to work to the island of Labuan (over a blissful clear sea) in either a Royal Navy or Royal Air Force helicopter from the already-mentioned long-fingered rock that gave us such splendid views from our balcony. If these failed for weather or operational reasons we took an Army Air Corps (AAC) Beaver, or a Single Pioneer of the Royal Air Force. All these had to be tasked by me, in fact for our long journeys the RAF made me sign as 'in charge' of a DC3 and I wondered what the crew were for? I also remember signing for a VIP Hastings when we flew to Hong Kong – I suspect I was really put upon. Mail was flown in daily, even at weekends, as work and operational duties were 365 days a year. I looked after four racial groups, at least, some of whom couldn't understand each other: the magnificent Chinese cook (Leon), kitchen staff, waiters, cleaners, laundry staff, maids, Gurkha soldiers and odd-job men to the residence. There were staff cars, pennants for VIP visits, Land Rovers and the speedboat of course; add to this the bear, monkey, gibbon and other pets which came or went, and one is beginning to comprehend the lifestyle. Perhaps all this seems in the remit of a competent young ADC but things went wrong on an almost daily basis and there was only one whipping-boy on whose shoulders the whip fell.

A well-oiled routine, however, was established for the collection of VIPs, VVIPs and royalty, some of whom were foreign diplomats reporting to their government on the confrontation. Generally speaking everyone was very amenable; we did get a few fast balls, especially when over-officious staff would ask for a seating plan for dinner, three months hence, with the hobbies and interests of those their bosses would be meeting. We were fighting a war and to obtain such commitments from important and busy people so far in advance was almost an impossibility. Other things which could trip a young ADC up were the order of precedence and seniority of guests. Invitation cards and thank-you letters had to be precise, punctiliously so right down to decorations, full stops and commas and heaven help you if you got one little dot wrong when it should have been a comma, let alone mix up a KCB with a KBE, KCMG or place it before or after a gallantry medal. So different today when people think my rank is my Christian name and more often than not I am addressed Mr Major in my letters. Actually, it has disintegrated to even more informality, when the twenty-year-old youth addresses me as Lawrence over the telephone, and we haven't even met!

In the UK one would have had a British sergeant to help but this was Gurkha territory then and my House Sergeant was a Gurkha infanteer, and I am not certain if he had ever been in a European house before this job. There were certain things which were taboo to someone so warlike and sensitive as him; consequently, womanly things were discreetly secreted in bedside drawers or bathroom cabinets by someone not so warlike and not so easily offended, namely me, together with the purchase of such … if Pam was away, which was quite often.

Fifty years on, the nitty-gritty of running such an establishment has faded, but we did set enormously high standards in dress, speech and manners. The details have faded, but the memory of our guests, in some cases, is still vivid. I rapidly formed collective opinions of the three services, for instance when a four- or five-star Admiral of the Fleet visited – Admiral Sir Varyl-Begg and Sir Frank Twiss come to mind – the General and I would collect them from Brunei airport. The journey back in the staff car was a pleasant run through the lush green vegetation of the countryside, sprinkled as it was with the local houses on stilts and the indolent water buffalo gently grazing. In the meantime, I would have bid my farewell and with the aid of a helicopter would dash the suitcases to Muara Lodge; by the time the motor car or cars had arrived I would be there to greet them again and together with the staff show them to their rooms. To the admirals, I would say, 'Admiral, your kit will be ready and pressed within half an hour.' They, the Navy, would respond with disarming charm for men of such seniority, 'Lawrence, how kind … what efficiency, wonderful service but no hurry, what do we wear for dinner tonight?'

To a visiting Field Marshal or General, I would say the same but the reply was different. 'Good, as long as it's no longer.' While to an Air Chief Marshal, well, they just broke down in tears of gratitude for no one had ever cleaned their kit! Over the months I pointed this out to General George, who came back with the question and 'why do you think that is so?' I propounded my belief, for what it was worth, that naval officers spent many hours thinking on the bridge, in their solitary night-time watches, looking out over a hostile sea, angry clouds and rough elements which in the blink of an eye could swallow their tiny ship, for what ship is big in such a vast ocean? They therefore have time to think and observe how vulnerable they are, indeed insignificant when pitted against omnipotent nature. They are therefore more humble, and in my youthful experience nicer for it.

We Army officers on the other hand, were more 'gung-ho' 'over the top' boys. We had no Mother Nature to restrain us and as such there was the feeling of natural superiority, demanding instantaneous obedience. We were just that little bit more arrogant with a tendency for pomposity ... not me of course! There were some mitigating circumstances; infantry officers had to have a different approach to say Royal Electrical Mechanical Engineers (REME): the former could not debate with their soldiers when going into the attack, while a REME officer with his craftsman or artificer would do just that in order to work out some difficult technical or mechanical problem. The RAF I never really fathomed; leadership is difficult when as a fighter pilot you only have yourself to lead, but as the younger service they were a little aloof ... or perhaps frozen out? For example, there is the Army & Navy Club, the Naval and Military Club, the Junior Army and Navy Club (as was) but just the RAF Club in Piccadilly in glorious solitude. Please do not think I am in any way biased, as my uncle was shot down in Bomber Command on 29 June 1940 aged twenty-three, while Uncle John was tortured by the Japs on the Burma railroad.

Now, there I do have a prejudice! Anyway, we are beneath the skin jolly good chaps ... and no mistake! (To quote 1940s black and white films.)

The balcony at Muara Lodge was as large as a battleship's bridge and like a ship it was surrounded by a heavy teak railing which prompted one to lean on it and pretend it was a ship, as one gazed out to sea. We gave drinks parties here on a grand scale and pre-dinner drinks whether entertaining or not, just *en famille*. Many nights we were in Red Sea rig, a dinner jacket (without the jacket) but bow tie and cummerbund. I sported a really meretricious waistband which had rather been foisted on me when I took the great and the good to Kampong Ayer (i.e. Water-Village) to the Sea-Dyaks spinning the gold kain (a cloth). The girls in the village on stilts, some who had never set foot on dry land, worked topless, and their light-brown unblemished skin on show meant that this was a VIP trip that always proved a delightful distraction. The only drawback being that no one ever bought any of the material and it was on one such occasion that I was forced to purchase some to make up for the parsimony of our guests. This I made into a heavy gold cummerbund which I still have. The Navy and Army officers put it down to the brashness of youth but an Air Vice Marshal thought that it was 'frightfully smart' and asked me to have two made up for him. This, I did but he never paid me ... bloody Brylcreem boys. General George was appalled.

It was on such a night as we waited for our guests that General George suddenly said, 'Oh yes, next month we have six generals all from the UK coming to stay for three days or so.' No problem there, for some of them were already known to me, but he then said, 'There is one particular friend of mine who I do need to brief you on ... there is just about time.'

'Major-General Peter Young is Director of Infantry and retires this year, now he is a funny old stick for not only will he shout at you but he appears to be highly irascible to the point of rudeness.

Every time you speak to him or ask him a question – and I mean every time – he will scowl at you and bark "What?" Now he doesn't mean to be rude but to those that don't know him it certainly appears so. He is tall and intimidating and a bit frightening but it all goes back a long way. It happened when he was in Colditz Castle as a POW. I think that he was probably the youngest POW there, a Second Lieutenant in the Oxford and Buckinghamshire Light Infantry...'

The escape committee met every week and contenders would put their names forward either with a good idea or to press their case for a fast-track escape. In some instances there was merit in this, as one officer may have had exceptional ability in a certain discipline, or another was an expert in something quite vital to the war effort. It therefore tended to be the more mature officers that were nominated to escape, those that had something to offer. As a wet-behind-the-ears nineteen-year-old Peter Young was just a novice – learning his trade as it were, and therefore right at the bottom of the list. He stubbornly persisted in harassing the committee and used his youth as the very reason why he should be pushed to the front of the queue – war was a young man's business, he contended. Eventually, he was so frustrated that he wondered out loud when he would get out of Colditz? His fellow POWs teased him: considering his age, experience and the fact that his name began with Y ... probably in the year 2000! It was then that Peter decided that drastic action was called for and once again he went before the escape committee with a brilliant idea – he was going to go deaf.

'What!?' they exploded. That would never do, as they simply would not allow it. For a start, 'it's not British – underhand and not fair.' What did Newbolt say: 'Play up, play up and play the game.' Good golly he would turn in his grave if an Englishman stooped so low. That's what could give the British a bad name, perfidious Albion and all that. However, Peter was set on his course.

Peter now followed a regime of fake deafness, which in spite of the advice and threats of his seniors he pursued relentlessly. For one so young it must have been incredibly hard to be ostracised, sent to Coventry, and as time went on mentally abused. A POW camp must be hard enough without being at war with both your enemy and your friends. They would taunt him by saying his sister was a whore and his mother the brothel-keeper, but whatever they said elicited no reply. There was no turning back when he discovered that his own brother officers had informed the Germans as to his behaviour. This culminated in a German sentry walking behind him and discharging his rifle ... but it produced not a flinch from the intrepid young man.

Eventually Peter, this remarkable, single-minded officer, won the day. The Germans repatriated him through the Red Cross, considering that his war was over. He must have felt victorious on arriving back on our shores, but he didn't wait long before reporting to the War Office in order to get back in the fray.

'Lt Peter Young reporting back for duty, sir,' he proudly saluted as he shouted.

'... But you're deaf,' came back the reply.

'What?' he shouted abusively.

'There you are again,' was the reply. 'You're deaf ... we can't take you back if you're deaf.'

General George finished ... just in time for us to hear our guests arrive.

Postscript

I met the irascible Major-General and we got on very well. He told me that it took him more time to convince the British Army that he was *not* deaf than it took him to convince the German Army that he was. In all events, 'All's well that ends well' to quote the Bard, for he was back in time to take part in the D-Day landings and to rise to Director of Infantry, but to his dying day he would still shout 'What?', and this is how I remember him ... but with great affection.

28

CASSINO

Luncheon called, and at 12:30 I walked out of my office, shouting to the chief clerk, 'I'll be back by 2 p.m.' The Austin Healey 3000, roof off, was parked on the square and I lazily drove it to the Mess – knowing full well I should have walked. There I manoeuvred it, nose in, to the space just outside the Mess. I turned off the engine and waited for the inevitable to happen, and sure enough it did. Fusilier Donaldson in his white jacket came running out, 'Major Hill's compliments, sir, but would you mind backing in your motor car?' he said. This little game had been going on for some time, and of course I always deferred to this very experienced soldier and turned the car around. Today, however, was different for I too was a Company Commander of D Coy, a position I was lucky enough to hold until I resigned my commission in February 1967. 'My compliments to the Major,' I said, 'but I think I will just leave it as it is today.' Now, all these years on, I blush at the thought of my ignorance and lack of respect. I got out of the motor and strode into the Mess, looked at my mail, washed hands, brushed hair and made for the bar. Major Kevin Hill sat there with his modest half-pint and beckoned me over. Instead of being nasty, as he could well have been, he sat me down and bought me a drink.

'You know Lorenzo, there's always a good reason why I ask you to do these eccentric things like backing into a parking space ... Oh good here's your drink. I was younger than you and like yourself commanding a Company of Fusiliers, the Company Commander and second-in-command had both been killed and at twenty-three as a young Lieutenant I found myself out of my depth and fighting for our lives at the battle of Cassino.' We paused to take our drinks and I thought of this dreadful battle when the Germans held this famous monastery and Polish and Commonwealth forces battered it unsuccessfully for months, swamped in sludge, covered in snow and plagued by intense cold, and when they attacked they scaled precipitous rocks to gain their objective under infernal fire.

'Well,' he said, 'we were called to a Commanding Officer's Orders Group for the Battalion to mount yet another attack against this seemingly impregnable fortress. We all drove into an olive grove and since we knew that the Germans from their lofty perch had us under constant surveillance, we backed into positions for a quick get-away and, tired as we were, we camouflaged up the vehicles as best we could ... well, the other Company Commanders did, but it took me all my time, in our lethargy, to get my crew out and "cam up" before they slumped back in the jeep, the driver at the wheel and my radio operator and runner asleep in the back. We were dirty, exhausted, unfed and we all needed a jolly good rest. It was not to be. We had hardly settled ourselves in the command post when Jerry's mortar bombs straddled us, the CO merely said, "disperse gentlemen" – we folded our maps, collected our kit and we were away, no thought of tiredness now, no heavy legs or dragging of feet, as the adrenalin pumped around the body and fear took control. The older, more experienced Company Commanders were in their vehicles and off, but I was left there in the clearing urging my lads to back out and flee. Matters were exacerbated by the fact that we had inadvertently gone into the mud and the jeep's wheels were spewing dirt and spinning uncontrollably. It was then that it happened, a direct hit from a mortar bomb. When I picked myself up and recovered my senses, I found that all three of my young crew were dead. I had hand-picked these Fusiliers as we all came from Bury. Their death was attributed directly to me and my war didn't end until I had returned home and seen their families and apologised. It was a burden I have always carried and I hope you now understand my passion for obeying the rules and carrying out routine drills, for they have an important purpose and one day could save your life. More importantly, by doing these things correctly you will safeguard those that put their trust in you.'

Postscript

Lt Colonel Kevin Hill MBE, MC became our CO shortly after this. A highly respected and devoted Lancashire Fusilier who served the Regiment until his dying day. He was probably the greatest authority and repository on all matters of our history and traditions and always gave sound advice. A devout RC, he wrote me a splendid confidential report, my last in the Army. I was flattered by his comments, the last sentence being the best – it stated, 'he is the most immoral officer that I have ever met.' I thanked him profusely for this before he replied, 'it is not meant to be a compliment, Lorenzo.' Nevertheless, he was pleased to see me marry five years later and attended our wedding, keeping my wicked reputation safe ... I think.

29

ARABIAN ADVENTURES

The deserts of Arabia, millions of square miles of yellow sand stretching like an ocean, are both beautiful and fascinating. However, my time there was not my happiest posting. Those empty expanses are not a natural habitat for man – certainly not *this* man, and the young officer chafed at the boredom. Now, more reclusive by nature, I might find greater appeal there.

What is more, I did not regard my own performance as an officer as being up to my usual standard, partially because of my imperfect command of the language and also due to the fact that it was hard to relate to the Arab soldier, to inspire and lead him. It was undoubtedly a struggle to drum up enthusiasm surrounded by the lethargy of the desert. A poor excuse, really, for it is an officer's duty to overcome such things and in my opinion I fell short of the standards set by my alma mater – 'Serve to Lead'. However, my life there did introduce me to another culture, indeed a whole new dimension on life, which can only be advantageous.

My first port of call was the Army School of Languages at Beaconsfield in Buckinghamshire. This was a total eye-opener for me, and under the auspices of the Royal Army Education Corps we were taught basic Arabic in three months. Their teaching methods were in my opinion way ahead of contemporary practice. For instance, I remember as a ten-year-old schoolboy studying Latin and the great poet Vigil's *Aeneid*, under my Latin tutor Mr Tamlin. Here we learned such masterly phrases as 'arboreal bowers', written before the birth of Christ for goodness' sake. The formality of the Latin sunk in, for I am often looked at askance, judged old-fashioned and out of touch in my speech. I have often used 'arboreal bowers' in everyday conversation and then asked my interlocutor whether they had understood the figure of speech. The answer is usually in the negative. I am, though, no linguistic genius, and during school French lessons I may well ofen have said, 'tomorrow your house I quickly come.' This *lapsus linguae* would always prompt Mr Ritchie, our French master, to execute a beautiful backhand swipe with his textbook; he must have been a table tennis player.

'You don't say that in English boy, do you? So why say it in French?'

The effect was to render one mute for fear not only of making a fool of oneself, but also of another slap. However, the teaching at Beaconsfield was entirely different. If I had said, 'tomorrow, your house I quickly come' the teachers there would be positively enthusiastic, no clout on the back of one's head, but rather a hearty pat on the back.

'Well done,' they would rave, 'tomorrow, your house I quickly come, I fully understand you … it doesn't matter, but, you could say, "I'll come quickly to your house tomorrow." Don't worry … you have made yourself understood.' This wonderful encouraging approach made one positively sparkle with pride and achievement and drove one to study even harder. They pointed out that people who read the tabloids probably use only 3,000 words in everyday speech, and as long as we learnt a similar vocabulary we would have the basis of the language mastered once with our units. Supposing one wanted to learn the Arabic for 'officer'? No need, one simply used the term 'soldier.' There were no such words as chaise longue, sofa, settee: 'Don't cluster your mind with such verbosity – just say chair,' was the line.

After three months one was able to pass the colloquial examination and hence arrive in the Middle East with at least a modicum of linguistic knowledge. As I said, I am not a natural at such things and had I been a star pupil I am certain that I would have been a better officer. The language itself has many variations and differing accents, and there is also a certain snobbery attached to it, as we have with English. I was always told that Egyptian and Jordanian Arabic was respected and looked up to, rather like Oxford English, but there again some would say Saudi Arabian was the purest form because of its closeness to the Koran and the pilgrimage city of Mecca, but remember Arabic is spoken over a vast area in many lands.

I arrived in Abu Dhabi, the capital of the Emirate now known as the United Arab Emirates, a place so different from today as to be totally unrecognisable. Then it had but one basic hotel and a mile or two of metal roads – the rest was sand. The shops consisted of shacks and corrugated roofs. The airport I would motor into without any restriction, right up to the BOAC VCIO (now renamed British Airways) and ask the crew to take my mail to England for posting there.

Later, I made friends with my bank manager at the National Bank of Abu Dhabi. Here in his air-conditioned office we would drink coffee and he would regale me with his tales of wealth, woe but ultimate success. It transpired that he had been seconded to run the new National Bank of the Emirate, successor to the now defunct Martins Bank. His London masters would constantly harass him, asking whether Sheikh Zaid had deposited his new-found oil wealth in his own bank. They quite rightly said that until the Sheikh had the confidence to put his many millions into his own bank, then how could one expect his subjects to do so? A reasonable argument. For some three years the manager pleaded with the ruler to place his money in the bank rather than keep it in piles in his palace. Now, the Sheikh had lived as a Bedouin in the desert for all of his life, until the country had become oil rich. He was also illiterate, but with all the Bedu traits of guile. Suddenly, out of the blue he announced to John that he was going to bring *his* money to *his* bank. John rang London with the good news, and was given an enormous pay rise in the instant. When he told this story he always smiled contentedly and looked to the ceiling, as if thanking the heavens! On the duly appointed day a fleet of limousines arrived, ten or more he thought, all filled with boxes of gold, dinars and Maria Theresa Austrian dollars, which were still accepted for their silver content even though she had died in 1780! In fact, I still have three of these, made into silver ashtrays by 'Sheikh Robby's' workshop in what was the tiny state of Ras al Kaimah.

With the money now safely in the bank, the bank did what all banks do: invest it in the money markets of the world. This was to have dreadful repercussions for my friend the manager, for some three months later Sheikh Zaid paid a visit to the bank in order to count his loot. I suppose the gold bars were still in situ, but there was a huge deficit in terms of cash. John was accused of theft, shackled and thrown into prison, no doubt to be executed for grand larceny.

'Well, what did you do? Why didn't you tell him where it was?' I said.

'Easier said than done,' he replied. 'You try telling someone who can neither read, write and who has never travelled outside his own backyard that his millions have been invested in the money markets of London, Frankfurt and Rome.' I could sympathise with the Sheikh, as I still don't understand how vast amounts of cash are distributed about the globe. Come what may, John feared for his life and languished in an unpleasant prison for some three days. His life was saved by his Chinese teller who was quick-witted enough to contact our High Commissioner in Bahrain who flew down to save John and also to explain to the ruler that his money was indeed safe and all accounted for.

My time in Abu Dhabi was short-lived, about a week or so, just sufficient to meet people, be briefed and obtain the necessary uniforms. From here I was to be dispatched to what the great explorer Major Sir Wilfred Thesiger (1910–2003) called the Empty Quarter, or Rub al Khali, an area of some 250,000 square miles bordering the state of Saudi Arabia. Thesiger had worked out that he was only the fourth European to get to where I would be stationed, so in terms of popularity it wasn't exactly featuring in Cook's Tours itinerary. Our job there was three-fold: to settle the Bedu (none passed our way), to safeguard the border (but no one knew exactly where this was) and to monitor the locusts (none ever seen). The area of the Liwa was also referred to as the land of the singing sands. My tiny aircraft landed on the '*subqua*', a small area of oasis and hard surface which always reminded me of a form of natural tar. The camp was silent, other than a soldier who met me and told me he was my servant or bearer. He hailed from Tehran in Iran, but like so many inhabitants of that area had come to the Gulf States to seek work, and indeed had married there. We strolled to my tent and I unpacked what little I had. It transpired that the Arab Officer Commanding had deployed the squadron into the desert but they would be home by nightfall. As I acquainted myself with the camp environs and the row upon row of neat tents, the eerie silence was broken by an ever-increasing noise of what sounded to me like a piston-engined bomber.

'Mohammed,' I shouted, 'what on earth is that noise … it sounds like aircraft.'

His black eyes looked puzzled. 'The noise,' I reiterated, 'can't you hear it?'

'But sir,' he replied, 'you are in the land of the singing sands.'

I felt somewhat foolish but had I noticed the slight breeze it may have been more obvious. The camp was surrounded by hills of pure sand, just like the type one gets with a sand-filled egg-timer. These are crowned on top by a single grain of sand, as sharply defined as a knife's edge. A breath of wind topples this grain of sand, then multiplied a trillion times as that one, and its kin, dislodge others in their path. The stronger the wind the larger the displacement, with every little grain adding to the rumbling noise of the running sand cascading down the steep dunes. Soon the rumble becomes substantial, culminating in what I thought was a piston-engine bomber coming in for an attack! This makes it impossible to map an area like the Rub al Khali, for any fixed spot inevitably succumbs to encroachment. My lean-to shower-and-loo at the bottom of the dunes would in time have to be moved to another temporary site, and so on. I suppose our dunes would creep upon us at twelve to fifteen feet a year. The desert here was very different to that over which the 8th Army had fought at El Alamein, where wadis and rocks were in great profusion.

Our camp consisted of some 500 Arab soldiers and 50 or so dhobi wallahs – civilians who cleaned, washed and cooked. The Arab commander left within days and his place was taken by a British Major whom I was to understudy for a few months. Roy Goble was a Yorkshireman belonging to the 14th Foot, The West Yorkshire Regiment (The Prince of Wales's Own). He had bright blue eyes and blond curly hair full of colour, but he was going bald early in life. He was an excellent officer, unambivalent and straight as a die. He had a good command of Arabic and his control over the soldiers, especially for a foreigner, was outstanding. He taught me to play backgammon and most mornings, as the sun climbed towards its apex and the heat grew intense, we would play for high stakes: pennies or matchsticks.

Life began early in the desert, about 5 a.m. when dawn broke and the heat was ambient. Our meals were simple tea and toast made freshly for us, but sometimes we would eat the soldiers' unleavened bread rolled up with jam or dates. If the Queen had ever come for dinner our fare would have been the same, the highlight of the evening being tinned pineapple rings and Nestlé's tinned cream. This was our 'luxury', so consequently we became quite thin. Every few weeks a Caribou transport aeroplane, a Canadian de Havilland I think, would deliver fresh rations and a dozen goats would be run off the aeroplane to be rounded up by a happy throng of soldiers. The Caribou had about the shortest landing and take-off of any aircraft I have seen. Totally misnamed in my opinion, for a caribou is a large mammal that certainly can't fly or carry anything at all, and I don't think it has ever been domesticated to pull a sledge – silly name! Rather, I saw it as a pelican, with a copious beak holding our rations.

Morning was also the nicest time of day; true, the sunsets there were red-blooded and magnificent, but dawn was fresh and one could see the desert in all its glory. Mountains of sand stretching as far as the eye could see. The sun as it rose overhead provided perspective, and one could see the view: fore, middle and background in three dimensions. The dunes reflected brilliant colours of yellow, white and tinges of rose. The crests of the hills were majestic, running curvaceously from top to bottom and traversing the landscape in a huge sweep reminiscent of waves. All this changed at midday when the sun was directly overhead. Its harsh, cruel light reduced everything to a one-dimensional backcloth devoid of any merit, an inhospitable hell. I often wondered how such beauty could change so quickly, just by the sun's movement and light, for it was still the same landscape.

‡

During training I noticed that the Arab soldier seldom thought of himself as what we would now call a 'team player', rather it was just the opposite. An illustration: on the harder 'tarmac type' surface of the oasis I would have three 4-ton Bedford trucks, each representing an infantry section, going at about 6 mph in a circuit. The soldiers had to perform in relays by running up to a Bren gun, stripping it, assembling it and then running up to the truck and scrambling on board, having negotiated quite a high tailgate. It required some speed and athleticism and was meant to instil competitiveness. However, the soldiers never got enthusiastic over such a race, no word of encouragement to their mates and never an offer of a helping hand. One was well and truly on one's own, and I can remember thinking that an Arab army, weighed down by this lack of unity, would be at a marked disadvantage fighting the Israelis.

It wasn't until some months later, when I had a camel, that I came to revise my view of this 'selfish' trait among the Arabs. I would ride off into the desert, always with my Browning pistol and sometimes a few tin cans for target practice. The first time I did this I was apprehensive as to how the beast would react. Perhaps I would be propelled at enormous speed as the frightened animal took off with me still astride it. I figured that if this happened a fall to the ground was the best option, for at least the landing was soft. In the event the camel paid no heed to the shot whatsoever and I must add that I was surprised at the discipline and good manners of my Dromedary, the Arab one-humped camel, as distinct from the Asian Bactrian, or two-humped, version. When I compare it to my horse-riding experiences I found that I seemed able to trust my camel far more than the more ebullient, frisky horses that I had ridden for many years. The two experiences were very different though: a horse accelerated like a sports car, whereas my camel was a sedate saloon, but there again I am told that to ride a racing camel is an outstanding experience.

It was on one of these solitary outings that I observed a speck in the distance. The sun and heat-haze could play havoc with the eyesight at times, but as I rode on I saw this black speck become a dot, then a blob and a blur … but there was no doubting that it was a moving shape. In fact, when I saw the film *Lawrence of Arabia*, it replicated my experience of a sinister black swirl emerging from the dunes. Eventually there was no mistaking that approaching was a fearsome-looking Bedouin, riding one camel, with a second in attendance bearing a large tractor inner tube, which he had somehow filled with water. I was happy that I was armed. For the last 100 yards or so he came at me at a fair-paced trot, suddenly stopping and throwing himself from his mount, saying as he did so, *'Tureed cigara?'* ('Have you got a cigarette?')

This was a huge breach of etiquette, for the Arabs are punctilious in their manners and in the ritual of greeting one another. The formula went something along these lines:

'Salaam al lakum.'
'Wa al lakum as salaam.'
'Kayf halak?'
'Ana bikhayr.'
'Ana mabsoot.'
'Al hamdu lil lah.'

Greetings.
And also to you.
How are you?
All is well.
I am so glad.
Thanks be to God.

… and on leaving a similarly polite farewell which can take some time…

'*Fi aman illah.*'
'*Ma as salama.*'

A ritual prescribed over the centuries, replete with religious connotations. However, this wild-looking unwashed man had contravened convention in a most unusual way, but on listening to his story one could totally understand this lapse of custom. I told him that I didn't smoke and therefore could not oblige him. He squatted disconsolately and after some silent reflection on his part we talked. It transpired that this man had not seen or spoken to anyone for some eight days. He had set off to cross one of the earth's most inhospitable deserts, relying on his own powers of navigation and his two camels. Now, I know that these ships of the deserts are unique in their endurance and tolerance in such an environment, and indeed they can travel the desert for three days without sustenance and can do so at a remarkable sixty miles a day – but even they can suffer from sickness and become lame. The risk he took in setting off into the unknown, relying purely on his own skill, judgement and an uncanny sense of direction, would be to many minds a great folly, but to me was an act of outstanding bravery. How many of us go twelve hours without speaking to someone, let alone eight days? His world was he himself and two camels. As a Bedu, he would have known of some of the water holes, but it is not always possible to locate them, especially if you encounter a sandstorm. So I had to rethink my opinion of the Arab, with his in-built self-reliance and propensity to act alone. Two different nations, two divergent philosophies, but both brave in their own way. In the end he arrived in the camp as a guest of the squadron, but to be honest he could have done without our company. The one trump card I held to convince him of our hospitality was that they would be cigarettes in abundance!

As a postscript to this, I hear now that the famed independence of the Bedouin may have somewhat faded, as many now own the latest 4x4, with incredible trailers and caravans to match, and they watch satellite television in the once-remote oases.

On the subject of oases, many of my friends picture these as deep pools of water, shaded by palm tree fronds, with nubile maidens dressed in seductive, diaphanous garments dancing for one's erotic pleasure, as depicted in Hollywood movies. Alas, nothing is further from the truth, for as often as not an oasis will have no visible water at all, but rather a subterranean supply, providing a well-head and allowing the growth of date trees and a prolific plant that grows to knee height, that we called the *ha'wa*. This, I imagine, belongs to the cactus family, though not viciously barbed, and contains a good deal of brackish water. Our date palms produced a most delicious fruit, which as it ripens can be picked prematurely, so half the date is browned and the remainder is about to turn. They were plump and juicy, with both a sweet and sour taste. They bore little relation to those we purchase at Christmas-time. However, the season is short and for the rest of the year the dates are compressed in large tins for all-year-round consumption. The palm tree itself can live for about a hundred years and has many uses: wood for carpentry, the stem-fibre for simple ropes, the leaves for matting.

There was little other vegetation about, more's the pity, for it provided the only shade for the guide's little donkey. How the donkey came to be in such a place I do not know, whether a favour from the Caribou pilot or a hazardous journey from Abu Dhabi, for he was the only one I recall seeing in the desert. Certainly, it was a long journey from the capital. Indeed I always found it amazing that, if a soldier took three weeks' leave we could also give him two to three weeks' marching-time home and two to three weeks to return. Now I suppose it is rather like the North Sea oil-rigs, where they are ferried by helicopter. Anyway, sometimes our little donkey would wander into our unfenced camp and the soldiers would feed him tit-bits, jump on his back and take rides. On a few occasions he would arrive outside my office tent and I was persuaded to amble back to the Mess tent on him. I must say it was quicker to walk, even through the slow-paced sand, and probably healthier too, for I suspect he was never groomed or de-loused. He had a lovely donkey nature, very placid and friendly, and he could have stepped out of a Walt Disney film for his 'toenails' (in no way did they resemble hooves) were huge curling-up things, giving him a cuddly-toy-like appearance, as he flopped about in the sand.

I hadn't been around very long, and perhaps my mentor Roy had gone on leave, for certainly I was the only European officer in camp. The recently promoted Lt Ateeq, an excellent and experienced man, had joined us from the Trucial Oman Scouts, but he always chose to Mess with the sergeants. Suddenly there was a commotion outside my tent, with about a dozen soldiers milling around. I turned from my desk, and a sergeant announced in Arabic that 'Mohammed the Kutch has ridden the little donkey'. (Mohammed the Kutch being our vehicle fitter, looking after our motor transport.) As I said, my grasp of the language was far from perfect, but I said that I had understood, and replied that I too had 'ridden the donkey from my office this very lunchtime'. Outside, the Kutch was being manhandled and I had to step into the fray to assuage strained tempers. The shouting persisted for another ten minutes before the Sergeant-Major appeared, and I told him that I could find nothing amiss in this man's behaviour. He then showed me his left arm, straightened it and then bent it quickly, simultaneously bringing his right fist into the left elbow in a quick, vicious movement. *Now* I understood.

The Kutch had, indeed, 'ridden the donkey' ... in a sexual fashion. I defused the incident a little, becoming more formal, gathering up my headdress and calling for Lt Ateeq and the Orderly Sergeant to come and see me. This duly happened, and the donkey, sporting an embarrassing erection, was paraded before me. I was then taken to the oasis with a hue and cry lynch mob following at my heels. Here, I was shown the palm tree with the rope tether-marks which had secured the animal while the Kutch had allegedly performed this gross act. He was then forced kneeling in front of me while a pistol was produced and I was invited to shoot his brains out. Apparently, this summary justice was considered perfectly acceptable for such a heinous crime. I looked at the piteous boy, probably no older than twenty. He had fairish skin, large brown eyes and a shaven head which at the time was unusual. There was no defiance in his rather sad face, but I think at that moment he thought that death was imminent. I knew that the nomads were bloodthirsty by nature and I recalled Thesiger and his time with the Danakil nomads, where they systematically castrated their enemy, one warrior claiming four sets of testicles in a bloody orgy and all in a single day (though this was in the Aussa Sultanate, so not quite local). However, there was no dilemma for me, as I knew that I would rather shoot myself than this young man, and no amount of crowd participation or bullying would change my mind. The Arab Lieutenant Ateeq was a source of strength, although he would have left me to carry out the execution, had it been my wish. We established a guard of NCOs to look after the soldier, with strict orders that if any ill came to him they would be held responsible. I asked Ateeq if he had ever witnessed a similar scenario when he was with the TOS. He had, and if a summary execution were not carried out then as an alternative the miscreant would be staked out in a loincloth at first light on the parade ground. He would not be cut down until darkness fell.

'But that is a terrible ordeal,' I remonstrated. The man would die a horrible death, his tongue swelling as the day progressed, eventually to choke him.

'Allah Kareen' (God is Good) Ateeq replied, 'for if he is innocent Allah will protect him and he will survive to live another day.'

Without doubting Allah too blatantly, I expressed the opinion that it was probably best to use the bullet, but I would choose another way. After much discussion, he told me that the soldiers' mood might grow rebellious as night approached, and that I should be alert and have my personal weapon to hand. I let it be known that I had found Mohammed the Kutch guilty and that a morning stake-out was to take place. This, I hoped, would please the more religious elements of the squadron, but I then frantically started to contact Battalion HQ in Abu Dhabi in the hope that I could get the holy man or imam to fly up as dawn broke and thus diffuse this terrible imbroglio. We had no radio, only Morse code, and this of course could be read by the Arab clerks and disseminated to the already outraged squadron. So we were certainly not out of the woods yet and I spent a fairly fretful night. Night-time flying was impossible as we had no airstrip as such, and no lighting. However, Battalion HQ promised that the imam would be off as early as was humanly possible, and hopefully he'd arrive before any irretrievable harm was done. This, together with a later morning parade, bought me some valuable time, and when I was confronted by those soldiers who were senior Muslims (those who had been on a Hadj, a pilgrimage to Mecca) I could safely say that the matter had been taken out of my hands and placed more appropriately with the religious elders. It wasn't the answer that they wanted, as they thought that retribution was mine, with they themselves the instruments of punishment. It was true that the prospect of an execution had brought excitement to our sandy, celibate world, so far removed from civilisation. However, the soldiers could not go against their religious superiors and happily for me Mohammed the Kutch did indeed depart safely with the flying cleric.

The establishment then became tight-lipped, for I never found out the young soldier's fate. However, I did hear that there was some form of feud between him and the local men in the squadron. They resented him because he was from 'over the waters', from the Rann of Kutch, the border area between Pakistan and India, cut by the Tropic of Cancer. Furthermore, he was clever and was a good vehicle mechanic, and to add insult to injury he was a competent footballer who only two days ago had barged an Abu Dhabian on the pitch (well *sub'qua*), knocking him to the ground. This type of vendetta was common enough, but I feared for his chances in a religious court, especially if one or two locals falsely testified to the alleged act. Islam is a severe master, and even I had been told before I left England that it would be foolish of me to take a Holy Bible to Arabia, sound advice which I followed. I wonder how we would be branded in the United Kingdom were we to ban the Koran from our shores.

It was about this time that I learnt, purely by accident, that two fellow officers had been murdered in their beds, which prompted my bearer, whom I liked and got on well with, to say that he wanted my forgiveness but that if he were told that he must dispatch me then he would do so, for otherwise his family would be in jeopardy. From this period onwards I always slept with my Browning pistol under my pillow.

This sad story had a funny ending, for me anyway. About three weeks later the commanding officer paid me a visit and over pineapple rings and a bottle of brandy he said, 'Bloody bad show about that chap buggering the donkey, Lawrence.'

'Well yes,' I said pensively, 'but if you had seen the animal … he was the sweetest little donkey that you have ever seen.'

'My god, Lawrence,' he positively puffed, about to explode. 'We've got to get you out … you've been here too long.'

I wished they had!

In Koranic law, so I was informed, the donkey or *himar* was now considered unclean, and the guide or *daleel* must therefore destroy it. He could also claim compensation from the wrongdoer for the cost of the animal. This is what I was led to believe had transpired, for I no longer saw the donkey in camp. Some two months later, when I was in with the guide a couple of miles from our camp, whom should I be reunited with? None other than the Walt Disney donkey. No doubt the guide had declared him slaughtered and quickly claimed the compensation – well, we were days away from the capital and who was going to tell anyway?

My *daleel* was a civilian who lived with his young wife in three tents, with five camels and a few goats. His wife was a black-gowned apparition who flitted like a ghost between tents, totally enveloped in her Arabic garb. I cannot even say that I ever saw her eyes, for the head was always cast downwards.

The *daleel* came to me after the birth of one of his children demanding a sackful of salt.

'Why does he need that?' I asked of the Duty Sergeant.

'His wife has had a baby and he may wish to use her soon,' was the boastful reply.

It transpired that salt in the womb, similar to salt on a snail or such, just burns it up and contracts the wound, or in this case her parts. The act seemed absolutely brutal but when I discussed it with an Arabist officer who had served in the Jordanian Army under Glubb Pasha for some twenty years, he concluded that this was the manly thing to say, but, it did have a medical angle to it, insomuch as it cleaned the womb and prevented infection. Still, a horrendous and painful experience for which the Arab women have no comeback or say, considered as they were purely chattels of their men. Two or three months later, he again asked me for more salt but this time I was told it was for him to carry out a female circumcision, for he was contemplating another pilgrimage to Mecca and his young wife was to be deprived of her erotic areas in case she was sexually tempted during his enforced absence. In Marilyn French's excellent book *War Against Women* (1992), she estimates that 22–30 million girls and women go through this degrading, hideously painful experience, not at the hands of a medic, or in a clinically clean environment, but by an unqualified 'butcher' of a husband who performs the act without any form of drugs or consultation with his wife, other than his own personal whim, and of course the salt I provided.

My guide was a gruesome-looking fellow, who had lived in the desert as a true nomad. His flowing untrimmed beard, pockmarked skin and small deep-set eyes (through constant squinting I deduced) did not make him a pleasant sight. However, it was to his feet that I was always drawn, for they resembled dinner plates and, I say this quite seriously, I only knew that they were feet because they were found at the end of his legs. Over the years, and being without sandals of any kind, his feet had spread outwards and were now over-large and roundish. I cannot recall his toes in detail, but there again I tried not to look at these misshapen objects. However, they served their purpose well, for the large area of the foot, rather like with the camels, gave him leverage on the sand's soft surface. At the same time these feet were so calloused that they gave him no pain when walking on the burning sand, a feat impossible for the rest of us, including the Arab soldiers. I remember his other unique attribute was his in-built 'sat-nav'. I recall looking at my map one day, which in truth had very little on it other than a village called Bayt al Abd, to which I decided I would lead a patrol, about three days' march away. With the *daleel* in the vanguard we set off, with my compass pointing due north, but off he went 360 degrees the other way – due south. No remonstration would make him change his mind, and as it happened he knew his stuff, for his tortuous route led us to where I intended to go, rendering my compass totally irrelevant.

My decision to go on patrol was not without a certain amount of self-interest, for I had figured that since this was the only village on the map there might be a cool drink there – a beer was too much to ask, but a refreshing ice-cold drink would revive my spirits. In about two and a half days we arrived and looked down from the top of the sand dunes to a flat area, not unlike our own camp.

'We are here,' the *daleel* said in his usual taciturn fashion.

'Where is the village?' I said.

'Well, he has gone,' he replied.

'Who has gone?' I retorted.

'Al Abd has gone,' he persisted.

'Where has he gone?' I demanded.

'To his winter quarters,' he said, still staring ahead.

Bayt al Abd, I should have known, meant the house of the slave. He *was* the village, and he had chosen to move with his wives, camels, tents, numerous offspring and goats, and there was nothing more to say or see or drink.

The soldiers were probably more disappointed than me, for I learned later that they had been looking forward to a feast. To be honest I was not a great devotee of these harmonious gatherings. For a start, the host would parade before me, as senior guest, some unfortunate animal, but usually a goat (and protocol demanded it should be his best) whose eyes I would look into knowing that some five hours later I would be invited to swallow it, the eye that is. Furthermore, sitting cross-legged on the floor played havoc with my knees, while the sole use of the right hand (the left being used for other purposes), rolling up and lobbing to others choice pieces of meat and balls of rice with dubious juices, wasn't my idea of haute cuisine.

It was also the custom to offer guests the nicest morsels and hard-boiled eggs were thrown around one rather like wayward ping-pong balls. However, in my neck of the woods the animal's head was placed on top of the rice, rather like the boar's head in England but ever so slightly less well presented. At my first feast my host had taken the skull and with great kindness had scooped the eye out with the animal's incisor, which he then used to gouge out the soft muscle tissue behind the eye as a delicacy for me. What turned my stomach inside out was in the handling of the head: the juices of the brain, blood and I know not what flowed out as a horrible black slick, spreading over and running down the rice. This was eagerly awaited by my fellow diners. The mucus-type fluid provided a wonderful and obviously tasty adhesive, handy for rolling one's rice into mouth-watering balls, which were diligently placed in front of me for my delectation.

No, I wasn't a great fan of the Arab feast but I did appreciate the kindness of the Bedu's hospitality for this was genuine and freely given from their slender resources. So after another night under the stars we returned the way we came, following the guide's circuitous route but with his uncanny sense of direction still leading us forward, just the breathless uttering of his favourite word 'kidda, kidda' (this way, that way) and his gnarled hand pointing this way or that.

I asked my Arab-speaking expert, when next in town, how the guide managed in daylight when there were no stars. He surprised me by saying that when he had come to town he was terrified and could not find his way around anywhere. Well, each to his own.

His three-year-old boy was a different story, and one I thought would end in disaster. The little chap had somehow drunk some kerosene instead of water and was rushed in to see me. It was night, but I knew that if we did not get him to hospital immediately he would be dead by morning. As it happened everything went well and everyone seemed to be in the right place at the right time, the doctor, the pilot and our Morse code all co-ordinating without a hitch. Now, we had never had a night landing before, as I explained, for our little piece of sub'qua had no landing lights or navigational aids whatsoever. However, an intrepid pilot agreed to give it a go after I had outlined my plan, which was to marshal every vehicle in the place, the Land Rovers and the 4-tonners, and to light up a strip, giving our aviator a visible runway. We also set off flares when we heard the aircraft's engine and a perfect landing was accomplished. The skill of the pilot was the lifeline for our young patient, and with the doctor in attendance the little boy was whisked off to hospital to make a full recovery.

What had amazed me, though, was the fact that the guide had actually sought out my help, for so often the Arabs adopt a fatalistic attitude to life. Sometimes the soldiers just seemed to cave in and let life roll over them. We were out in the desert in my Land Rover when the driver tipped the vehicle over. Normally we always patrolled in two vehicles, in the hope that one would at least be serviceable, so I don't know how we came to be alone. After sweating our guts out trying to extricate ourselves and watching our dwindling supply of water, my driver suddenly gave up and announced that we would die here, and 'it was Allah's will', which is also why any order given to them or accepted by them is always followed by the caveat '*inshallah*' – if Allah wills it.

Here was a case where 'God willed it', and we could try no more. I of course did not go along with this sophistry and shook the man physically while putting a shovel in his hand and arousing him from his lethargy. As it is evident we made it home, but it was unpleasant and it was not the last time I was to experience this type of thing. This fatalism in the Arab mind was also linked to a lack of urgency, brought home to me one morning when we had our coffee. Our coffee ceremony was a daily ritual, either in my tent, the Sergeants' Mess tent or elsewhere. One sat in a circle on the floor and drank from small handle-less cups which held a mouthful or two. The host stood around the circle holding the ornate brass coffee pot, the one we have all seen with the swan neck and large brass handle. Sometimes dates were served or other little delicacies, and if the ceremony was held in my tent my servant performed the host's duty, but it seemed to be very egalitarian, with senior personnel happy to perform this task. One only ever accepted three cups, as I remember, before uttering the words '*shukran, shukran, shukran*' with a little shake of the cup signifying one was replete. The coffee had no milk or sugar in it, unless a little had been added during the making. What was common to all their coffee was the cardamom seed and the capsules of several tropical plants of the ginger family, which made the coffee more spicy and less 'coffeey'.

I remember on one such occasion Lt Ateeq had come and joined us for coffee, still dusted with desert sand fresh from leading a patrol. He had some thirty men, two 4-tonners and some Land Rovers.

'Salaam al lakum.'
'Wa al lakum as salaam.'
'Kayf halak?'
'Ana bikhayr.'
'Ana mabsoot.'
'Al hamdu lil lah.'

We then proceeded to drink our coffee and exchange pleasantries, for perhaps half an hour or so. Lt Ateeq eventually asked to be excused and I said, 'Well, you'll probably be tired and need to catch up on some sleep after that arduous patrol.' 'Oh no sir,' was his reply, 'I need to go and rescue the 4-tonner, it tipped on its way down and I think the driver may have broken his arm as it went over on its side.'

Again, it would have been a severe breach of protocol had he rushed into the tent and shouted, 'Quick help, Fusilier Snooks is trapped in the 4-tonner with a broken arm,' as we would have done. Everything in good time. Well, life among the dunes of the Empty Quarter was slow-moving and nothing was that urgent to upset the sedate, ordered life of our community, with its time-honoured manners and the old order of things. Rather charming really, as long as you weren't the soldier trapped with a broken arm ... not as yet confirmed of course.

It was about this time that I had a severe trauma, and of course it had to happen at night. Mohammed had brought me my customary bowl of hot water to wash and clean my teeth. I was still dressed in uniform but had flip flops on my feet. I remember I went outside the tent for a quick walk about and to say goodnight to the stars. I then walked over to my table to perform my ablutions. I had just placed my hands in the water when I was hit by a pain so searing, so totally hideous, that I gave a blood curling cry and jumped – well I think 'rocketed' would be a better word, as my body took off skywards before crashing on the ground. When Mohammed came rushing in he saw me doubled up and holding my stomach, but I had gained the safety of my bed. I must have been ashen-faced but all I could say was '*Jeeb Tabib*' (bring the doctor).

The doctor was an Arab Corporal who had done a six-week medical course, and Mohammed duly departed to walk to the medic's tent. I had time to think what had happened, but not for long, for I felt an excruciating pain creeping up both of my legs and freezing my blood, a total and terrifying paralysis. By this time Mohammed had returned, a total time which we established later of about eight minutes. Apparently, he had got to the medical tent and said something like, 'The OC must have a pain in his stomach for he is clutching it with both hands.' This prompted the Cpl to give him two tablets which by the time he got to me were melting and had to be scraped from his sweaty palm. I can't remember taking them, although they were well on their way to being dissolved! I could only scream to him again, 'Get me the bloody doctor! I am dying.'

I think at this stage my bearer had at last begun to take me seriously, for he quickened his gait and looked anxious. On this occasion I think that he may even have trotted to the medic's tent. All the while the paralysis got painfully worse and was insidiously creeping up my legs, and I thought that once it got to my heart it would freeze all the working parts and I would die quite a slow death. I also remember half-comforting myself by thinking that if it got to my 'manliness' first, then of course death *was* preferable. A jumble of emotions raced through my mind; now thinking back on it, had the paralysis frozen my gonads then presumably they could have been unfrozen or un-paralysed, but not so the heart? Surely a paralysis meant just that: paralysing the heart muscles and death. The pain kept on progressing upwards and I began to retch. The doctor appeared and other faces gazed over my heavily perspiring head with my body jumping quite involuntarily in pain. My legs were now bent at the knee and I could not straighten them.

The doctor looked down in terror, and I remembered the word for scorpion: 'Agrab', I uttered. His brown face turned green as he fled from the tent to collect his medicine. The journey time (all worked out retrospectively) was getting shorter: 8 minutes, 5 minutes and now in this instance a creditable 4-minute mile, as he duly appeared with syringe and morphine. He was shaking as he injected my left big toe and my right heel. The time was now about 2200 hrs and the camp had been alerted with the senior NCOs, indeed a veritable crowd, all pushing around to see me in my tent. It reminded me of a biblical scene painted by one of the great masters, when they cram onto the canvas every detail and hordes of disparate characters, for by now the soldiers were mostly dressed in their white robes and some carried their beads. I had two severe stings, and the fact that the injections had taken so long to administer, probably well over half an hour, meant that their efficacy had been somewhat or totally negated. There was turmoil around, but I somehow had the presence of mind to send a signal, about midnight, to Battalion HQ that 'sunray call sign 4 bitten by two scorpions. Request casevac [casualty evacuation] ASP' which prompted the reply, 'is sunray call sign 4 dead yet?' I was hanging on but could I hang on until daybreak and rescue by the little Cessna? I also remember thinking that this will have enlivened the pace of life in base HQ, but the drama would not have the same effect if I survived. At least if I was dead they would have something to chat about at the bar. Oh well, I would hope to disappoint them.

In the meantime, I picked up snippets of the sergeants' conversation which cast doubt on my goodness. I heard one definitely say, 'I thought the Englishman was quite a decent fellow, God is good and one can be forgiven for being bitten by one scorpion ... but to be bitten by two ... well.' The inference being that I had hoodwinked them all, and in reality was an evil sod! The paralysis seemed to stay around the top of my legs and lower stomach and I wondered (as I have already said) whether I would ever perform again. I remember hearing stories of the two world wars, when wounded soldiers would use their helmets to protect their genitals rather than the heart or head, so at least my preoccupations weren't as unhealthy as one may think. Sickness followed and an all-night vigil was kept by my bed. I know soldiers held my hand and mopped my brow and I remember thinking that there was after all a gentleness to these men that I had not previously witnessed.

Dawn broke and I was still alive. Back at base I was placed in a sickroom and pumped with lots of things, including morphine I suspect. As I slowly recovered I noticed that there was a glass case, not unlike a fish tank, on the window sill. It contained a small snake and a mouse, and I wondered what possible pleasure people derived from keeping a tame, or even untamed, snake in such a place. The mouse ran from corner to corner, always sniffing and sometimes becoming quite brave and even running over his 'companion'. I thought perhaps there was a happy ending to this little scenario and someone was going to tell me that they were the best of friends, but there wasn't, for on the second day the snake got bored or hungry and ate his cellmate. I never found out why such a macabre thing was in a sick bay of all places – perhaps to remind me how tenuous life is and how lucky I was.

Over the weekend my girlfriend (later to be my wife) arrived and I remember her asking me why I couldn't remember all my words and how I appeared unusually vague. I can't remember my answer, but what I did find out from the experts was that I had stepped between two mating scorpions and quite rightly they had expressed venomous anger at having their nookie interrupted. What always amazed me was that they had struck so absolutely as one, a total blitzkrieg, simultaneously.

When I returned to the UK and tried to impress everyone with my (remarkable bravery) knowledge of scorpions, I was thoroughly undermined. It appeared David Attenborough had made a programme on these arachnids, and everyone knew that they performed a sort of square dance in their courtship, and it was during this dance of death almost that my feet had got in the way, one to the left and one to the right. I was flabbergasted that creatures so vile could be so caring as to perform a delicate quadrille between my feet before mating! Here they had the better of me. Had I been required to perform such a complicated dance before mating I think that I would have lost interest or moved on to fresh pastures with someone who shared my passion for reaching a rather quicker conclusion.

After this weekend I spent a few days in Abu Dhabi and went to see the bank manager, knowing that he would have some ice-cold beers hidden in his refrigerator. I was in uniform and had hardly got out of the taxi when two attractive young women came running towards me.

'Excuse me, excuse me, please,' looking a little flustered and somewhat furtive.

'Excuse me, but you're important aren't you … you're an officer or something?' they said in harmony, giggling.

'Well, I have never been regarded as important,' I joked, 'but if it pleases you, I am happy to be so.'

I thought that I would prefer their company to even that of a cold beer, so I wanted to prolong the conversation as long as I could, for who knew where it would lead?

It came about that these young things, one brunette, and the other blonde, belonged to an ENSA-style cabaret. They both hailed from Scotland and were about twenty years of age. When they had arrived in the Emirate, the Sheikh in charge of passports and immigration had his staff keep the passports (they didn't like the word 'confiscate') of some people, normally women, and it was always happened to be the attractive one, just in case they had a dubious past, which might hopefully continue into the future. I can confirm this, for many of the airline stewardesses had a similar and repetitive experience. I should also add in the majority of cases it resulted in the girls, and indeed the rest of the crew, being invited to perfectly innocent beach parties. Unfortunately, the Sheikh's sons had laid claim to these rather naïve dancers, and who wouldn't for they both had lovely figures and were attractive to behold. Anyway, the authorities were reluctant to return their passports to them and the girls were left in no doubt that their documents would not be forthcoming unless their relationship developed into that of a boy and girlfriend. This, indeed, had happened and the boys, whom I think I had met, were pleasant and generous. However, as happens to most young men, they had over the months met others and intended to explore pastures new. The two young women were concerned, in fact sure, that they were about to be passed down the line, perhaps to older men and so it may have continued until they had become part of the white slave trade. (This really interested me for in my evil mind I had always wanted a lovely slave and these two were ideal candidates ... just a pipe dream.)

Their question was unequivocal: could I get their passports back and negotiate an escape? Well, who better to confer with than John the Bank, with his experience in prison and his line to his saviour, the High Commissioner in Bahrain? I couldn't promise anything but I took down their details and, if I remember correctly, they were both 36-24-36 or thereabouts. I would try, but I was quite circumspect in not giving them my details, for I didn't want any nasty recriminations. So that was a labour of love ... 'to labour and ask for no reward'.

Until about six months later, and on my way home through Beirut, what should I hear in perfect sing-song harmony but 'Excuse me, excuse me ... well it's us ... do you remember us, the girls you rescued from ... we owe you a big favour.' So there is justice in this world, well sometimes! So I was rewarded for my unselfishness, diligence and altruism in rescuing these fair maidens. Needless to say, I had a wonderful week in Beirut and strangely enough I still have a rather dated photograph of the cabaret pair, long-legged and saucy, but happy memories to conclude my time in Arabia and the Middle East, for after that Beirut would become another ugly war zone, so far removed from the old sophisticated city I remembered, with its wonderful French legacy and intriguing Arab souk, all rolled so conveniently into one wonderful capital.

30

GINGER

I once had a friend who was very tall and slim, but his one overriding feature was a great shock of ginger hair. His name was Peter Robinson and he was extremely clever. Indeed, when I knew him he was a young and up-and-coming lecturer at London University. Peter quite simply excelled at everything he did, and he seemed to do just that – everything. He had fingers in every pie. He accompanied rally and racing drivers on the circuits and wrote exciting articles about them. He wrote for learned journals, newspapers and magazines, and no smart party at the most expensive hotel was complete unless he was there. Invariably, he would end up in the glossy social columns, photographed with the good and the great. In short he was most annoying, especially to someone like me whose only preoccupation was the fair sex and expensive dinner dates. Nevertheless, one was inexplicably drawn to him and I couldn't help not only admiring him but also liking his company, for his mind was active, his brain fertile and his company a challenge.

Peter also had a social conscience, for every Friday on his way to work he would give money to the blind man begging outside Gloucester Road tube station. The man was there in all weathers and it would take a harder heart than mine not to be saddened by the sight of him. His dirty clothes and dishevelled looks were not enhanced by a matted and overgrown beard, with dark sunglasses further adding to his aura of gloom and despondency. If only he could have seen himself I am certain it would have spurred him on to take charge of his appearance, but one could only sympathise with his plight. The notice around his neck proclaimed him to be 'Ex-serviceman, blind and war-wounded'. It also supported a tray with a few match boxes and the usual jumping beans, no doubt to catch the eye of passing mothers with children.

'Why Friday?' I once asked when accompanying him on his journey.

'Pay day dear boy,' he said. 'I do it religiously every week on Friday. We always pass the same time of day and over the last five years he knows not only my voice but can hear me coming – hears my step I suppose.' I thought him even more annoying now – charitable to the blind too.

Now it happened one stifling summer's evening that Peter was jammed solid with the rush-hour commuters. He was sweating profusely and, as he commented, 'had an unwashed armpit in my face'. It was then that he questioned his lifestyle.

What am I doing with my life? Why do I put up with this? I am an idiot … a nut case … a total nut case. The syncopation of the railway lines seemed to match a lyric he had been turning around in his head as he swayed along in the heat. By the time he had surfaced from the subterranean torture he had already formulated a famous advertising ditty. Lesser men would have rationalised that, truth be told, it didn't really amount to much after all and by the time the first thirst-quenching pint was downed all would be forgotten. Not Peter. He returned to his flat and assiduously turned out twelve advertising plates, all neat, coloured and professional. These he posted the next morning. Three or four months elapsed and then one day he telephoned me.

'Remember my advertisements?' he laughingly jibed.

'What of them?' I replied.

'You'll never guess, only a cheque for a very large amount of money. It arrived yesterday, yes Friday,' he said. 'I am rich, so come over for a drink then dinner at Fredianos.' He explained that he had picked up the morning mail on leaving his flat for work. Normally, he opened it in the office over a cup of coffee but the firm's advertising logo had caught his eye and the temptation was too great.

'I was over the moon,' he laughed, 'and so full of bonhomie and largesse that I rolled up the only note I had, actually a week's spending money – well £10 to be exact – and with a little difficulty squeezed it into the round hole (as opposed to the coin slit) when I passed my beggar man and his rattling tin.'

'Lucky chap,' I remarked.

'Yes, he thought so too,' he reflected pensively. 'He gave me a huge grin and said, "Thanks Ginger."

'He wasn't there when I returned a couple of hours later,' his voice trailing off somewhat sadly.

Life's deceptive at times.

31

MODEL GIRLS

I was sitting having breakfast in Chelsea Barracks, Lower Sloane Street, London. In the 1960s it was the ugly home of the Brigade of Guards, who took it in turns to perform public duties from there. I say ugly, for it conformed to the much-loved breeze block and reinforced concrete 1950s style of architecture. The type that reminded you of prisons, and within five years already looked dated and hideous. I remember how the rain, soot and general pollution of the capital soon reduced its white ribbed concrete to unequal lines of black-stained grime, while the 'ammo' boots with the obligatory thirteen studs per sole reverberated on the stone stairs and provided ice-skating conditions for those guardsmen in a hurry to get to parade.

Happily it has recently been razed to the ground and only the rectangular-shaped walls testify to its existence. The MOD thought fit to sell it, and soon from the concrete dust of the barracks will rise splendid new flats, so highly priced that only foreign potentates will be able to afford them, thus continuing the tradition of expelling Londoners from London and rehousing them in Milton Keynes, Thetford, Croydon and Crawley. Meanwhile the poor old soldiers patiently commute from Windsor and even Aldershot on occasions, but what is another four hours added to their working day? They are not paid overtime so it's a saving to the taxpayer in all events. Anyway, I had played an early morning game of squash with my Grenadier friend of Sandhurst days, and he must have noticed my gaunt bachelor appearance, hence his invitation to breakfast. Now breakfast is normally taken in silence as one chomps on one's toast and reads the salacious broadsheets. This morning the silence was broken by a subaltern reading *The Times* for he suddenly said, 'My goodness Lawrence, here is just the job for you.' I should quickly explain that the front page of *The Times* contained all the Situations Vacant, all the Flat Sharing facilities and general personal advertisements, hence its popularity and of course this was before the days of recruitment consultants and job centres. He read excitedly, 'Wanted: ex-ADC to run 30 of London's Most Beautiful Women.'

It gave a few conditions before categorically stating that before one could apply the Latin, or was it Greek, phrase appended must be translated and given to the MD's PA (the lovely Ruth McDonald-Hill) before one could speak to the man himself. There must have been a Wykehamist present, for we soon had the translation sorted and before I could say bacon and eggs I was in the telephone booth being put through to the boss. Our telephone conversation went something like this: 'Well, Mr Stacey, I would appreciate it if you could come immediately, for we don't have a lot of time.'

'Well, sir, that is a little difficult as I will need to go home and change.' In the back of my mind I thought that I must not prejudice the job and envisaged that this was a pinstripe and bowler hat type interview.

'Why?' he persisted.

'Well, I am only in my blazer and greys, having just played squash,' I replied.

'Oh, far too overdressed for us ... just get in your motor car and come at once,' he laughed. His PA gave me explicit instructions and within minutes I was driving my Austin Healey 3000 towards London airport. I noticed that all the traffic was going into London while I was able to speed unhindered in the opposite direction; going home would therefore be as convenient but in reverse. Things were soon to get even better, for as I cut my throaty engine in the office courtyard I was confronted by a most handsome and avuncular man, moustached and with a paucity of hair on top but ample curls on the side and back of his head rather in the monastic fashion. He was big, nicely dressed in a conventional way and he smiled broadly as he took my hand heartily, and looking at the Healey, announced, 'Of course, we will run this for you.'

That car barely did fifteen miles to the gallon – he was my friend for life ... and indeed so he became.

Christopher Ulysses Williams was in his late thirties at the time. He was a Cambridge rugby Blue and bob-sleigh champion, before it went Olympian. His father had been a Harley Street man, a surgeon I think, and his brother an RAF flyer, becoming a senior officer in time. The brothers honed their golf skills with their famous drives up and down Harley Street – he explained that there weren't as many motor cars around in the late 1940s so damage was negligible! He had also been a Major in the Honourable Artillery Company (HAC), an elite TA formation, hence his wish to employ an ex-regular officer. He led me around the office which was filled with former models, now administratively employed. It was easy-going and looked like fun, and as we progressed from room to room it became clear to me that I had the job. You will be responsible for this ... you will do that ... and I expect you to report back to me on the following.

After an hour or so he sat me down and said, 'Well how do you feel about it?' I was floored on hearing what my salary and expenses came to, but more than that flabbergasted by the models, the client base and the type of work the agency undertook. I had come to the conclusion that I would do the job for nothing, but here I was being paid more than a Major-General. What had I done to deserve such a break? It was like putting a little boy in a sweet shop, for I knew I couldn't help but touch the goods. Adam and Eve all over again, I thought.

It transpired that Christopher's wife had died just a couple of days before and that he had landed the biggest contract ever given so far in the modelling world. The client, Rothmans, had insisted that they needed thirty women of model quality to carry out a campaign of sampling cigarettes in up-market outlets. We were to be given thirty Hillman Imp motor cars, rather racy little things, all in a special livery. The job was to last three months, all of us put up in minimum three-star hotels. For a lot of the girls, three months of regular work was a great bonus; many got huge emoluments, but often for only one or two days at a time. The standard was therefore high and we were able to pick and choose, with a mixed proportion of genuine models and some experienced promotion girls who knew the ropes (for example girls who were competent in-store demonstrators). It was a strange sensation. All my working life I had been among licentious soldiery (and here I willingly include myself), often unwashed and vulgar ... well certainly the latter. Swearing was endemic and everyone was referred to as a 'bastard' – clearly some were, but lots weren't. 'How do you remember all their names?' I asked Chris. 'You will get to know quite a lot of them gradually but in the meantime just call them darling,' he laughed.

The other angle, which bothered me, was that I had noticed another Cambridge man who was the statistician and had been with the company since its inception, as indeed had others. Why was I superseding these people?

'Well, I want a soldier ... for a start I know that you will work twenty-four hours a day. For instance, if, one of the girls can't carry her suitcase to her room, I know that you will oblige; if one of the motor cars has a puncture, I know that as a soldier you will roll up your sleeves and get on with it. In short you will be all things to all men ... in this case women! Most importantly, I wanted an ex-ADC who knows the form, who is *au fait* in dealing with senior personnel, able to converse intelligently [debatable] and maintain standards and uphold general etiquette in my absence, and this is all reflected in your pay and conditions.' In short, he wanted someone who was able to make decisions and stand by them. I subsequently discovered that his second-in-command, so mild-mannered and correct, had a drink problem and would disappear for days on end.

His remarks were prescient, for it was only a few days later that I saw a petite secretary, one Wendy Rona (subsequently to become a very good friend of mine), struggling with a very heavy typewriter. They were rather cumbersome in those days, so I took it from her and placed it in the transport. On asking her head of department why he hadn't helped her, he confidentially whispered that he was 'executive', and wasn't paid to be a coolie. I also couldn't help but notice that when the administrative team, the 'leaders' if you like, were called upon to have dinner with the clients, followed by a late-night drinking session, they viewed this as working time, added it to their regular sleep pattern, and thereby surfaced for work around midday. I don't think that they ever came around to my military way of thinking: an 8 a.m. briefing for the girls meant them too.

Formalities being completed I drove home, totally elated and not believing my good fortune. I was to pack, sort out my affairs and be at a country hotel near Maidenhead by 7 p.m. the following day. Tomorrow couldn't come quick enough.

I arrived at the hotel, only to be told that the briefing had started early, so I was to secrete myself into the room. This I did as surreptitiously as I could. I opened the door an inch, to see a most lovely girl at the end of the line. Another inch and the next girl so revealed seemed even lovelier, and on it went, each improving in beauty on the last. There were thirty young women there, each with her own brand of sex appeal and aura. Some willowy models, others with curves befitting the most glamorous of film stars. Hair in a variety of scintillating styles. Eyes of blue, sultry brown, challenging black and hues indeterminate, flashing smiles of pure femininity with girlish laughs all designed to entrap one.

Where was one to begin? Indeed, to this day I still couldn't design my perfect woman. I don't particularly care for short hair, yet I know many attractive short-haired members of the opposite sex who defy my prejudices. All this was impressed on my subconscious in a matter of seconds, and I hadn't as yet even discovered their personalities. Looking back, I suspect that I thought that I was in heaven and life could not be improved upon.

In the bar I was approached by an attractive blonde who expressed a desire to see my motor car; apparently she had seen me drive in and since her boyfriend had an exotic marque she was a bit of an enthusiast. She ended up in the driver's seat before taking it for a short spin. Now, as everyone knows, space in a sports car precludes basic, let alone advanced, techniques … until I suggested the bonnet. This was a calculated risk, for I had decided that I really should talk to all the girls first, and it wasn't as though Maureen would have been my first choice. But as it was all a little public, I expected that she'd refuse. So she did, and I was let off the hook.

After drinks there was a most convivial dinner with all the girls and the clients; the menu went unnoticed with so many conflicting perfumes and bewitching wiles. Then it was into the merry-go-round of work, such things as fitting uniforms, allocating motor cars, drivers and passengers, who had driving licences and who had not, contracts, photographs and cash floats, all under the benign eye of the clients, men with gin and tonics in their hands and contented happy smiles, all of who graciously admitted that had it been thirty men doing this promotion, they certainly would not have found the time to attend!

It was about 11 p.m. and I was with a line of girls, ticking something off on my clipboard and genuinely trying to be good, when a bustling Clare, whom I had briefly met, burst through the mini-crowd and said, 'Lawrence, before anyone else reserves you, you're sleeping with me tonight, room 340. We should be finished in about thirty minutes ... say, midnight ... see you then,' and off she went to the catcalls and laughs of the others. Clare had formerly modelled clothes but discovered that she had a flair for designing them and turned her attention to doing just that, building up a thriving business, and with her riotous, extrovert personality she had became something of a celebrity in the rag trade. I felt that she could have become a comedienne par excellence, possessing as she did such an outstanding character. She was only with us for two days and would not accompany us on tour. She had huge blue-green eyes, long reddish hair and a fair complexion. Her qualities dictated that, in all she did, she was in the driving seat and worked your controls. Unusually I don't remember being allowed to speak too much, as one quip followed another, and the more I laughed the more I encouraged her. She was a tonic by any standards. Married briefly, she had a son whom she sent away to public school, and if he was anything like his mother I would love to know, for he surely would have a future as a stand-up comic.

Life on the road was fun, by and large. We started in Cornwall and Devon and generally stayed in each town for five days, the weekends being given over to travel and, for some, a quick dash back to see boyfriends in London, time permitting. Life was always busy, not only on the business side of things, promoting the brand, collecting feedback from vendors and the public, but also with man-management problems. Personality clashes, motor car bumps, girls missing boyfriends and others re-evaluating the job ... some temperamental outbursts but generally few and far between.

My secretary Kate was a most enchanting girl, whose family I still know. She knew everyone in society and was much in demand for social events. She was a true dilettante, in the nicest sense of the word, and could have been a first-class model, indeed, probably anything she cared to turn her hand to, but she saw little reason to apply herself to anything. Why should she? She was always popular, an asset wherever she went and therefore saw no reason to worry about anything. She was a total one-off, not conventionally beautiful but possessing that rare quality of making one stop and look. She was as if from another world – 'unusual' is not strong enough – and I hope that I have vaguely conveyed her spirit. She had immensely long legs, which seemed to emanate from her neck. I don't know if she had a body, like a foal she seemed to be just legs. Long cardigans or short dresses sufficed for her wardrobe, accentuating her limbs, but never vulgarly so. She was quite pale, with long grey hair, an immense and pretty smile with good teeth and a lovely mouth, which housed many a cigarette. She was too lazy to participate in the promotion and thought that as a secretary to me it provided an easy option. Everyone used to say 'Katie, I just love your hair, who did it for you? Was it Vidal Sassoon or …?' 'No darling, Daddy was a Judge and begat me at sixty-seven, and that's why I have grey hair.' It was perfectly true, as brother Nigel would testify. There was another element to this extraordinary girl, and that was her voice: low, slightly breathless, bordering on the laconic, as if too bored to say much. A fascinating creature by any standards. Her friend Janie was as scatty and as jumpy as Katie was sloth-like, yet they made an incomparable pair, akin to a comedy duo.

Janie was louder, still boasting an aristocratic accent, always late, always in trouble and was given two or three warnings by me in as many days. I would berate her as nicely as I could, but still wishing to put my point across. She would give me some wonderfully lame, and on one occasion lachrymose, excuse and then with a flick of her long thick hair apologise and swear that it would never happen again. It always did. Finally, it came to the crunch when Janie was again out of step with the others.

'That's it, Katie, she has let me down again, she is sacked,' I said, 'unless of course she wants to sleep with me.'

'That is so unfair Lawrence,' she drawled lazily, 'it would be different if you were nice-looking, then it wouldn't be such a horrendous experience. No, she would rather be sacked than go through that.'

Well, it was worth a try, and of course I relented or else Katie would have made my life hell. Janie later married a Duke, not named Mr Duke but a real duke. I believe she was the last in a line of seven who bore the title. That was comforting for me, for I then rationalised that she probably had an Electra complex to explain away her indifference to me ... well, we men always need some excuse! I saw the Duchess Janie once more at a very jolly reception, but I hid behind someone tall, just in case she exposed me.

‡

Dear Katie died recently in Australia. We hadn't seen her since 1972 when Jillie and I were on our honeymoon trip around the world, but even that was not without its drama, with the usual sprinkling of humour. We were waiting outside Sydney airport, and true to form Katie was late. Suddenly, we saw a smart chocolate-brown Rover 2000 backing down the one-way circuit at speed, hotly pursued by a police car. The driver of the Rover seemed to be oblivious to the commotion, or if aware of it was totally unfazed. On stopping, who would emerge but Katie, and without regard to the constabulary she opened the back door and took out a baby. This neatly coincided with the arrival of a young policeman and a perfect pair of arms to cradle the infant bundle.

'Just take Emma while I collect my friends,' she exhaled with a contumacious coquetry. Needless to say the policeman obliged, and on our return we all thanked a blushing young patrol-man profusely before driving off in the right direction this time. It just seemed a natural thing to do: in Katie's philosophy what were policemen there for anyway … to help one of course!

We spent a week in Sydney, eating, drinking and generally in a wonderful stupor.

'Darling Jillie, what would you like to drink for breakfast?' She would disinterestedly yawn.

'Coffee or tea would be fine,' was the reply.

'No, gin or vodka, I meant,' accompanied by smoke swirls.

After her liquid breakfast, it would be time to call for her beautiful red setter, let loose down the street.

'Fanny, Fanny … oh where is my lovely Fanny,' she would call without a trace of self-consciousness, much to the amusement or perhaps chagrin of the residents of the suburb of Paddington. On yet another occasion at a dinner party held for us, her husband Geoffrey Crutchley-Crundle (a character her equal, who made wine) suddenly announced that dinner had finished and off we went to bed while the others dispersed. Ten minutes later Katie appeared with two glasses of wine and announced that the dinner party had been re-convened and the whole thing had been a ploy to get rid of some obnoxious people who had imposed themselves and, frankly, 'bored' her.

‡

It was during the first week of the promotion tour that I got to know the girls and their personalities. One pair seemed to share my sense of humour and general outlook on life, but even this was a problem for they were identical twins. Both were obviously beautiful, but individually identifiable, for Pamela was blonde and Frances auburn. They thought alike and shared an uncanny telepathy, especially if one was in trouble. They both had dimples, they both spoke alike, laughed alike and no part of their mien wasn't lovely, attractive and devastatingly appealing. Pamela had a boyfriend, as did Frances, who appeared to be older than her, but both led roller-coaster lives, living in expensive flats in central London but having no ambition whatsoever. They were much in demand for modelling work, but not if it conflicted with their social life. They had even been persuaded to cut a record, covering a popular ditty at the time. The title evades me but the chorus went 'And then I go and spoil it all by saying something stupid like I love you.' It was more a naïve than virtuoso performance, but therein lay its charm. But they couldn't be persuaded or bothered to promote it. It was just another laugh, and in fact as I write I am looking at a *Daily Express* article on this matchless pair. No matter – life was for living and only today counted. It was a great pity that I could not have gone out with both of them, but troilism was too advanced for our bourgeois upbringing. Anyway, Pamela succinctly summed up the situation by rightfully declaring that her sister was more ladylike and appropriate for someone as conventional as me. This proved to be true, for many months later I was eventually to meet Michael, Pam's current boyfriend. I'd seen his money for myself, often round at Pam's flat she would throw in the air bundles of large white notes, a veritable snowstorm of fivers (our largest denomination at the time).

'But how does Michael come by this?' I would ask agape.

'He's in publishing,' she would reply.

It was inevitable that we should meet one day and we, Frances and I, were duly invited to a club which vied unsuccessfully with Annabel's. It was called the Revolution and catered for a younger, more independent clientele. I was in a bottle-green smoking jacket and Michael a leather one. It was no doubt expensive but neither the jacket nor the man was to my liking. However, for Pam's sake I tried my best to be civil to him. We had finished our main course and the girls were otherwise engaged talking to friends.

'What publishing house do you work for?' I enquired.

I knew of Macmillan, Chatto & Windus, Penguin and Oxford

My friend and the founder of a most successful advertising agency. The urbane Chris Ulysses Williams – a man of many talents, Ch. 31.

A lovely girl and the bull terrier, all 'snout and mean-eyed', Ch. 40.

Promotional and showbiz events in Cambridge and Torquay.

International beauty and model Tanya, Ch. 31.

The delightful Frances Laird-Henry. Her twin Pamela was identical, apart from the fact that she was blonde, Ch. 31.

The first – or illegal – Mrs Stacey. Gentle, lovely Marjorie (1964), Ch. 17.

Playtime … again. St Ives, Cornwall. Three months away … and imagine I was paid for this holiday!

Joan Harkness

Versatile and beautiful. Joan Harkness, one of the agency's favourites and a highly successful model. She is a life-long friend, and godmother to our daughter Antonia, Ch. 31.

One half of the rescued cabaret act. I
later met her in Beirut, Ch. 29.

On the left, the charming 'Dolly
Brolly'; right, my irrepressible and
long-legged secretary Katie, Ch. 31.

One of our models sporting a characteristic hair-do.

Durban, on the
promenade,
1965. Jenny was
to follow me to
England, Ch. 17.

My Healey 3000
seen in Curzon
Street. However,
see Ch. 28 for the
Cassino story.

Old College Dining Hall, Sandhurst. It was on a Mess night such as this that my regimental interview took place, Ch. 10.

Our Rolls-Royce. Born 1960 into the family. Owned by me for thirty-six years. Its back seat has more hidden sins even than me! (Ch. 36.)

The ever-patient and enduring real Mrs Stacey (1988). Forty-two years married and still going strong. Ch. 40.

My family. L–R: Jillie, Hugh-Oliver, Warwick, Antonia and Danielle. Mougins, France, c.1989, Ch. 40.

University Press and a few others, and expected it must be one of the big boys, considering his surplus cash.

'Well, dirty books and lots of porn ... yeah, loads of bloody seedy shops in Soho,' he replied ingenuously.

'Oh yes, and you expect me to believe that all this is condoned by the police,' I said, half-mockingly.

'Believe it or not it is, I just pay them off, scores of them. They tip me off when they are about to do a raid, my shop manager pays a statutory fine and I open another outlet the same night.'

I was aged twenty-eight and still believed in the inviolability of the armed forces, the judiciary and the police force. I was incensed by such blatant lies and told the twins, who had re-joined us, that I was not prepared to sit and listen to a man that peddled such diabolic lies and with that Frances and I left. It was a quite a stand to make in support of the establishment, for I had noticed the sumptuous dessert trolley that was to come, and in those days puddings were my Achilles' heel. Nevertheless, it was the principle that society insisted I stood for, and a sacrifice I had to make ... such *noblesse oblige*!

There the matter should have ended, but some five years later a scandal of biblical proportions broke as the media exposed a certain born-again Christian with a previous life as a porn baron. It was headline news, all over the press and radio and TV news, and the key character was none other than Michael himself, and his involvement with Commander Kenneth Drury of the Metropolitan Police. Some sixty to seventy policemen were charged, twenty or so eventually given prison sentences. The press detailed holidays dispensed by Michael in the then highly popular island of Malta, yachts in St Paul's Bay and high living, all handed out by my acquaintance, who in spite of his dubious and shifty past had told me the entire truth.

In retrospect, I wish I had stayed for dessert.

Frances was a wonderful girl, and on the last night of the

promotion at a fabulous thank-you dinner for the girls it was announced that the two of us had got engaged. I don't know who thought this up, I was probably a little inebriated at the time; however, I was immensely proud to think that I had the most beautiful of girls and would indeed have been proud to have married her. In fact I wonder if she would be surprised to learn that her photograph is only an arm's length away on my desk, and has been all these years.

If only I could have stayed settled, but then along came the Christian Dior girls. Then a fabulous three months with the swimwear people (I know the name but can't spell it). All six girls in bikinis, beach buggies, games of boules against showbiz personalities and more lovely hotels. Too much to eat, too much to drink and, as my wife says with a sigh, too much of the other!

With the swimwear firm we had a very large American shooting brake which accommodated the six models and me. Each day was like a holiday as we lived in smart hotels and frequented the lovely West Country resorts. My summer idyll was heightened by the presence of my girlfriend of the time, a very successful model by the name of Joan Harkness. Joan was an exceptionally beautiful girl who had twice graced the cover of *Vogue*. Her natural attributes were enhanced by a bubbling personality with a sense of humour to match. Originally from Belfast, her proud but somewhat eccentric parents were religiously inclined and followers of the Plymouth Brethren. They never knew that Joan smoked, drank or stole a kiss from her many ardent admirers. Consequently, whenever they visited her all alcohol was banned or certainly well hidden, no trace of cigarettes or even an ashtray allowed and any aftershave that appeared in the bathroom was removed forthwith. This is not to say that her mother and father were prudes, for the laughter that reverberated around the room was deafening, and their outlook on life was so typical of most Northern Irish families: unpredictable, generous and always endearing.

One thing that became apparent to me was the law of supply and demand. Here was I living with six utterly wonderful girls who under normal circumstances would not have looked at me twice, but now in some way I was fêted by them. Dinner was taken communally as we all got on so well; however, they would purposely arrive early so when I came down to dine they would all stand up for me, perhaps pull away my chair, all designed to make me blush and to draw attention to this heavenly enclave. They would then embarrass me further by discussing whose turn it was to dance with me, much to the amusement of the hotel orchestra. They ate sparingly and I was the recipient of many unwanted courses, especially greedy (as I mentioned) when the desserts came along, certainly two or three a night, and on one particularly voracious occasion allegedly four! I was therefore getting fatter and fatter, and not having the height to hide it became positively bouncy. It didn't seem to make any difference to them ... as there was only one man then we may as well all flirt with him. Poor Joan, stuck with a little fat fellow who was having double everything.

For the whole three months I can't remember any unpleasantness, no jealous remarks or any form of female nastiness as occurs when women are held in close commune. In fact, I think just the opposite, as they seem to be so supportive of each other. I should also remark that not all models are the dizzy blondes that many men take them for. Diane Argent, most lovely both in looks and nature, held a Cambridge Maths degree and had been a research graduate on about £1,100 p.a. She and her legs were 'discovered', and so they should have been, multiplying her insignificant salary at least ten-fold. Her elegantly long and luscious legs were the focus of the most prestigious nylon manufacturer in the country and could be seen in every glossy magazine and the many advertising hoardings that graced the country. Oh, halcyon days ... why, how did I become old? Then there was the perfect lady: softly spoken, silken seductress Dolly Brolly, Mickey and Veronica. All of them simply adorable, what a pity one couldn't be marooned on a desert island never to be rescued.

I have discussed with my sons, Warwick and Hugh-Oliver, our preoccupation with the female form, especially legs. Both are connoisseurs on the subject and sport comely wives themselves. For my part I put it down to an experience I had when being taken to prep school in the late summer of 1948. My mother and I had emerged from Piccadilly tube station and were halfway across Regent Street, stuck on the traffic island watching the taxis flash by. The old London black cab had doors then that opened the 'wrong way', with the handles facing forwards. I was standing patiently holding my mother's hand but was aware of a nice young woman who was close next to me. She must have been positioned side-on, and was wearing an elegant wraparound black skirt, popular at the time. Suddenly a taxi went past her, evidently too close for its door handle became involved with the wraparound skirt, which duly performed as the designer had intended it to, neatly unwrapping her and whisking away the said garment. I suddenly beheld this apparition of shapely legs with black suspenders adjacent to my nose. Now, I cannot say that this made an impression on me at the time, but it must have entered the deepest recesses of my subconscious, passing into the darkest corners of my mind and bursting out like poisonous boils in a manifestation of depravity years later. All this exacerbates the sad condition brought upon me by the thought of the lovely Diane's legs. I don't know what my sons' excuses are. I think that they are just naturally perverted. Thank goodness nothing to do with me ... perhaps I should have a chat with their mother? But where was I, oh yes, models.

Amid all these beauties, there was only one who, had she told me in a casual conversation on the number 19 bus that she was a highly-paid photographic model, I would have found it difficult to believe (although of course I would have commented 'How wonderful'). One day Chris had said to me that one of our girls, in the super league of world models, had been diagnosed with cancer, which was then a death sentence. She was returning from a very famous French fashion house, from where she had been contracted to see us.

'I am dreading seeing her, she was such a super girl – so please be around to lighten the load when she comes. We'll have to have a drink, irrespective of the time – just to keep things as happy as we can, given the circumstances,' he said ruefully.

Two weeks later I dashed into Christopher's office: 'The girl with cancer is here,' I shouted in great agitation. I had seen her coming up the path, a thin gaunt face, legs which looked like Lowry's matchstick figures, likely to snap into two at any time. Her hair was fine and in the style of an urchin cut, no doubt it had all been shaved off at some stage. Her cheekbones were no doubt prominent because of her weight loss, accentuating her large deep-set eyes. Her teeth and smile, so far unseen, were dazzling when I met her. She was slightly bowled over to be entertained so well and so early in the day. Chris was marvellous and we chatted happily for ages. I was full of admiration for a once beautiful woman who could so easily face death with such equanimity. Eventually we were interrupted by a telephone call for me, which I deemed best to take in my office, so I used this as an excuse to escape. Chris quickly joined me, pretending he needed to borrow some cigarettes ... not that I smoked!

'That's *not* the girl,' he said, 'that's Holly, she's doing a job for us,' he happily declared. In fact Holly was the girl with whom I'd had the imaginary conversation atop the number 19 bus (the one that goes King's Road, Sloane Square and Hyde Park Corner ... but you don't need to know this).

It was about a week later that I was called to the telephone to discuss a photo-call with a model named ... you've guessed it, Holly. The photographer was unknown to me but I recognised his voice. A weekly comedy programme called *Life with the Lyons,* starring Bebe and Dan Lyons and featuring their children Richard and his sister, whose name now evades me, was highly popular and featured on the Home Service. Perhaps they were Canadian, for they certainly had North American accents, and in the intervening years Richard had become a successful photographer. Suffice to say that we all met in Curzon Street, at the Washington Hotel bar, with Holly bearing that disconcerting look that had so thrown me when I'd first met her back in the office. I had brought a full blonde wig for her, and she appeared some thirty minutes later absolutely radiant. The barman shook the cocktail, I (off photo, other than my hand) offered her a menthol king-size St Moritz cigarette, in its fetching light green box, Richard said 'smile'. The dazzling smile reappeared and was held for as long as it was needed and the eyes remained large and unblinking for an eternity, or so it seemed. The result was a stunning photograph, which went national, of a sophisticated, appealing woman with alluring deep-set eyes and classical high cheekbones. All in all the perfect example of the wealthy, upmarket woman who could afford to smoke such a prized and expensive cigarette. How wrong could I have been? I don't know what happened to Holly; she was an eminent politician's daughter or niece, who could look like the girl next door but with a consummate approach to her profession as well as a benign modesty.

Sometimes, our clients held fashion parades in the smartest London and provincial hotels, special occasions with expensive dinners for us and the models. We often had to stay the night, and one time I remember creeping down the hotel corridor well after midnight. I distinctly recall gingerly carrying my Chelsea boots in front of me, rather how Jeeves the butler would bring them to your room. Chelsea boots with their elasticated sides can sometimes be difficult to put on, well until such time as the elastic becomes malleable, and mine were still newish. Anyway, as I proceeded down the thick carpeted passageway, with a big smile on my face,

I turned the corner and literally bumped into Christopher. It was rather like a Brian Rix Whitehall farce, for we both recoiled and in a second or two of catatonic horror involuntarily cried out ... not a word was spoken though, as like ships in the night we passed and went our separate ways. Was he steaming towards the same harbour in which I had found refuge? Or perhaps he may also have thought that I was on my way to his little haven? We will never know. Next morning at breakfast, as he had his first cigarette with his coffee, smilingly he said, 'Well done, dear boy. It's good to see you haven't lost your Army habits ... looking after the troops, eh ... bedding them down for the night ... what!' Well, such was my devotion to duty.

Talking of the Army, for two if not three years running I was invited to the Lansdowne Club for luncheon by my old commanding officer, a Major-General who was then the Director of Army Recruiting (Later Lt General Sir James Wilson). I was offered Adjutant to my old Battalion in Hong Kong, by then amalgamated as the 4 Bn Royal Regiment of Fusiliers (RRF), and other good career jobs. He was keen to see me back in uniform, though in fact he was quite an irascible man when aroused, and since I had enjoyed his largesse I always compromised and gave him a little bit of hope. 'I will just do one more summer stint and then consider your offer,' I would say. He eventually gave up on me. He never understood why a chap like me, or indeed anyone, wanted to spend his time being with beautiful women when one could be sitting in the shivering cold and mud of a trench, unwashed, constipated and tired in a snow blizzard on some godforsaken windswept plain in northern Germany, and all for a pittance. I suppose it takes all types to make a world.

I learned later that his grandfather was Field Marshal Sir Henry Wilson GCB DSO, who was shot on the doorstep of his Eaton Place house by two IRA men in 1922. Ironically, they had served throughout the Great War in the British Army. He never told me this during our luncheons, but had I known this when I served under him as a Lieutenant it certainly may have inspired me to do the same, for he led his officers a merry dance. Interestingly, he managed to be football correspondent for *The Times* newspaper; some of us thought that this was not quite proper, but would have been perfectly at ease if his game had been rugby union. It was he who almost caught me having my illicit weekend at the Army & Navy Club in Pall Mall when I pretended that I was married. Actually, he was very good to me really, a clever man who ploughed his own furrow in the Army and for this he had to be admired.

‡

It always appeared odd, during my time working in the 'fashion industry' or in my case its environs, that I was considered an 'expert' – at my tender age and with little experience. One can become a celebrity for a miscellany of stupid reasons. It matters little if one is infamous or lacking in any form of scruples (which explains my brief glory). Indeed, the bigger the mouth and the more outrageous one is, the more appealing it is to society, which puts you on a pedestal and treats you as a role model. See footballers, pop-stars and some actors and actresses.

Then we come to politicians, who make promises that they know they can never honour, deflecting retribution by behaving like schoolboys in the playground and shouting at the opposition in endless retrospective blame. Cabinet ministers become experts in their posts in a matter of weeks; months later they assume another ministerial post, acquiring a new field of interest. Was it John Reid to whom Tony Blair gave seven Cabinet posts in eight years? Imagine going for a brain operation and the surgeon saying, 'It was toes last week, but today I think I'll try my hand at brains.' This would really instil one with confidence, but we trust our politicians to meddle in complex and difficult subjects for which they are totally unqualified, and in many cases woefully ignorant. Other people in public life set low standards which the public accept for spurious reasons, but pity the man next door who might fall into the same category – he would certainly not be offered the same tolerance. The press promote such things and we, the public, are in their dubious hands.

I am not saying that my status was anything like the examples above. It was on a much lower strata, but nevertheless I was indeed invited to comment on women on commercial radio, or asked to join Miss America's party and escort them to Annabel's. I remember an American actor, Robert Vaughan, who was famous at the time. I argued furiously with him over the war in Vietnam, for he was very anti and I very pro. In retrospect, he was right and I was very wrong.

On another occasion the telephone voice, frightfully cultivated, asked whether I would co-host a young lady who was probably twenty-one at the time? Her name was Princess Anne and her father the Duke of Edinburgh, Prince Philip, to whom I had been local ADC when he attended the independence parade in Malawi in the early 1960s. It was a Grosvenor House Hotel ball, I think, and the poor girl felt very aggrieved at her recent treatment by the press. I must add that the Royal Family were perhaps not as popular then as they are now, but nevertheless no one should harry and pester such a young person, who has no right of comeback. It is hard enough coming to terms with life at that age, let alone with the press on your back. I knew that she had recently acquired a Reliant Scimitar GTE, and since my dancing is pathetic I relied on my interest in motor cars to get us through the first dance. Yes, it was the same Tamworth firm that built the Robin Reliant three-wheelers – remember Del Boy in *Only Fools and Horses*. Well, they also introduced to the world a new genre: a sporting estate. This model had an all glass-fibre body and was therefore rust-free, and to my mind very smart. It was also pretty nippy, but try as she might, Princess Anne could never drive it correctly. If she went at the statutory 30 mph down the Mall, the press boys shadowing her every move branded her a goody-goody for holding up the traffic. If she went at 40 mph down the same stretch of road then she was an irresponsible Jehu for driving too fast. My sympathy was entirely with her. Strangely enough, she was to borrow my Rolls-Royce on occasions when I was in BAOR, but was unaware as to whom it belonged. I also learned much later that my flatmate for a short while, a young man named Piers Weld-Forrester, was a great friend of Princess Anne and had even entertained her in my flat – but this may be apocryphal. Sadly, he died very young, a rich young man addicted to fast motor cars and motorcycles, which proved to be his ultimate fate.

Anyway, it was all great fun back then to be an 'expert' on the weaker sex, and comment glibly on their virtues, strengths and foibles. Now I find myself in my seventies, married to a woman for forty-two years (I think we need to stress this in today's present climate). I have also brought up two intelligent and beautiful daughters, not to mention three adorable granddaughters. However, no one – not a single soul – now seeks my advice on women. Yet with forty-two years of marriage behind me, and having treasured and brought up my girls, am I not infinitely more capable of talking now, as opposed to my wet-behind-the-ears approach all those years ago? Obviously not, as the torch of wisdom has no doubt been passed to some spotty youth aged twenty who got his childhood sweetheart pregnant behind the bicycle sheds at school and is now a monosyllabic footballer perchance ... or lead guitarist in some pop band heavily committed to drugs. Sour grapes, I hear you shout.

‡

I must stress now that not all these lovely girls fell at my feet swooning adoringly. True, I was at a great advantage in working with them and in the fact that we got to know each other quickly by travelling together. This did provide some exciting opportunities and late-night assignations in quite exotic places – similar to airline crews when they travelled the world and had extended stays in romantic venues – but sometimes I had to work quite assiduously in pursuit of my prey. One girl really did catch my eye and proved a hard nut to crack. I needed to prove to her that I was no fly-by-night, but like her a true romantic. I hit upon the idea of rising with the lark ... well, to be honest I may have been roosting elsewhere on occasions, but nevertheless it should not detract from my genuine ardour. I would then drive all the way from my Knightsbridge flat to Putney where I met the milkman and deposited a red rose on top of her gold-topped pint of milk. Over the years I have come to fantasise about this little ruse – believing that the milkman was in fact the cheeky Benny Hill 'who drove the fastest milk float in the West'. I could see him posturing over the bottle, laying the rose then turning to camera with his inimitable smile. Well, I actually did this for some time ... two weeks or so, until it became ... well, unnecessary.

Life was also very expensive as we dined out somewhere every night. Indeed, sometimes I would never go into my kitchen, perhaps for a week at a time, not even to make a cup of tea. Hence, it was a perpetual space of neat and tidy living. I suppose my lifestyle demanded this, for I never seemed to take the same girl out twice. Well, perhaps a bit of an exaggeration, but first dates meant dressing up, and being fashion-conscious models they needed to be seen. What is more it didn't matter where you took your date. I remember taking someone to Le Caprice then on to Annabel's, which cost a small fortune. I thought that next morning on the catwalk she could hold her head up high – but not so, as she reported later. Philippa's boyfriend flew *her* to Paris in a private jet after taking her to the Moulin Rouge, and returned the same night! One couldn't win. I suspect we were all out to impress the world. What a far cry from my Sandhurst days, when the lovely little Annie Standage, complete with her Hermès headscarf, sat in the back of the taxi. 'But Annie,' I remonstrated, 'you have got to give me a kiss.' 'But why should I kiss you,' she pouted. 'Cos, I have just spent a month's pay on you at the Blue Angel in Mayfair,' I replied.

Well, life had progressed a little … at least now kisses were more freely given.

Laundry also proved expensive. I soon found that I needed two bedrooms which I used alternatively in order always to have clean sheets – perfumes being a give-away. Sunlight Laundries (now sadly defunct) did a roaring trade with me and I got on with the two old ladies, one of whom had been with the firm since about 1937. But I never persuaded them that I ran a B&B and therefore qualified for a trade discount: 'Mr Stacey, you're such a tease to be sure,' they would laugh.

It was during these days of blissful debauchery that I discovered from a visiting telephone engineer that there was a way of dialling yourself, quite simply, with just two digits. They used it to test that your telephone was functioning correctly. This was an invaluable asset and saved my life on numerous occasions. If for instance some young thing lingered too long, or if a particular lover was flying in from somewhere (I always encouraged everyone to telephone me first), I would simply ring myself, making sure that my *amour* heard the conversation: 'Oh my goodness, so-and-so has arrived and is on her way now,' I would shout in agitation. This seemed to suit all parties, protecting us from being compromised, perhaps by her friend (in a few instances), or certainly me in being caught red-handed in their flats, as happened once or twice. One of my friends had forgotten to tell me that she had a fiancé. I knew that she had admirers, but that was to be expected. I can laugh now at the episode, but it was terrifying at the time and very reminiscent of a Peter Sellers *Pink Panther* scene when his oriental karate-style valet launches like an Exocet missile at him. In this instance, the fiancé, a huge man well over 6ft and muscular with it, gave a blood-curdling cry of death as he literally charged into the room and dive-bombed the bed. It was in all events a good move for it totally devastated a lovely old sprung bed, with its heavy wooden headboard crashing on top of us. So heavy was the fall that plaster came away in the downstairs flat. However, my lover was able to turn this all to her advantage, first in pain, then in sheer anger at her beautiful bed being destroyed, before finally berating him for breaking into her flat. In fact, we had inadvertently in our passion left the front door open! By this means she totally defused the situation and it was her fiancé who left first and not me. She was a most astute girl and he obviously doted on her. In fact, they got married exactly a week after I did.

I suppose this was child's play compared to one moonlit night when six shots narrowly missed me. I won't dwell on this scenario for it is the stuff of nightmares and looking back on my life it certainly wasn't worth dying for. I probably thought so at the time – but imagine, I wouldn't have known my children and grandchildren, *quel dommage!* Such was and no doubt still is the impetuosity of youth. All I can say is that such fiery passion was in so many ways a great affliction. I have admitted what a terrible dancer I am but what I must be fair and honest about is that I am very good at the 'smooch', being small I fit into the contours of the average-sized women (or did then, now they are all Amazon-like), thus it was knee cap to knee cap, nibbling their ear, inhaling the sweet scent of their skin and the touch of soft hair. All accomplished without ever moving an inch! Superb dancing, but putting things into perspective, as I usually don't condone crudeness, I was always apologising for the packet of polo mints in my pocket ... as I said, it was an affliction. Well lots of men drink and become pot-bellied, some gamble, giving their wives sleepless nights of worry, others smoke with dreadful consequences. I suppose my weakness was natural and over-the-top ... but healthy.

With so many perks it seems unfair to add another but we were the recipients of a splendid villa in St Paul's Bay, Malta. High on the hill we looked over the bay with its constant blue sky and the floral decoration of the garden with a bower over its arched gate and the subtle smells of flowers unknown. I never enquired too closely whether it belonged to Christopher or to Rothmans, but it seemed to be in some way a joint venture. It became famous, I think, for the first Dulux paint advertisement featuring the Old English Sheepdog, you know the one that doesn't appear to have any eyes but resembles a thick pile rug in motion.

Going back years later it was a shadow of its former self, but for now it was palatial. My brief was simple, no more than seventy for a buffet, take who you want for two weeks at a time. It was a fantastic gift but in the sixties and early seventies expense accounts were over-liberal and tax avoidance for such things all seemed to be legally done. We had Kate, a wonderful young woman, cooking for us, a driver for the motor car and speedboat, as well as the local staff of cleaners and a gardener. Some of the girls from the agency would appear, which also seemed to attract the men from the passing yachts. I took my future wife and I remember she asked to stay the extra week, which at the time upset me as some of my old team were coming for a holiday and of course I didn't want to be branded a cissy! Besides there was still a lingering attraction for one or two of them!

Still, it was indubitably a holiday to remember: we were all young, happy and footloose, the bathing beautiful, while those of us who could tested our water-skiing ability to its limits in the azure sea of the bay. Kate was an accomplished cook by any standards, and only in her early twenties. Her father had been an Army officer and her education had been at a girls' public school. I point this out for I believe that with her genteel upbringing she was totally unsuited to cope with the uncouth behaviour of the few.

We had been asked to give hospitality to a yacht and its crew who had recently arrived in Malta, perhaps a business associate, I don't know. However, I do remember the owner well: no doubt successful and monied and aged about sixty. He was a big bulky man, grey wavy hair, red-faced with a Bacchanalian disposition to go with his red nose and loose tongue when replete with food and drink. He latched on to Kate, both physically and verbally, declaring her the most beautiful and fattest creature he had ever seen. Kate did indeed have a beautiful face to match her winsome nature and although she may have been overweight such language and boorish manners were and always will be obscene. Unfortunately, his presence was encouraged or perhaps he just turned up, either to invite the girls to parties on the yacht or for dinners. His 'playful' persecution of Kate, as he put it, continued until in the end I took him to task over the matter and told him he was no longer welcome. His bad behaviour, though, seemed to have impressed itself on Glen, our young driver, for when on our last night I took the staff to the Phoenician Hotel for dinner, he flatly refused to dance with Kate: 'She's too fat,' he told me. Had she been more vulgarly robust she would probably have told him and Joe where to go, but her upbringing and education were not of that style.

It was some three weeks later, after I had written her a wonderful reference, that I was told it would not be needed. Her parents had dutifully put her into a London teaching hospital as a private patient, due to her unhappy experience with us. Within three days of commencing her treatment she was dead, leaving Jillie and I devastated, indeed, all who knew her ... but imagine the impact on her doting parents and family. It seems an odd note to close on, especially when this was the happiest period of my bachelor days, but perhaps it is a salutary one, for I have without this tale espoused the virtues of beauty, yet here was a beautiful person whose grace shone in a different way. Here was no vanity, here was a friendly smile and laugh that greeted us constantly and here was a girl who may not stroll the catwalk but produced in you a glow of admiration and blissful satisfaction.

32

MY LIFE'S PARADIGM

When I was a young boy at prep school, our contraband was comics: *Dandy*, *Beano*, *Hotspur* and others whose names I now forget. Our lofty magisters, all products of Oxford and Cambridge, would hunt down and destroy such scurrilous publications, for were they not for the semi-literate, the ill-bred and the uncouth? The very antithesis of all that was their educational aim, their mantra pursued as religiously as some Marian martyr driven to the stake. For that was the comic's fate, confined to the housemaster's grate.

Later, at public school, we were allowed to buy our own Sunday newspapers, but again these were confined to the 'quality press' and I only remember *The Observer* and the *Sunday Times* in those far-off days. I do recall one Sunday newspaper called *The Reveille* which featured well-endowed 'pin-ups' on the front page, indeed on every page; the cut of their costume may have been revealing but there was no nakedness. Some of the more daring chaps would have the newsagents secrete one of these into the 'proper paper', and by such methods we were able to see how the other half lived and pursue our fantasies. There was also a rag called the *News of the World*, which contained very little news of the world but a great deal of petty scandal, infidelity and titillation. I remember in a Sixth Form debate how we decried such journalists and those hacks who pedalled this nonsense. It was, however, what the great British public wanted but it has at last met the fate it should have suffered back in the fifties. If these lecherous publications were ever discovered great was the retribution, for it was tantamount to the devil himself possessing you, and caning was the ultimate deterrent, used to purify one's decaying soul. The whole undertone of school was one of religiosity, and a constant crusade was waged against such sexual deviation. Now the pendulum has swung so far the other way: lewd advertisements in public telephone boxes, skimpily-clad girls proffering their bodies for the sale of motor cars, drinks and miscellaneous goods which have no possible connection to the female form. I hear children of twelve or so have access to pornography on the internet, which in my day would certainly call for expulsion, nay execution!

With these thoughts in mind, our schoolboy world was turned upside down one morning at assembly in 'big school', a beautiful oak-panelled hall. The headmaster made his way on to the stage, flanked by his housemasters and senior staff, all gowned and impressive. After the normal formalities had been competed, he then paused and began (I now paraphrase):

I have just returned from the Headmasters' Conference, which was held this year at Stowe. It was an interesting meeting where fellow headmasters swap ideas, formulate policies and put forward plans for the coming year. This time, though, we took a highly unusual decision which was strangely enough almost unanimous, considering its controversial nature. I refer to the status of the comic. There has entered into this arena a man of great foresight, a man of Christian principles and impeccable morality. A man of the cloth whose aim is to educate our youth in a fashion which upholds all that we hold sacred and good, bearing in mind our past history and traditions. In the spirit of nobility and emulating our great leaders, but not steeped so much in the past as to withhold progress. Indeed, he has shown himself to be that rare being, a man of God who combines the past with progress and modernity. His name is the Reverend Frank Fenwick and his impending comic, well, let us call it a boys' newspaper, is to be called *The Eagle*. This publication will look into the future with space travel, it will be educational, explaining a multitude of the earth's mysteries. It will depict the Bible in easy-to-read pictorial form, bringing alive the daring, dash and bravery of the early martyrs, and it is with pleasure that I now announce together with the other great public schools that this weekly paper may be sent to you by your parents.

We thought grown-ups then were always wrong or, if not wrong, totally out of touch with our likes and dislikes. The new comic was obviously to the headmaster's liking, ergo it would not be to ours. In the event *The Eagle* comic was to set new standards and take the youth of the country by storm. For a start it was in colour, and the editor true to his word. More remarkably, as our headmaster had predicted, it produced articles which made dull biblical stories come to life with amazing clarity and interest. I still remember the 'Life of St Paul' which appeared on the back page every week. The Editorial, following the form of 'real' newspapers, appeared in the middle of the magazine and treated us like adults. The drawings were by some of our best artists and cartoonists, while the cover page became a sensational story of Dan Dare in his battle against the Mekon in outer space. It was, in a word, superb and young schoolboys like me lived for the Tuesday post when our *Eagle* arrived. In fact, it held a double surprise, for in it my mother would hide a chocolate bar, or certainly a Penguin biscuit, until the ending of sweet rationing. This comic, boys' newspaper, magazine, call it what you will, went on under various publishers until 1969 but is still remembered with great nostalgia by so many of us. It also re-entered my life at about this time, not that I was reading it then, for Dan Dare had been replaced by the girls from *The Reveille* – well, not quite, but by those lovely girls of the model agency.

Now, Soho is situated very near the fashion shops of Oxford Street and the couturier workshops and salons of the 'rag trade', as it seems to call itself. It was here that one of our girls must have been modelling, and I had agreed to take her to luncheon at the Gay Hussar in Soho. The luncheon must have been good and we consumed more wine than we should have, for it obviously fuelled our passion in an intemperate way. A farewell kiss in a doorway led to more, which led in turn down a backstreet and to ardent whispers and ways of fulfilling such post-lunchtime desires.

'I have my Mini here, just off Greek Street – let's go there,' she urged.

For once, I promise you, it wasn't me that proffered the suggestion, but her pleas were urgent and I, of course, needed little encouragement anyway. We gained her motor car but even for me this seemed not only dangerous but also very public, besides a Mini was low-slung and every passer-by would have a clear view of a fornicating couple.

'I can't,' I said, disbelieving that I had uttered these words, but then I pictured a throng around us, perhaps cheering us on, or worse, offering advice, while the little motor car shook on its springs. It was all too much and for once I said so.

'Don't be such a defeatist … this is after all a den of iniquity … it's Soho for Christ's sake,' she urged.

'Let's go home,' I said.

'I haven't got time,' she retorted, still kissing me.

'Well, I can't, not here, and not in a Mini … nor can you,' I said, distraught, for who knew if this opportunity would ever return?

'I can,' she said, 'and I have. I have done it in a Bentley about this very spot.'

'Never, who would do it here?! No one in their right mind would perform here in daylight,' I cried.

'Well, the Reverend Frank Fenwick did, clever dick. He had more balls than you have,' she shouted in desperation.

I think that ended everything for me. Not that I minded following in the Reverend's footsteps, but my mind went back to all those years before in our hallowed, silent hall, where we heard with bated breath our literary liberation with the coming of a comic that was acceptable to the Headmasters' Conference, and all because it was founded at the behest of a fine Christian gentleman. If only our esteemed headmaster were here to re-evaluate his wonderful eulogy to the talented man of the cloth. Now it so happened that I got to know, or perhaps already knew, the Reverend Frank Fenwick for, although still a clergyman, he was then with a publishing firm. Hultons were no longer, but IPC may have been his employers and I think that their offices were in the area. Perhaps I am conflating time. In any case, in my dealings with him I found him to be a thoroughly good man, innovative, clever, possessing drive and charm. In fact, I got to know all of his family, including his beautiful wife, who I think had been a notable actress. Their home in Limehouse was one of the first of the docklands warehouses to be converted, I remember that it was right on the river, and here his wife and three daughters gave wonderful parties. Jan, Kate and Sally, in order of age I think. Indeed, Kate married Christopher Ulysses Williams, and Kate, Sally and myself all worked together at various times in the agency. It is a small world.

In conclusion, I would like to think that the good Reverend and I had a great deal in common as true lovers of mankind ... well, fifty per cent of it anyway!

33

MY BEST DATE EVER

The Hon. Mrs Fiona Fitzgerald-Simpson-Symmons was an extremely lovely woman, about ten years older than me. We had met at a smart fashion show at the Grosvenor House Hotel in Park Lane, where she bought expensive clothes most nonchalantly. She telephoned me one day.

'Darling, I am having a birthday party for Lascelles [her husband], a week on Thursday, 7.30 p.m. Can you come?'

'For certain,' said I.

'Promise?' said she.

'Present?' I said.

'Just yourself,' she said, purring.

I turned up dead on the dot with flowers as a thank-you, as etiquette demands.

'Oh dear,' said I, 'I'm the first one here,' all embarrassed.

'You are the only one here darling ... how does that suit you?'

'Perfectly,' said I, gulping and not believing my luck.

Now that's a party! Sadly only once in a lifetime.

34

THE ROTARY CLUB
TALKS

My friend Francis Willinger had about fifteen years on me; we had met through his attractive younger wife Andréa, who became a friend of ours. He was an extrovert character of Viennese Jewish extraction, but I was never aware of his background when I knew him. Only after his death did I learn from another source of his flight from the Nazis at a young age.

He owned a plastic factory in South London along with another business partner, which did rather well judging by his possessions. A flat in Kensington, unreliable Jaguar S-type (as they were in the sixties and seventies but emphatically not now) and a nice five-seater light aircraft, which he flew all over Europe in a most cavalier fashion. Unhappily, it was this that was to prove his downfall, not in the air as some expected but by walking into his own propeller when giving joy rides to deprived children from a home. He may well have tried to rescue a child whom he thought was in danger of running into the prop. In fact it was his charity work that brought us together; he was chairman of the Kensington Rotarians and he invited me to give a talk to his branch. I think at that stage I was still happily working, well that's a misnomer, *enjoying my hobby* in the model agency business. Francis, however, was not so interested in hearing me tell risqué stories of nubile young women.

'They are too old for that, probably give them high blood pressure and heart attacks and we can't have that after a good luncheon,' he had jocularly remarked. So what he would like was something military, anything war-like or British Army traditions. 'Perhaps Mess night antics,' he declared. So it was with this brief that I planned my lecture. 'Just one,' he confirmed, 'that's all.'

I quite enjoyed the switch from female to male company (well, three hours was enough), lots of gin and tonics before luncheon and wine with, but here I was careful not to imbibe too much as I didn't wish to slur my speech. I can't remember exactly what I spoke about, but forty minutes later I remember everyone patting me on my back with congratulatory words: 'well done', 'most enlightening' and 'very enjoyable'. Francis seemed satisfied too, for not so long after I received another invitation to talk to his fellow Rotarians.

'But you said it was customary for only one appearance,' I protested, 'now you want me to prepare a second talk.'

'Well, it is by popular demand – they want you back,' he said flatteringly.

So it was that the club was given another session of scintillating subjects from yours truly. I am happy to report that the outcome was the same, so I went home rather smug, believing that I had a future as an after-dinner raconteur. Two or three months had elapsed before I received yet another invitation to appear before them, and this appealed to my vanity so much that I again accepted. Francis introduced me as 'the man that needs no introduction', all to eager applause. Thus began my masterpiece. I was about halfway through my fascinating saga when I dropped my slide and whispered to the chap on the side to turn up the dimmer for a second. Unfortunately he hit the lot, flooding the room with light.

There in front of me were forty men all blissfully asleep, indeed so blissfully asleep it seemed a pity to wake them. Some smiling with arms folded, heads lolling, mouths open and one or two lightly snoring.

Actually it was not all bad, I rationalised. After all, I was their most popular lecturer, whose dulcet tones could lull these stressed businessmen to a restful state of sleep. It transpired that the members did genuinely request my presence ... but perhaps for the wrong reasons!

'No, no, you are not boring,' insisted a chastened and embarrassed Francis, 'it's just your lovely mellifluous tones that put us to sleep. It was warm, the food heavy, the drink drowsy and a perfect setting for dreamland – but definitely not boring!'

I didn't ask him how he knew that I wasn't boring, since like the rest of them he had slept through all three sessions. Furthermore, their offer inviting me to join them, out of guilt, fell on stony ground. I wouldn't want to join that indolent lot.

Come to think of it, my wife has always said that I bore people – but that is because she has heard all my stories before. If there were any truth in it, then none of those lovely models were actually awake. All my passion and ardour poured into deaf ears, into sleepwalking dolls who had been bored into submission long before their heads hit the pillow. Oh my goodness, could that be construed as a technical ... you know what? My God!

35

THE NAKED LOVER

Nakedness has never particularly bothered me. At the age of eight I remember, on rain-soaked summer days, all the house of some fifty prep school boys running to the school swimming pool. It involved a sprint across the extensive playground of some 400 yards and plunging into an unheated open pool, much to the amusement of any of the female domestic staff who may have been watching. It did not strike me as odd that we had no swimwear or towels – what would be the use of such trivia? The towels would be left on open benches to be soaked by the rain and any wet bathing trunks would present a logistic problem in the drying. So, consequently we swam naked all the time but took towels or wore shorts if the weather was nice. Later, communal showers and rugby sports tubs were the norm and one soon developed a non-modest approach to nudity. The Army only reinforced such habits, but I was always aware that many people did not share my views and preferred their own privacy, which I respected.

As I have grown older and lost the bloom of youth, I am not too fond of people seeing me even a little exposed, as I feel for them having to see something less than perfect. Nude or topless bathing in Saint-Tropez is wonderful if you have the body beautiful, but recently I have been aghast at some of the obscene sights of gross obesity I have been forced to witness on beaches around the world.

Nudity is a very personal thing and something that can acutely embarrass us; take for example the use of the humiliation of nakedness by torturers, gaolers and those in authority who wish to bend us to their will. The use of such tactics reinforces their superiority and degrades good people. I worry about such things, perhaps due to my preoccupation with the Nazis' treatment of the Jews, with torturers who resort to such tactics and, as happened to a lady friend of mine, internal body searches at airports, which appear to be carried out crudely and coldly. I have a recurring dream of being totally naked in public. Or could it be my past coming back to haunt me?

I was with my beautiful Frances in a Westminster flat just off Horseferry Road. What we were doing there, apart from staying the night, and to whom the flat belonged, I have no idea. But there we were. In the morning Frances had to be at Heathrow airport to fly to Munich for some job or other, and so a taxi was called for 7:30 a.m. It duly arrived and Frances climbed in before turning to me and saying, 'Come and give me a kiss then.' My naked body was hidden from the taxi driver by the front door but she persisted, 'Come on, don't be shy, you won't see me for three days ... a kiss please.' I cast around, but there was nothing to hand that I could wrap around me. A dash to the kitchen produced a small hand towel, with which I covered my essentials parts. More inducements followed: 'Quickly, we're going.' A furtive glance down the road revealed that my chances of stealing a last but not too lingering peck were favourable.

I dashed to the now closed taxi door and the waiting lips of my lover, poised at the window. We kissed, a pure innocent farewell caress as the taxi pulled away and the face was replaced by a wave of her bespangled hand. In those fleeting seconds on the pavement

I turned to see the door swing shut. I had pushed it well back and it seemed secure, but perhaps an open window and a sudden inrush of air had projected it towards its frame and barred my entrance.

It was like no other feeling I had ever experienced. It is bad enough when you lose your keys or lock yourself out, but then you are usually dressed and can climb on a bus and collect spare keys from someone, or call from a telephone box or run to a neighbour for help. Here I was in a strange area, knowing no one, no pocket full of money, no hardy shoes to walk anywhere, just the terror of being naked on a London street. Perhaps there was a law against such lewdness? Perhaps I would be arrested for flashing – let's hope so, the privacy and comfort of a Black Maria seemed in that moment infinitely better than standing there naked with a half-stuffed towel hiding my 'what's its'.

By now a few people were approaching; if they saw me they crossed the street, others kept their heads down, obviously embarrassed, some smiled diffidently. I backed up against the door and in between gaps in the passers-by checked what I already knew – a small hand towel was insufficient to spread around my girth. Luckily it was June, but even so my feet were getting cold and other extremities more so; soon I thought there wouldn't be too much to hide anyway, and then I would be seen as some freak, a eunuch. I felt so vulnerable but knew that I must appear confident, normal and treat the incident as an everyday event. Take the bull by the horns and ask for help. A woman may see me as some pervert trying to seek early morning favours. On the other hand a man might see me as a raging homosexual carried away by what the youth of today apparently call 'morning glory', although there was no evidence of this, rather the reverse. Perhaps an older woman may feel more disposed towards my predicament, but my decision was made when some young man of about my age came along with a huge smile on his face. He looked promising.

'I say,' I said. 'I have just locked myself out while kissing my girlfriend goodbye,' (that made me look normal at least). 'Do you know where there is … ?'

'A fire station,' he concluded my sentence for me. 'Yes, end of the road turn left onto Horseferry Road and it is on your left. You can't miss it.'

What an inspired chap, for my initial idea had been to ask for a police station, but the gods were kind to me that day, for what better place to seek help than from the fire brigade?

Although highly relieved, the walk there was something I have put behind me. So I rarely talk about this incident, and indeed this story only appears because I was asked if I had included it. Perhaps this is the reason I still occasionally dream of being naked in public, because I have not vented my insecurity by discussing it openly. Horseferry Road was busy, the old Routemasters trundling by in convoy to Victoria or Parliament Square. The passengers approaching from behind would have seen a totally naked man walking up a busy thoroughfare, while the motorists and pedestrians just stared in astonishment. You can imagine their opening remarks on arriving in the office, taking off their jackets and saying, 'Guess what I've just seen? A raving lunatic walking the street stark bollock naked, he should be locked away.'

Well, at least I'd broken the monotony of their daily routine.

I gained the sanctuary of the fire service where no one blinked an eyelid. I even rode in a big red fire engine but have little recall of this, having tried to erase this awful memory. I do know that the ladders were raised, something that normally I would have been thrilled to witness, and within seconds I had regained the safety of a flat to which I suddenly felt affiliated. However, I don't particularly like Horseferry Road and it probably doesn't like me.

My embarrassment, however, pales into total insignificance compared to the following incident. I must say I cannot entirely vouch for its accuracy, but I did know the man, and in fact we became 'chums', inasmuch as any NCO does who brings along a young officer when he joins his Regiment. Sgt Trouble, my *nom de guerre* for this likeable rogue, was with me when I first joined the Lancashire Fusiliers. I think he was Orderly Sgt and I was probably doing, as was my wont, extra orderly officer duties. Now, over the 24-hour duty one often wiled away the time over a mug of Army brew, listening to the folklore of the Regiment. These tales were often totally bizarre, always hilarious and sometimes unbelievable, and through the telling of them over the years no doubt suffered from hyperbole. The guardroom was a hive of activity, but at 3 a.m. it was the perfect time and place for a young subaltern to fall under the spell of an old soldier, and so it was.

Sgt Trouble told me that he had joined the XX in 1949 and was soon posted to Ismailia, about the time that trouble began in October 1951. The Egyptian Government had just abrogated its treaty with Great Britain and Colonel Nasser was to rise to prominence when he closed the Suez Canal. L/Cpl Trouble had just got his first stripe and was something of a blue-eyed boy, so much so that his Company Commander called for him one day and said, 'L/Cpl Trouble I have a special job for you. We are shortly to have a detachment of Women's Royal Army Corps (WRAC) coming here and we want them to feel at home. I want you to build a row of latrines that will do them justice.' The young NCO with his small working party began his first project. He dug a beautifully proportioned pit some five feet deep. Although a pit is just a pit he nevertheless dug it with pride: nice vertical sides 'all precision like.' In his lunch hour he would shelter there from the heat of day, relaxing with his Woodbines. He decided that these lavatories would be his signature work of art. He painted signs, made borders of stones, obtained hessian and compartmentalised the lavatories. His thunderboxes were beautifully varnished, and he devised a hessian door which would provide some measure of privacy for these homesick girls. Lavatory paper was somehow obtained, as opposed to the usual torn-up newspaper that were the lot of the

Fusiliers, and these he had suspended on cord. 'Palatial it was,' he declared proudly.

Perhaps our hero became too involved, for he found that during the week he was loath to leave his creation, settling down in the cool pit to snooze and smoke. It was to be his undoing. When it was that he decided he couldn't leave his project is not known, but he thought it would be nice if he could see the loos in action, and to this end he awaited the arrival of his first customer. At the appointed time the transport arrived, and with it the sweet alto tones of the WRAC girls. As the first lavatory seat was raised an effulgent shaft of sunlight announced the arrival of girl number one.

'I couldn't help it, I hadn't seen a white fanny for ages,' he said. 'I was there like a shot to witness a pert white bottom about to sit on my loo.' He may have been a little more soldier-like in his description, but as the comely derrière was about to be seated, was he suddenly overcome with jealousy at his creation being defiled? Or, as the prosecution maintained, 'a strong sense of carnal voracity projected his hand upward to grab the female part'. The terror of the girl must have been indescribable, for here was not the 'arm clothed in white samite, mystic, wonderful,' rising from Arthurian waters to retrieve 'the brand Excalibur' but Woodbine-stained fingers clawing in lust at a part of the body that women rightly claim to be their own. It must have been a moment of Draculean terror – imagine anyone going into the privacy of their loo and sitting down in what one would expect to be a safe and secure environment when suddenly a hand grabs one's ghoulies. A subsequent court-martial confined him to a military prison at Shepton Mallet, for how long I know not.

It wasn't to be the last time he was busted, for I later met him in Bury, together with another of our fraternity, a ginger-haired Irish man with an equally ready smile and cheeky disposition. Let's call him Sgt O'Naughty. Sgt Trouble, who I remember loved dressing up in cowboy garb complete with guns, was great muckers with Sgt O'Naughty and they often took leave together in the regimental town of Bury where they lived. They invited me to The Two Tubs next to Castle Armoury, the regimental pub of the Fifth Battalion Lancashire Fusiliers HQ, for a beer or two.

'How come you are so flushed?' I said.

'Made a pile today sir,' they echoed.

'But you are on leave, how can you make any money on leave?' I asked, knowing I shouldn't have asked, just as the words came out of my mouth.

'Simple sir,' they laughed. 'We've worked at lots of big firms around here – still have mates there. We know the layout, we know the form and working together we get away with murder.'

'But how?' I interjected.

'Well, it's all a matter of bluff you see, having the confidence to carry it off. So, I walk into the typing pool at Mather's, brown storeman's coat, clipboard, official forms like the Army 1052 and say something like, 'Hello girls, your lucky day today, cor luv, you're a corker ... well, what yer dun to deserve new desks and typewriters then?'

'Nothing,' they would reply.

'Well, yer down for new office equipment here ... look let me check ... George ... it is here the typewriters are for?'

Here Sgt Trouble, now *Mr* Trouble, would appear similarly dressed with top pocket full of pencils and biros; another flattering quip and winsome smile was flashed.

'This is it ... the new IBMs,' he would add. So it was that the senior girl would sign forms which looked official in triplicate. 'One copy for you luv,' while Mr Trouble would call some callow youth, perhaps a teenage son or nephew, to help them move the desk, chairs, typewriters or anything else that was to hand. One day they disappeared with a very nice old wall clock. These were whisked away to Rochdale, Oldham or Bolton where they had already been spoken for. They would then go into fits of laughter and discuss the merits of the girls. 'Cor, I fancied that dark-haired woman who offered us a cuppa … she was lovely,' they would sigh. Other observations followed, like wondering how long it took the firm to realise they'd been swindled. They actually thought that the girls would love them as some form of latter-day Robin Hoods, for they must have got the day off as they had nothing to work with. It wasn't outright stealing, you understand, just a little fun. Anyway, all these offices could do with a makeover, so in a way they were promoting trade, encouraging the economy to move on.

I concluded that it certainly required a good dose of *sang-froid*, but one day their luck would run out. They were great characters, not at all the bellowing, bully type one associates with infantry sergeants, but both seemed to have yo-yo lives, and by that I mean fluctuating in rank. There were other scams which they perpetrated, but by now we were on the whisky and it all became a little hazy. However, I had a most unprofessional approach to the pair for every time I saw them all I wanted to do was to laugh … and I still do.

36

Our Rolls-Royce

In 1960 my uncle was lucky enough to afford a new Rolls-Royce Silver Cloud II. The cost then seemed negligible, a mere £2,600, but of course everything is relative. However, some of the young, wilder elements of the community took exception to his affluence and would hassle him, spit on the motor and generally vandalise it at every opportunity. This, coupled with failing health, forced him to sell his pride and joy – to me. Sad for him, and of course his antagonists didn't take into consideration the fact that his purchase ensured employment for a highly-skilled workforce that still exists to this day. Moreover, it also preserved complex trades which don't exist in other motor car factories. Justification seems superfluous as one only need look skywards to see the reliance one places on Rolls-Royce engines, foreign-owned but still designed and made in Great Britain.

I was then serving in West Germany, where petrol was cheap to those of us serving in BAOR. On 16 February 1979, my six-year-old son Warwick and I had the adventure of our lives as we ferried, trained and collected our new purchase. The drive back to Rheindahlen in West Germany was equally exciting, and since then my family and I have nurtured a life-long love for this splendid motor. It has featured in our family weddings, prominent parties and served most functionally for the transportation of the six of us on high days and holidays. I also felt, as others did in the garrison, a certain pride in seeing a Rolls-Royce grille glide along German streets, outclassing the BMWs and the Mercedes-Benz. Well, in true partisan fashion that's what we thought. Having said that, the Germans felt no inclination to take their jealousy or wrath out on an inanimate object (though I don't think of it like that – it will come to heaven with me) and the only problems we had were grease marks on the windows where foreheads had rested, as they admired the rich leather seats and the fine veneer woodwork.

In fact, now I think of it, we did receive a censure while filling up in Nuremberg. I was paying for the petrol when the children rushed up to me saying that a German mechanic was washing the motor car. Indeed, he had taken exception to the fact that the white walled tyres were no longer white and took the liberty of cleaning them, mildly telling me that a beautiful motor car deserved better treatment.

Our time in Germany in so many ways was blissful: wonderful trips and holidays, weekend outings with the children down the River Moselle with its vineyards and castles and glorious picnics served from the capacious boot of the Rolls – ah, halcyon days.

On one occasion we were stuck for what could have been hours on the German-Swiss border. We had all the children with us and it was unbearably hot as we wiled away the time with our engine off. Suddenly, a border guard whistled and beckoned us forward a good 500 yards or so to the head of the queue.

'This is it,' I said to the family, 'we will be taken apart bit by bit.'

'Why Daddy?' chorused the children.

'Because they think we are rich,' I said. However, I need not have had any qualms, for it was because they thought we were rich that we had been called forward to avoid the queuing.

'Lovely car, sir, beautiful children, would they like some toffees?'

They crowded around like bees at the proverbial honey pot. 'And where are you going sir?' they smiled. 'The Rosensee, ah lovely hotel, have you a map … take this one it's better,' they continued. To cut a long story short we drove away with toffees, a better road map than I possessed, a parking disc and much goodwill. The Swiss, you see, as I quickly learned, love rich people. They sustain the economy, and no doubt they still had the misconception that as a British officer I was there to deposit another million pounds in my hidden Swiss bank account, and that was all to their benefit. The downside to the story was that the following year we repeated the same journey in an ordinary blue Triumph 2000, but being smaller the paraphernalia of nappies, pushchairs and teddies was all too evident. Here was an ordinary family man scraping together the money for a holiday in Switzerland … and they did take us apart, literally. Indeed, they discovered that we were a bottle of gin over and an open bottle of whisky which I explained was for our own consumption, but my good fortune of the previous visit caught up with us now and we paid the excess begrudgingly. The moral of the story is self-evident – when travelling in Switzerland travel in a Rolls-Royce.

Travelling in Honecker's Communist East Germany was far more prosaic, and a little frightening too, for we were deep in the days of the Cold War and to us war was always just around the corner, with the thought of total oblivion in the form of nuclear strikes omnipresent. Indeed, people forget West Berlin was an island then, surrounded by its inimical Communist neighbour. The East German border guards weren't that keen on a Rolls-Royce passing into the land of the Trabant; I suspect it showed the contrast between capitalism and communism too starkly. I learned later that they had thought of technicalities either to hold us up or bar us altogether, and had it not been for the Royal Military Police (the Redcaps) slipping them a few *Playboy* magazines we may never have got though Checkpoint Charlie.

Our journey down Hitler's old autobahn was none too comfortable for I seem to remember the surface being 'rucked' cement and potholed – and it had to be completed at exactly 50–55 mph. We heard dreadful stories of what had happened to those that went too fast, too slow or broke down, and to some who had exited the autobahn too early. Anyway, we made it into West Berlin and safety. West Berlin was vibrant, exciting and one felt one was living on the edge, a frenetic existence with the communists on the doorstep. We took the motor into the forbiddingly grey East Berlin, with its dour, repetitive blocks of flats and the fine old buildings of a bygone age, still pockmarked by Russian bullets as they forced entry into Hitler's last stronghold. We were told just how empty the shops were in East Berlin but the first one we saw was full of cereal packets which belied the rumour. However, the rest of the shop was totally devoid of any produce, and we also had our suspicions that some of the boxes were empty anyway. On returning to the Cloud we found a crowd of about twenty, many of the men wearing black leather jackets with the women similarly dressed in drab, dull colours, but pleasant enough. I suspect that they had never seen such a large vehicle which prompted them to ask me, '*Sind Sie ein Koenig?*'

Was I a King? Sadly, on this occasion the Rolls-Royce disgraced itself, as a hole appeared in the silencer box and we motored back into West Germany, after an interesting weekend, sounding like a tractor. Oh shame! I still blush at the recollection.

While we were in Germany, the adjutant of a rather smart Regiment telephoned me to ask, 'Sir, is your Rolls-Royce available this weekend, we would like to borrow it, if we may?' I said that it was and asked why. He explained that someone near and dear to the Regiment was arriving and that they would love to use it.

'Feel free,' I said.

It was duly collected by the CO's driver who returned it fully valeted three days later with a thank-you from the Regiment which was to be found in the boot. It was a most appreciated gift – a case of Bollinger. Some months later the exercise was repeated with the same result and when on the third occasion I was asked, I responded with, 'Why not have it for a few weeks?' The thought of a car full of champagne really excited me. However, on this occasion the motor car was returned pristine as always, apart from some mud on a tyre and the wheel arches.

'What happened here?' I asked the young Corporal.

'Well sir, the young couple took motor car onto the ranges after the ball.' I presumed it was really for a kiss and a cuddle, and good luck to them, I thought. A little mud on the tyres was nothing when I could later reveal to my children, 'Royal bottoms *may* have sat on these very seats.'

When I was in Bielefeld I was commanding soldiers and therefore had a dedicated driver for my Land Rover. I always preferred driving myself, but for both tactical and practical reasons this wasn't possible. However, in the evening at purely private functions one usually drove oneself, and since drink-drive rules were now being strongly enforced it behoved officers not to be caught in such a situation.

One day, my driver said to me, 'You know, sir, I would love to drive you and your wife to your dinner parties and social engagements in the evenings, and it would be a good idea, just in case you had a drink and were a wee bit over the limit, as it could end your career.'

If only I could have foreseen the potential disaster. L/Cpl Parish, as we shall call him, went beyond the call of duty. For a start, he would always dress in his best uniform and service dress hat, a peaked cap with a red band embracing it. 'I must look the part,' he would say. He was also very daring. On one occasion we arrived at the Commander-in-Chief's residence, where motor cars other than the Ambassador's official Rolls-Royce Silver Shadow were banned. It was in the early days of the IRA when one exercised extreme caution. All the other officers were on foot walking up the drive but when the sentries saw the Rolls the gates swung open, salutes were exchanged and our Cloud stayed alongside the Ambassador's Shadow all night – just the two all snug.

I think this was the time that His Excellency pointed out that his Rolls-Royce was newer than mine. I, of course, was too diplomatic to point out that I owned mine but his had to be returned at the end of his appointment – so my wife Jillie said it instead!

Then came a ceremony in which we were to be granted the Freedom of the City. We all drove to the venue, a large stadium, and were due to park and proceed on foot. L/Cpl Parish, however, greatly embarrassed me as he simply followed in the exhaust fumes of the Minister-President of the region, in tandem with his official Mercedes, rolling into the stadium itself, blithely saying, 'But sir, we are in a Rolls-Royce.' He got away with it because he was always in uniform, so it looked official, and 'important' figures could be vaguely seen hiding in the back of an imposing limousine. Sometimes though, our behaviour didn't go down too well as older, more senior, officers resented a mere forty-year-old with a pretty wife being allowed such privileges.

'Every dog must have his day,' to quote Swift, and these were mine. But they were not to last. L/Cpl Parish would disappear after dropping us off at the party, returning to our married quarters where our pretty babysitter Lucy took his fancy. He had a great personality, a supreme gift of the gab and a soldier's sense of humour, in all aspects a winsome fellow and I am sure she enjoyed his company, but no more.

One very hot Saturday afternoon, I decided that since L/Cpl Parish was on leave I would clean the motor car, cleaning being something of a fetish of mine. If I were to appear in *Who's Who*, my wife agreed that my first entry under 'hobbies and interests' would be 'cleaning', before my other considerable interests; a little sad really but there it is, and we are all made differently. One bit of cleaning led to more – wash, chamois, wax and polish, chrome, black tyres, hoover rugs and hide-cream for the leather. Well, I had got this far so I may as well remove the back seat to do it properly. This I did and beneath uncovered a veritable cornucopia of women's make-up, hairpins, hair slides, a vanity mirror or two, eye shadow, lipsticks, powder … in fact it would be easier to list what *wasn't* there. Suffice to say that I carried the above carefully into the house, where I thought a grateful Jillie would thank me profusely for reuniting her with her lost cosmetics. Instead, all I got was suspicious looks and scurrilous remarks about my morals, or rather lack of them. I convincingly pointed out that I would not be the perpetrator of my own downfall, we agreed that it was probably my aunt's from a couple of years back and there the matter rested, but not before Jillie had jettisoned the offending items.

Now every September we had a unit barbecue or 'smoker', as the boys called it. It was a lovely balmy evening and those soldiers who were married brought their wives along, all looking remarkably pretty. The cook-house did a wonderful spread as usual and there was a general air of bonhomie and conviviality. As the evening drew to its end, the 'marrieds' drifted homewards while the beer-drinking bachelors lingered in the shadows of a dying bonfire.

'Well, where do we go for the girls then?' I heard one say.

'What about the lay-by,' I heard L/Cpl Parish reply, 'you know the one that runs alongside the woods.'

'What about …' and here various clubs were mentioned, before they agreed that you had to buy more drinks and perhaps pay an entrance charge and that guaranteed you nothing.

'No the lay-by is the place,' said L/Cpl Parish, overriding all opposition. 'Listen, I tell you, I take the old man's Roller down there regularly … I tell you the girls love it. I take them on a jolly around the town or somewhere and chances are I get a free jump,' he continued. 'Just take something decent to impress them, anyway, I know them all, and you'll be all right Scotty if you take me.'

'The old man's Roller,' Scotty added, as if in disbelief.

'Ya, the back seat's better than a double bed, there's more leverage.'

They all laughed, but it was curtailed as I emerged from the shadows. 'I hope you haven't, L/Cpl Parish,' I said, half-smiling.

'No sir, of course not,' he laughed, 'but I had thought about it.'

My appointment was actually coming to an end and the party had been held in tandem with the two events, my farewell and the annual barbecue. It was on our way home that the cache of cosmetics was explained. We initially had a little giggle, 'Gosh, we could have started a make-up shop with what the girls provided,' Jillie smirked, but our mirth was short-lived as we envisaged the enormity of the acts that had been performed on our virgin back seat. It was then we decided we needed steam cleaning and deep leather therapy (was there such a service?) to remove the immoral things that the back seat had witnessed, and then there was the fact that our beautiful, innocent children had sat on those very seats, how rough and vulgar compared to those genteel royal bottoms, we mused. The terrible betrayal, as my wife saw it, was that I always paid my driver handsomely and Jillie more often than not would say to L/Cpl Parish, 'Go home if you wish, there's food or sandwiches for you there.' I guess he preferred 'soldiers' PT' (their polite euphemism for fornication) to the food – well, soldiers will be soldiers.

In time, and after the 'spring clean', it became a great dining-out story when back in England. Until such time as my chum, the late Colonel Chris Hughes, ex-Intelligence Corps, said to me, 'But that's a terrible story and extremely serious, in fact very detrimental to you. First British Corps is our only fighting corps and as such is the target of a huge amount of espionage.'

'Well, of course I knew that,' I interrupted, 'so how would it have affected me?'

'The security boys would have had you covered night and day, especially in your position as OC and Corps Reconnaissance Officer, and running around in the largest most distinctive black and gold Rolls-Royce carrying German prostitutes in droves ... what do you think you were doing?'

'It wasn't me,' I protested.

'Yes, I know but the security boys probably didn't, for a start there were different shifts, many operatives, and all they saw was your flashy car driving into dubious woods, dark alleys and scantily-clad whores getting in and out. If that isn't a security risk I don't know what is. You are open to all kinds of pressure and so easily compromised, you are so vulnerable. What a disaster,' and he didn't laugh, or even smile.

Well, we still tell the story as you see and somewhere in my file in MOD Whitehall there will be a big black mark saying that 'When commanding troops he set a deplorable example and showed a total lack of self-control and immoral behaviour, added to this and even more serious is that he could have jeopardised the integrity of First British Corps by being a target of corruption and a grave security threat to us all,' or words to that effect.

Postscript
Thanks L/Cpl Parish. So that is why I didn't become a General! Bloody RR!

37

INTEGRITY

The Army places an enormous emphasis on integrity in every sphere of activity, social as well as military. Well, it did in my day. Now, in common with society, the boundaries seem somewhat blurred. To quote Tennyson:

> The old order changeth, yielding place to new,
> And God fulfils himself in many ways,
> Lest one good custom should corrupt the world.

What was a heinous crime when I was in the services has today become the norm. It was a serious offence to harbour a woman in one's room – perhaps a court-martial even. Suddenly, from the sixties to the seventies this changed and was perfectly in order. Indeed, one could find the next-door room was occupied by a young female officer who seemed totally unnerved by sharing the male ablutions. Something I always found distasteful on the very few occasions I experienced such proximity.

I also found that the military were unjustly treated in so many ways, compared to civil servants, bankers, diplomats and certainly the police force, to say nothing of MPs with the recent expenses scandal. In many instances one used one's own motor car for duty and was told that no claim was permissible. Indeed, I was informed that I must pay my own hotel bill and run my own motor for some three weeks in 1962 whilst leading a team of young Fusiliers in Keep the Army in the Public Eye (KAPE). After all, it was for 'the good of the Regiment' and who could argue with that?

When I was in my first term at RMA Sandhurst a young officer-cadet travelled to London and paid for a journey on the tube to Hyde Park. However, since his friends were going to Piccadilly he extended his journey, thus incurring a further two pence on his ticket. He was caught and reported to the authorities at Sandhurst as defrauding the London Underground of, in modern money, about £2 or so. He was promptly expelled and a salutary warning given to us that, if he was likely to cheat on £2, how much greater the temptation would be when the stakes were raised and he was looking after company funds of £500? I could see the logic behind this, but this young man was straight from school where it was probably an act of great daring to place a worthless washer into a vending machine and obtain a bar of Fry's Five Boys chocolate or some such delicacy. Perhaps the powers that be should have shown more leniency and given him the benefit of the doubt and assumed 'that he had intended to pay the modest excess at the other end'. In all events he lost his chosen profession and learnt a very hard lesson. However, his judges had been brought up to even more exacting standards, similar to people of my age now, victims of our own upbringings, always a generation behind. Even so, it still rankles that if we in the military were convicted for drink-driving and fined by the civil courts we were then punished by the military for bringing the service into disrepute. So different to two policemen who went on an expensive and physically demanding white-water rafting holiday in Canada with a friend of mine.

'How did they afford that?' I asked, 'and the time off?'

'Oh, they had a six months' paid leave with bad backs,' he

retorted, 'besides they both ran a business back home!' All right for some.

‡

When I was serving in Borneo I was asked by my General to oversee the making of an enclosure for a honey bear. Barloo was his name and his photograph is still to hand now. It shows him mischievous, cuddly and sporting a white furry V-shaped necklace, and he was to be the children's favourite pet. As the bear's playground was completed and paid for, the Chinese contractor very kindly made me a gift of a small book on honey bears. It cost 10/- at the time, or fifty pence in today's money. At dinner that night we were discussing the habits of these creatures when my General asked me how I was suddenly such an authority on honey bears.

'Mr Ong gave me this book,' I told him, 'and it gives ...' but before I could complete the sentence: 'He *what?*' roared the General. 'You have accepted a present. Do you know that you are now beholden to this man; it is tantamount to taking a bribe. Officers, however young, should know better.'

It was 11 p.m. when the staff car dropped me off in Brunei town to return the present to Mr Ong in his steamy little restaurant. He was as sad as I was chided and chaste. We parted still as friends but what was on his part an act of kindness was seen by my superiors as undermining an officer's sacred duty to be incorruptible. It was a lesson to learn and stood me in good stead. From that day on I was authorised to repay the postage cost of anyone who wrote to complain or gripe about the military. It was thought that by doing this we would be inconveniencing the writer as little as possible and showing ourselves as being as fair and honest as one could be.

‡

I was standing in civilian clothes (the mode of dress for all military air trooping flights) when the tannoy system at the airport announced: 'Would Mr Stacey, Lt, Lancashire Fusiliers, please report to the Air Trooping Office?'

This I duly did. I was confronted by a Warrant Officer, Class II or Sergeant-Major, from the now defunct Royal Army Service Corps (RASC).

'Sir,' he said, standing up from behind his desk, 'we have a slight problem. British Army of the Rhine's pay was incomplete this week, somehow they were short and we need an officer to take this money over. It's quite a lot I am afraid but you will be met at the other side by a Major in the Royal Army Pay Corps who will take it off your hands ... about £50,000 I think.'

I can't remember signing for it but I must have done. In any case, I departed from the office with this burdensome briefcase. I recall that not only was it weighty but the gold royal cipher was well worn and the black leather cracked. The flight was then delayed for a good two hours and I found myself with nothing better to do than admire the numerous female ground staff of the many airlines that were beginning to move into the expanding Gatwick airport.

I didn't think it strange that I was given no escort, indeed I didn't consider it an odd request, just all in a day's work. After all I had already done some funny duties, like carrying a baby in its tiny coffin in the back of my motor car for some 200 miles or so in West Germany. This I did think slightly eerie. How on earth did that come about? I can't recall.

I arrived in due course at RAF Gütersloh and handed over this large amount of money. I thought no more about it ... well, until twenty-five years later when I was doing officer recruiting. My duties involved a variety of things, but mostly lecturing at universities and University Officer Training Corps. One day, a young undergraduate brought up the subject of integrity and how the Army manifested it. I was at a loss for a good paradigm until

I had a flash of inspiration and used the story recounted above. The young man came back at me, and there followed a good deal of group discussion, principally about the present-day cash value of the contents of the briefcase (a few million pounds). That was what really preoccupied them, and my integrity seemed to impress them not an iota. In fact, I found myself bombarded by inimical questions.

'Sir, what were you thinking? You try to tell us that you never thought of walking across to Air Argentina, Air Spain or some other country with no extradition treaty and flying off?'

'Do you think that is integrity?' another queried. 'It's just plain stupidity.'

'Sir, you plainly had a duty to grab your one and only chance in life, to get enough money to live forever without any financial worries,' another shouted.

Such was the tone of my youthful audience. To be honest I was aghast, for at their age I'd had no idea that countries had extradition treaties or whatever. We argued the toss for the next half an hour, but I was unable to convince them that what I did was correct. The fact that it was the state's money (didn't they rob us – they certainly waste our resources?) as opposed to something more personal ensured that they didn't see it as an act of larceny. 'You didn't take it, therefore you are a loser, an idiot' was the consensus. Some of this I put down to bravado and perhaps having a tilt at authority. On subsequent lectures I introduced the topic less sententiously but my action of all those years ago just seemed to invite puzzlement and mild incredulity at my naïvety.

What a long way we have come in life from our grandparents' Victorian ethics to our brash new world. As one American put it, 'In the States it doesn't matter how you make your money as long as you make it, buddy.'

So there, General ... was I still wrong to accept Mr Ong's book?

38

MISTAKEN IDENTITY

It was a very pleasant summer's day, probably too hot to be in a three-piece blue pinstripe suit, with rolled umbrella and trilby, but I had set out in the early morning when the dark clouds had looked foreboding, and if I carried an umbrella it was my little gesture at making other people's lives happier ... it wouldn't rain. My duties that day had taken me into the City of London, all neatly coinciding with a regimental luncheon at H.M. Tower of London, still the headquarters of the Royal Regiment of Fusiliers.

Many gin and tonics later, luncheon, and a rarely-taken brandy had given me a flushed face and a wonderful bonhomie towards my fellow men. I stepped from the cavernous underground and entered the sunny world of Sloane Square, which marks the beginning of the famous King's Road, Chelsea, the haunt of a select tribe of people called the Sloane Rangers. The head of this tribe is one called the Earl of Cadogan, who seems to own quite a lot of it. The Earl is much bigger than I am, much richer ... well actually, much, much, much richer than I am and perhaps a little older. However, we conform in one thing. Whenever I have seen him he has a similar blue pinstripe suit on, perhaps a club or school tie, an unfurled umbrella and, I'm pretty certain, a Locke's trilby.

I leisurely crossed the road and went north parallel with Sloane Street into the heart of the tribe's HQ. In fact it was Cadogan Garden Mews, which afforded me just a little more shade. I was confronted by some dozen or more burly workmen in their yellow hats and grime-covered overalls who suddenly showed not only a great deal of interest but also respect. The foreman, perhaps recognising my regimental tie, said in an Irish brogue, 'Ah and a good afternoon to you, sir.' Touched by such affection, I raised my hat and, smiling as graciously as I knew how, said (hopefully in not too slurred a fashion): 'Well good afternoon gentleman, what a pleasant surprise,' as I reviewed my line of 'troops'. I just wanted to say, 'Stand at ease, carry on Sergeant-Major,' but I didn't. However, I must admit I found the experience edifying. I had not gone more than a few paces past them, when I heard one of their number saying, 'Who the f*** was he?'

'You don't recognise the boss ... that's f***ing Cadogan, yer fool ... bejesus!'

I thought that the episode was rather amusing but I didn't have a great deal of time to dwell on it, for suddenly my heart rate increased as I saw a chauffeur with his hosepipe, bucket, sponges and chamois leather cleaning a certain motor car that I had long wanted to see. The garage had hidden its contents well, save for the bumper and over-riders which protruded from the swing-down door. I guessed it to be a Rolls-Royce Silver Cloud and as I quickened my pace in eager anticipation I saw a beautiful Cloud, bodied by one of our great coach builders. The motor had a very low mileage and had been lovingly maintained. There followed an animated discussion on the merit of the Cloud I, with its relatively uncomplicated straight six engine, and the later models with the larger V8 engine. In all, we chatted for well over a half an hour, and it transpired that my new-found acquaintance had driven it for over twenty years and was clearly attached to it. He then paid me a great compliment.

'Do you know sir, I can't think of anyone I would like to have this motor car more than yourself. Indeed, I would go as far as to say that if I had a word with Mr Finkelstein ... who is now in his nineties and needs to sell it, he would do you a very special concession, especially to one of his own.'

This set bells ringing, was he an old soldier perhaps? 'What do you mean by that?' I enquired. 'One of his own?'

'Well, one of his faith,' he replied, 'a Jewish gentleman.'

'But what makes you think I am a Jewish gentleman?' I smiled dryly.

'Well, aren't you sir? I thought your hat was a give-away.'

I had travelled less than 150 yards in the space of two or three minutes and been identified as the Earl of Cadogan and a Jewish gentleman. If only I had half the money of either the former or the latter I would have been very happy.

39

WHAT'S IN A NAME

This little story should really be told by my great friend and my younger son's godfather. Sadly, he died of cancer a few years ago but I am certain that he wouldn't mind me stealing it.

It was a warm summer's evening as we prepared for the fathers and sons dinner at the Royal Military Academy, Sandhurst. This rather nice gesture and modern tradition was new to me as no such thing happened in my day. I sat on my son's bed watching him frantically getting dressed, red striped blues trousers with Ministry of Defence braces were squeezed on, the braces tightly covering a clean white shirt. He then sat on his chair to place on his feet a funny sort of boot – sort of half shoe and half Chelsea boot. A total compromise really for it had laces but only two pairs of eyelets.

'Do you know what that boot's called?' I said, proudly smiling.

'Of course I do, I've been bulling the wretched things for a year now,' he said, applying himself robustly to the task in hand.

'I bet you don't know why it's called that,' I teased him.

'Haven't a clue,' he said uninterestedly.

'It was all your godfather's father's doing,' I said.

'Really, how?' he said with a little more enthusiasm.

I continued, 'Well, Nick's father was a Major-General at the end of the war and in charge of dress, uniforms, headgear you know, all forms of garb, total dress code.'

'I didn't know that,' he smiled.

'Yes, in 1945–6 there were all kinds of things happening. Regiments were being disbanded, others amalgamated, lots of things happening in the TA, as well as a general update and review of all the British Army dress, and I bet you didn't know that the old King, the Queen's father, was the most ardent disciple of all things military. He took an interest in everything he loved: the Army, its traditions, the uniforms, the bands, their music, our medals – everything about it – seriously. No doubt he had the same respect for the Navy and the Royal Air Force, but just think they have only a standard uniform for all branches, but we in the Army have hundreds of different styles, colours, headdress, badges, a host of idiosyncrasies.'

'That's true,' he mused.

'Well, the King used to insist on Nick's father seeing him every week at the palace, I think every Thursday over tea, to discuss the various changes that were taking place. It wasn't a one-sided discussion, the King would suggest this, veto that and as I said was totally immersed in the minutia of it all.'

'Go on,' he said earnestly.

'Well, you know the Mess Wellington which you will shortly be acquiring.'

Here I must pause and explain that the Mess Wellington isn't a Wellington at all. True the Iron Duke introduced the Wellington boot but Mess Wellingtons are different: thin leather boots worn underneath very tight Mess overalls. In the days of batmen or servants they would be a great help in putting the wretched things on – and of course the spurs.

I continued, 'To overcome these awkward things and for use on more informal occasions the King suggested and designed the boot that you are putting on now.'

'Well, well,' he laughed, 'that is interesting.'

'Ah, but I haven't finished yet,' I said. 'The pair designed the boot to their satisfaction, drank their tea and the General took his leave. He had got to the door when the King called out, "General, what should we call the boot?"

'"Well, sir … I shall have to give it some thought," he said.

'"Hang on," the King continued, "my name is George, your name is George – let us call it the George Boot!"'

And so it was.

'Never,' said my son, astonished.

'As true as I am sitting here,' I concluded.

‡

My friend and my son's godfather was Major Nick Payne 13/18 Hussars and later of the Army Corps. His wife Jutta and two sons Martin and Charlie Payne are still great friends of ours.

40

JOLIE MADAME

My younger sister has constantly decried my lifestyle with the accusative: 'And what have you *ever* accomplished in your life?'

I suspect, as you have reached this, my last little tale, you probably concur with her sentiments. Certainly I lived a hedonistic existence, in my younger days devoid of any ambition other than the sweet dalliance, and the attendance of as many parties and other frivolous pursuits as possible in later life. Certainly, there is scant evidence of anything serious or substantial accomplished in my journey through life with its wastrel ways. Except ... except for my family of whom I am inordinately proud ... and it was all to do with balmy nights in the scented gardens of the already mentioned Muara Lodge, the old Sultan of Brunei's summer *istana*.

Drinks and entertaining were alfresco on the huge curved balcony of the house. Its magnificent view looked seaward. The floral aromas drifted upwards to mingle with the expensive perfumes of our female guests as they lounged on the polished teak balustrade. There was, however, one who seemed to outdo all others, as its wearer weaved her way amongst her guests, leaving a trail of desire behind her. Over the months I found the scent heady and romantic, coupled with the fact that the woman in question, the much admired Pam Lea, was highly feminine, petite and with a personality to match. Now before people's imaginations take flight, I was not in love with her, for a start she was twenty years my senior and my General's wife. However, I did find her attractive, as I am certain all men did. It was after such a party when the guests had departed that we sat on the veranda admiring the silent starlit sky. Pam, who loved her gardening, was extolling the beautiful fragrance of some flower or other when I said, 'It doesn't compare to your perfume.'

I can't imagine I was so bold to ask her what it was, as these things are rather personal to women. However, the information was forthcoming in any case, and perhaps it was George Lea who elucidated. I can't remember, suffice to say that it was from Parfumerie Balmain and it was *Jolie Madame.*

We move from the seductive nights of the Far East to London, a world away in climatic terms but exciting and vibrant nonetheless, especially for a young man such as myself. I had been invited by my friend of Borneo days, Squadron Leader Denis Stoten, RAF, then retired and flying out of Heathrow airport with British European Airways (BEA). He, as a bachelor (well divorced really) with old-style charm, had at his bidding a bevy of airline stewardesses, young and attractive. I should point out that in those days standards were high and selection difficult. A dinner party was on offer and he had a lovely girl whom he thought I might like to meet. In the event I took along my current Greek girlfriend, called Katie. The girl who could have been my date was just like a younger version of Pam, small, pretty with a divine figure and I remember noticing her lovely hands – just right for me. She didn't like me though; in fact, when asked to describe me, she went for 'Bull Terrier', all snout and mean-eyed.

Some weeks later and after many telephone calls I invited her out on a mid-afternoon rendezvous and I took her on my mucker's

Army bicycle, a sit-up-and-beg type in war-department green with a parcel shelf behind the seat. She sort of rode side-saddle behind me, which wasn't very comfortable but quite original for a first date. I was pedalling along High Street Kensington on a sunny summer's day when the local constabulary gave chase in a Panda car. We outdid them though by cycling to the entrance of the Royal Garden Hotel where we disappeared among the throng of American tourists who frequented London in their droves in the sixties. From there we made our way, still by bicycle, to the Scarsdale, a popular tavern at the time – perhaps it still is? Be that as it may, such proximity to this delightful, soft thing brought back the starry nights, the sound of the adjacent jungle and the lapping of the sea that was our lot when relaxing with a drink on the veranda back in Muara, cocooned in warmth and with the intoxicating floral scents assailing us – and yes, that glorious smell that outclassed even nature, the sensuous, erotic odour of Balmain.

'I just love *Jolie Madame*,' I said, 'it just does something that turns me inside out,' and so it did, weak at the knees and gooey.

Suddenly, like the biblical blind man, 'the scales fell from her eyes' as she beheld me afresh. All previous ill-favour from my passenger, one Jillie Carlson, was transformed into delight. That someone so arrogant, boorish and resembling a pretty unattractive dog (let's face it, they may be good with children but what a cross to bear) could display such a sensibility! Well, a metamorphosis occurred, or rather a chain reaction. What was once despised was suddenly acclaimed, this new-found sensitivity, this hidden knowledge of female intimacy and all coupled with such good taste – Balmain! Who would have thought that one so ignorant could be pardoned so quickly? So it was that the mother of my four children was seduced, nay impressed, by one random mention of some rather inconsequential information: the name on a bottle of perfume.

Five years later we were married. In the intervening years, a prolonged spell one might think, I was occupied with the model agency job, which landed in my lap the very next week. Still, it is appropriate that I pay homage to my wife Jillie for her patience and devotion to our children and me. We are not virtuosos in anything really (well, Jillie in cooking) but I can and do maintain that there was no finer mother, with a better instinct for bringing up children, than my wife. She has been totally selfless in all that she did for them. She demanded nothing for herself and never has done. Her generosity is boundless and her legacy is daily with us.

Our four children are in constant and daily conversation with us, still best friends and companions and with an outstanding example of motherhood now passed onto them and our grandchildren – eight so far. We spend happy weeks together in summer-time France and big family Christmases.

So from the ramblings of a rascal there is some justice for all those that toil, like the vast majority of mothers who devote their lives to their families. To womanhood in general whom I admire enormously – God Bless Them. As for me … well, as Jillie and the song say,

> I have always been faithful to you, darling, in my fashion,
> I have always been faithful to you, darling, in my way.

So it shall continue till death us do part.